Prison Land

Prison Land

Mapping Carceral Power across Neoliberal America

Brett Story

University of Minnesota Press
Minneapolis | London

The University of Minnesota Press gratefully acknowledges the generous assistance provided for the publication of this book by the Margaret S. Harding Memorial Endowment, honoring the first director of the University of Minnesota Press.

Portions of chapters 1 and 2 were published in "'The Prison and the City: Tracking the Neoliberal Life of the 'Million Dollar Block,'" *Theoretical Criminology* 20, no. 3 (2016): 257–76. Portions of chapter 1 were published in "Against a Humanizing Prison Cinema: *The Prison in Twelve Landscapes* and the Politics of Abolition Imagery," in *The Visual Criminology Handbook*, ed. M. Brown and E. Carrabine, 455–66 (London: Routledge, 2017). Portions of chapter 3 were published in B. Story and J. Schept, "Against Punishment: Centering Work, Wage, and Uneven Development in Mapping the Carceral State," *Social Justice: A Journal of Crime, Conflict, and World Order* 46 (forthcoming in 2019).

Published by the University of Minnesota Press
111 Third Avenue South, Suite 290
Minneapolis, MN 55401-2520
upress.umn.edu

Printed in the United States of America on acid-free paper

The University of Minnesota is an equal-opportunity educator and employer.

26 25 24 23 22 21 20 19   10 9 8 7 6 5 4 3 2 1

Library of Congress Cataloging-in-Publication Data
Names: Story, Brett, author.
Title: Prison land : mapping carceral power across neoliberal America / Brett Story.
Description: Minneapolis : University of Minnesota Press, 2019. | Includes bibliographical references and index. |
Identifiers: LCCN 2018045509 (print) | ISBN 978-1-5179-0687-0 (hc) | ISBN 978-1-5179-0688-7 (pb)
Subjects: LCSH: Prisons—United States. | Prisons—Canada. | Discrimination in criminal justice administration—United States. | Discrimination in criminal justice administration—Canada. | Corrections—Political aspects—United States. | Corrections—Political aspects—Canada. | Capitalism—United States. | Capitalism—Canada. | BISAC: SOCIAL SCIENCE / Penology. | SOCIAL SCIENCE / Human Geography. | SOCIAL SCIENCE / Anthropology / Cultural.
Classification: LCC HV9471 .S843 2019 (print) | DDC 365/.973—dc23
LC record available at https://lccn.loc.gov/2018045509

For birdie

Contents

Preface

I came to the prison, at first, indirectly. Not through arrest or conviction at all, but through eviction. The first time I was evicted, it was the mid-1980s and I was a child living in Toronto with my mother, a single parent on social assistance. We shared a bedroom in a house with a group of other, mostly low income, women. The real estate market in our neighborhood had just begun heating up, and the collective rent paid by the tenants in our house didn't match what other apartments in the neighborhood were starting to rent for. So our landlord took advantage of a loophole in the municipal rent-control rules to evict all of us. Modest single-family homes in that same neighborhood now sell for millions of dollars.

Almost twenty years later, I found myself facing eviction again, under similar circumstances, though as a student rather than as a child. I'd moved to Montreal in the late 1990s, just as its independent music scene was exploding and the hangover of Quebec separatism still guaranteed cheap rents for working people, artists, and activists. The province's flight risk (manifested as late as 1995 in a province-wide referendum on independence from Canada) made the terrain too unstable for real-estate capital, which was good news for everyone I knew. It meant we could work part-time jobs and spend our *real* time doing political organizing, making art, and building community. But that eventually started to change, and the real estate developers descended. When my landlord evicted my roommates and me in a legally suspect move with echoes of the eviction I'd faced as child, I decided to make a film about gentrification and its consequences.

During this period, my social activism also became more closely focused on access to housing and on challenging the displacement of the poor and working-class from Montreal's downtown core. In trying to make sense of how the city was transforming, I discovered the scholarship of radical geographers, and particularly the work of gentrification theorist Neil Smith. Through organizing and studying, I came to understand the two evictions of my life not as a coincidence, nor as a consequence of personal failure, but as expressions of capital. I learned how to read the city itself as a landscape of power, and I began to make alliances with others whose experiences of poverty, often bound up with structural racism, conditioned their vulnerability vis-à-vis both the state and the market.

One cannot organize against housing displacement and urban gentrification without confronting, almost immediately, the role of the police in urban space. My little personal film about eviction became, necessarily, a bigger story about urban policing, about the criminalization of poverty and homelessness, and about the power of real estate capital in determining who gets to be in certain spaces and who doesn't. When police swept up homeless people and used new laws against panhandling to move or jail them, it was at the behest of the tourism industry or a condo developer, or both. I had not encountered the prison directly, but I was face to face with the processes of urban class conquest, for which the revanchist technologies of police and prisons are often put to work. This seemingly indirect route is also the path taken by this book, which proposes that we examine the U.S. prison system from the external geographies that fuel its reproduction and its growth.

There is a long history within geography of demystifying everyday landscapes, excavating the forces, relations, and structures of power hidden within a given spatial field. I remember first reading the geographer David Harvey describe how construction cranes in the urban skyline tell us how capital is moving through real estate in the form of new building development, thus signaling the importance (or lack thereof) of that particular city to the global economy. I now see construction cranes along a skyline differently from how I did before; they've lost their innocence. Similarly, when economic geographer Ruth Wilson Gilmore describes prisons as partial geographical solutions to political crises, she is asking us to take seriously the *spatial* dimensions of the prison industrial complex (where prisons are built, for example, or where prisoners come from) as clues pointing to the actual crises (rooted in capitalism), rather than the spurious crisis (so-called "crime," or lawlessness) for which prisons are claimed as deputized solutions. Space, it turns out, matters a great deal. The work of these thinkers, foundational to my own analysis and activism, underscores the importance of geography (of landscape, of territory, of spatial processes and relationships) not just as an object of study, but as a *method* of investigation, as a way into thinking differently about the present condition, including the role of the prison within the landscape of our social order.

I am a geographer by academic training, but a nonfiction filmmaker by practice. From 2014 to 2016, while researching and writing this book, I made a feature-length documentary film called *The Prison in Twelve Landscapes.* The formal conceit of the film is simple: it is a film about the U.S. prison system in which you never (or almost never) see a prison. Constructed as a series of twelve vignettes that unfold across the diverse geographies of American life—a coalfield, a wildfire, a chess park, a long-distance bus—the film invites audiences to think about the prison spatially and systematically, as an institution both produced out of, and productive of the forces that govern and organize the existing social and economic order. It is a film less about crime and criminal justice than about racial capitalism and its consequences as dispersed across the landscapes we inhabit and call home.

The film was released publically in the spring of 2016 and was, to my surprise (given its formal premise and political orientation), something of a success as far as these things go. Reviewed favorably by the *New York Times* (where it was a critics' pick), nominated for a Canadian Screen Award, and broadcast on prime-time television on PBS's *Independent Lens* series, the film has gone on to screen everywhere from church basements to law schools and from art galleries to penitentiary classrooms. I'd like to think the film has resonated so widely because what it tries to say and, certainly, what it tries to ask are matters of common sense: Why *do* we lock so many people up? Who bears the consequences? What interests does the prison serve? That the answers to these questions lead to at least an incipient abolitionist politics, opening up a way of imagining a society that can exist without prisons and other like structures of violence, is my greatest hope.

It is important to point out that the film emerged alongside this book and in collaboration with it. The questions asked and the methodologies developed in the making of these two artifacts are necessarily bound up with one another, even as their final forms differ. In some cases, the methodological overlap is overt. Many of the interviews I conducted for the film and the scenes that I observed alongside my cinematographer make their way into the chapters that follow (with the permission of their subjects, of course). For example, when I travelled to eastern Kentucky in the summer of 2014, it was with a small film crew and at the invitation of justice scholar Judah Schept, whom I'd met at an academic conference in Tennessee the previous year. Just as there is a chapter in this book on coal decline and prison construction in eastern Kentucky, there is also a section in the film that visualizes the dreams of the region's workers as they are animated by the promise of a prison boom. In other cases, the relationship between the writing and the filmmaking unfolded in the reverse. For example, it was after travelling the route to Attica on a chartered bus for visitors from New York a number of times, as fieldwork for this book, that I decided to ask some of the people I met whether I might bring along a camera and film the journey. That footage now opens and closes the film.

Nonfiction filmmaking and geographic inquiry have much in common: they are both endeavors invested in questions of seeing. Specifically, each asks how we see, and might see differently, the world that we make and that in turn makes us. The realm of representation is a fraught one, and the work of aesthetics, in its original meaning as "perception through feeling," is intimately tied to the reproduction or transformation of hegemonic ideas. For me as a filmmaker, there are the questions of what is unseen and how cinema might be harnessed to reveal it or help us see it differently, and then there is the problem of what *is* seen, and what all that seeing does or doesn't do. The artist Trevor Paglen, also a geographer, has described his photographs of the so-called "black world" of classified defense activity as a kind of counterimagery. He speaks of his practice as trying to push vision and perception as far as possible, even to the point where it starts to break down. He describes trying to create new vantage points that we can use to look back at ourselves with different kinds of eyes.

Within conventional prison documentaries, the task of making the problem of incarceration evident is almost always conceived of and executed as the production of images *of* and *within* the prison itself, as if there were no other way of making the prison or its captive subjects visible, and as if visibility involved nothing more than the state of being able to see and be seen. This has always frustrated me. Over and over again in many of these films, one is offered the terrible inside of a cell, a caged black man or woman, and a story of innocence, redemption, or excess suffering (or all three). However emotionally moving they might be, I wonder what we learn from these films other than how a few people might be rescued, in our imaginations and occasionally in real life. Conceiving of the solution to the invisibility of incarceration and the disappearance of prisoners as simply a matter of exposing the prison's internal scenery does little to denaturalize the prison as a reified fact on the ground of modern capitalist life, nor does it upset the carceral order as a legitimate system of social differentiation. Worse, a visual focus on the human in a cage can limit our very ability to grasp the social relations, historical processes, and material logics that come to bear on the prison regime's existence and its continuation.

What is at stake in both the making of a film and the writing of a book is the construction of popular knowledge about the functions of the capitalist state and the legitimacy of its most oppressive institutions and activities. Political transformation has always required multiple strategies and forms of intervention, including rigorous scholarship and disobedient art. I have been a life-long participant in and student of social movements and continue to learn from freedom fighters, both inside and out. Both the film and this book are offered as small contributions to the long struggle they and we are engaged in, the struggle against poverty and racism, forced confinement and forced migration, and the exploitation of labor and of land. The struggle for freedom is a struggle not just against cages, but against a society that could have cages. Let us look everywhere, so that we can act anywhere.

Introduction
The Prison out of Place

Anyone who has ever struggled with poverty knows how extremely expensive it is to be poor.

—JAMES BALDWIN

Samantha Jenkins, a fifty-year-old African American woman from Missouri, once stole two steaks from a local grocery store in the city of Jennings, a small town just seven miles outside of St. Louis. She was homeless and she was hungry. Over the next fifteen years, Jenkins would be arrested and incarcerated in the Jennings jail nineteen separate times, all for that one theft. Having accrued a court fine that she was unable to pay, she was arrested over and over again, accumulating new court fines in the process, which in turn begot new arrest warrants. In and out of the overcrowded and unsanitary local jail, denied legal defense and refused forgiveness on her debt, Jenkins repeatedly lost jobs and lost homes, caught in a never-ending cycle of poverty fines that ended only when she became the lead plaintiff on a landmark settlement in 2016 that saw the city of Jennings pay out $4.7 million to over 2000 class members. The city was found to be locking people up illegally, in contravention of a 1983 U.S. Supreme Court ruling that declared that incarcerating someone for being unable to pay his or her debt is unconstitutional.

One of over ninety small municipalities carved into the outer suburbs of St. Louis, Jennings is a majority-black subdivision of 15,000 people, forged out of redlining and other discriminatory housing policies that embedded racial segregation into the postwar landscape of greater St. Louis. Zoning rules that classified white neighborhoods as residential and black areas as industrial or commercial, that segregated public housing projects from whites-only real-estate markets, and that bulldozed through predominantly African American neighborhoods in the name of urban renewal have, over the past century, produced one of the most highly balkanized greater municipal areas in the nation. Municipal boundary lines, some of them enforced by actual street barriers like large concrete balls or gates, formalize class and racial segregation, ensuring the non-distribution of resources and tax revenues among the dozens of discreet "towns" of St. Louis County. These towns range in population from thirteen residents to over 50,000, together forming a patchwork of what the urban historian Colin Gordon calls "postage-stamp municipalities." They are situated so close together that a person driving a four-mile stretch of one major road would pass through eight separate cities. Each of these municipalities is likely to have their own police force.

Public attention became newly directed onto these small, otherwise seemingly nondescript communities, like Jenkins's home of Jennings, late into the summer of 2014, when a young black man named Michael Brown was shot dead by a local police officer in the adjacent St. Louis County suburb of Ferguson. Brown's was one of a number of high-profile deaths of African Americans at the hands of police to spark public outrage that year. As protests erupted in Ferguson and its neighboring communities and international media descended on the area, reports began to circulate about a systemic practice of overpolicing in the most economically neglected of these subdivisions. Like elsewhere, middle-class white flight and economic deindustrialization are at the root of some of this woe, but local tax policy also figures prominently as a key cause of the area's financial problems.

Municipal tax revenue in St. Louis County is limited by the Missouri constitution, specifically a clause called the "Hancock Amendment." The amendment was written in 1980 by the founder of a group called the Taxpayer Survival Association, Representative Mel Hancock, and radically *limits* the ability of local municipalities to raise money through taxes, even from commercial enterprises. Any increase of local taxes must be approved by a city-wide referendum, which has proven difficult at best. So constrained, local governments turned to a more reliable source of local revenue: their traffic cops. Each equipped with its own municipal code, its own police force, and its own court, many of these communities, including Jennings and Ferguson, now lean heavily on municipal fines to fill their public coffers, systematically incentivizing a widening net of po-

Traffic stops and police fines are frequent occurrences in St. Louis County municipalities. Photograph by Maya Bankovic.

lice crackdowns on the most minor and anachronistic of offenses (Balko 2014b). Finable infractions include driving with a suspended license, failing to provide proof of insurance, and being found in a residence without an occupancy permit on hand.

Defense attorneys in the St. Louis area call these "poverty violations" and describe how it is the region's poor black residents who bear the economic brunt of this extractive system of municipal financing (Balko 2014a). Because indigent defendants are not provided with public defenders, many of those who do not have the resources to pay their fines avoid showing up in court at all out of fear of the penal repercussions. Police are then legally able to issue an arrest warrant, setting off a chain of events that can lead to jail time. In 2014, the city of Jennings issued an average of more than 2.1 arrest warrants per household, mostly in cases involving unpaid debt for tickets. In Ferguson the same year, the police handed out an average of three arrest warrants per household (Drum 2014). Municipalities may also imprison individuals for ordinance violations and keep them detained until the fine and cost of the suit against them are paid, a practice tantamount to running debtors' prisons. In Jennings, over 2,000 people languished nearly 9,000 days in the city jail during 2015 solely because they were not able to pay traffic tickets and court fines.

The town of Ferguson became a flashpoint for the Black Lives Matter movement and a metonym for the national epidemic of state violence against black individuals and communities. But the suburban munici- palities of St. Louis County, including Ferguson and Jennings, also call our attention to the complex racial geographies of what I in this book call "carceral space": the sites and relations of power that enable and incentiv- ize the systematic capture, control, and confinement of human beings through structures of immobility and dispossession. In other words, the local geography conditions carceral practices, including police harass- ment, arrest and court proceedings, and incarceration, in various ways. Indeed, the modern debtors' prisons that proliferate throughout the towns of St. Louis County are made possible by a historical alignment of policies, forces, and crises that coalesced to produce a particular socio- economic landscape and organize the relations that govern life within it. Those relations include private property, work and waged labor, and race and racism. The space produced out of these forces in Ferguson and its neighboring communities is one in which police harassment, court bu- reaucracy, and the specter of detention dominate the conditions of life for local residents. Questions of where and why people live where they do, what resources are made available or taken away from them, and who is rendered vulnerable to state injury are written into the very power re- lations that design and govern this inhabited landscape.

The ways space is organized, used, and rendered meaningful are al- ways socially determined. Critical geographers have long argued that the spatial organization of everyday life is a social product arising from and mutually constitutive of purposeful social practice.[1] What this means is that space is political *and* ideological. It conveys existing power dynam- ics and the governing logics that make sense of them, and it also struc- tures those dynamics into being. As David Harvey puts it, "Space and the political organization of space express social relationships but also react back upon them" (1973, 306). To examine the determination of space, therefore, is to ask how power operates materially and ideologi- cally within society, to demystify the social relations that organize every- day life and inhabited space, and to critically deconstruct the historical contingencies that condition the present situation.

To return to the example of Ferguson, then, the story of so-called incidental or exceptional police violence that emerged after the death of

Brown can be recast as a broader narrative about penal infrastructure and the very production of carceral space. The political economy of St. Louis County's urban landscape—how these municipalities came to be in the first place, how resources are distributed among them, why police are so powerful here, and who is adversely effected by their interventions—exposes the kinds of social and economic relations that actually underwrite the local penal system. Here, tax policy and the racial vagaries of residential zoning are as salient to the production of carceral control as are the so-called criminal-justice-system or public-safety concerns, if not more so. St. Louis County offers a point of departure, then, for investigating the kinds of social relations that produce and reproduce the carceral regime across the United States more broadly.

By "social relations," I refer specifically to the relations of power over the productive forces in society. If the forces of production are the technologies, inputs, materials, and tools we use to transform nature, then the relations tell us how people fit into those processes. Social relations tell us, for example, how people relate to each other vis-à-vis the ownership and control of productive assets, who works for whom, and who controls and benefits from the surplus created. The social relations that organize contemporary life in the United States are, of course, capitalist relations, and the prison system, as a mechanism of control and discipline increasingly central to the state's operations, can be understood as an expression of, and means of enforcing, those relations.

While the term "mass incarceration" is most often invoked to indicate the proliferation of structures of captivity and the inflation of the prison population, one core argument of this book is that mass incarceration also points to how the U.S. carceral system has become increasingly bound up in matters of finance, electoral politics, land use, racial ordering, labor deregulation, citizenship, gender governance, and urban restructuring, among other processes. In other words, the prison is more than just a building or the numbers of people inside that building, but rather, as many have established, a robust and extensive "industrial complex" that is fully implicated in the functioning of the contemporary capitalist economy. As its influence as a structure of power has grown, its complex interrelationships with other social systems and power relations, from real-estate finance to union deregulation, have also deepened.

It follows, then, that any productive analysis of the prison system's functions, meaning what it is actually doing as a central institution of the contemporary U.S. state, requires a broadening of the political and social fields within which it is normally examined.

Prison Land attempts to expand the boundaries within which we assess the criminal-justice system by restaging the prison as a set of relationships dispersed across a set of landscapes we don't always view or conceive of as carceral. It is precisely because relationships are necessarily made up of contingencies that mapping their complex geographies can be so useful to social struggle. I try to do some of that mapping by casting carceral space as encompassing the whole continuum of relationships that make up the prison system: from the sites of criminalization, arrest, and conviction to the landscapes of building construction; from zones of immobility and social control to the spaces deployed for the forced circulation and transfer of bodies. Yet it also encompasses something broader than these penal nodes. Carceral space constitutes those very social relations and geographic practices through which the state's capacities of containment, displacement, and dispossession are put to work for "racial capitalism," a term that acknowledges that, insofar as capitalism requires inequality to function as a system of exploitation, it has always also relied on racial categories to enshrine that inequality as natural rather than produced (Robinson 1983). The U.S. capitalist state's dramatic investment in its carceral machinery over the past half century has less to do with crime and criminals per se than it does with broader social dynamics in the economy and race relations. These dynamics and relations are always at once spatialized and spatializing, and it is to their complex geographies that this book turns its gaze.

Directing our attention to a set of carceral spaces as understood here, this book offers a new framework for thinking about the role of the prison in the contemporary social order. The spaces examined in the following chapters are themselves "produced" in the sense that they are manifestations of social constructions and practices (see Smith 1984; Lefebvre 1974), but they are also productive of a capitalist order in which prisons are increasingly "what the growing neoliberal state is made of" (Gilmore and Gilmore 2008, 143). The neoliberal state is itself an evolving entity, and thus this book suggests we look to the spaces *beyond* the penitentiary in order to comprehend it and the work of carceral logics and practices more broadly.

Prison Land situates its investigation in the unfolding and contradictory present of the post-2008 financial recession, as state budgetary crises across the United States fueled bipartisan initiatives for cost-cutting penal reforms. Throughout these pages, I return to the question of whether these reforms portend the demise of the carceral state, or simply its repackaging. To answer this question, I propose that we take an expansive view of what constitutes carceral space by uncoupling the prison from both crime and punishment in the analytic imaginary and by interrogating the less visible social relations by which carceral space both manages life and makes that life disposable. Framing the prison as a set of relations allows us to ask about the production of new carceral forms and correlative carceral practices across the landscape of contemporary reform efforts. To that end, it is worth briefly looking back at the long relationship between reform, place, and space in the evolution of the U.S. prison system.

Rethinking Prison and Place

Place has always been central to what a prison is, and to what it does. Developed in the United States at the turn of the nineteenth century, between the Revolution and the Civil War, the modern penitentiary system was premised from its very inception on the dedication of a discrete locale for systematic punishment. Up until this time, the state's interventions against those found guilty of lawbreaking consisted primarily of corporal punishments, usually floggings or executions, enacted out in the open and within full view of the sovereign's subjects. These subjects were the intended audience. It was to instill in them a fear of the state and obedience to the law that the offender's body was publicly displayed while the wrath of the sovereign performed violently upon it. Not all, however, went as planned. Officials began to notice that these public acts of corporal brutality would often produce an inadvertent effect on the crowds who gathered to take in their spectacle. Witnesses would become riled up, unruly, and even riotous. Worse yet, that rowdy collective energy would sometimes be infused with a *sympathy* toward the condemned subject, rather than the antipathy anticipated by the punishing state (Foucault 1977; Smith 2011b).

Openly displayed bodily punishment was facing its own crisis of legitimacy, as the Enlightenment period in Western Europe and the new republic heralded humanist ideas about the redeemability of certain subjects. The era's governing elites, increasingly anxious about growing sympathy among the poor for the penalized and the possibility of common cause among them, joined with Enlightenment thinkers in imagining a new apparatus for the meting out of state punishment. The penitentiary as a *place*, by which I mean a discrete and enclosed architecture of confinement, was subsequently introduced in Philadelphia and then in Auburn, New York, with the deliberate intent of taking the practice of penality out of the public square and relocating it somewhere *less visible*. The emergent penitentiary form served, at least partly, to foreclose the risk of public sympathy by hiding the violence of the state behind closed doors and high walls. Thus concealed, criminals could continue to be represented to other sections of the possibly empathetic poor as dangerous and wicked, neutralizing their potential alliance.

The built form and urban siting of the penitentiary served a secondary function as well. The edifices themselves were designed to operate as terrorizing public spectacles for those on the outside. The literary historian Caleb Smith describes how the awesome gothic facades of Eastern State Penitentiary in Philadelphia, for example, were crafted to elicit the fear and dread one might have in relation to the dungeons of the old world, even as the prison reformers who championed this new system wanted to describe what was happening inside them in Enlightenment terms of humane correction (Smith 2011a). The nonincarcerated subjects of the new republic were meant to encounter the prison edifice regularly in their everyday movement throughout the city and be both menaced and disciplined by the penitentiary's specter of terror.

At the same time, the prison has always been much more than just a place. The nineteenth-century emergence of the penitentiary as a system of punishment signaled a new era in American state-building, one in which the prison would play a pivotal role as an apparatus for subject production. Much of this disciplinary work was (and is) elided by the reformist agenda that conjured the penitentiary into being in the first place. Couched in terms of "humanism" and "correction" by the penitentiary's Enlightenment champions, the prison's revolutionary promise was the rehabilitation of those who had broken the law. But as Foucault demonstrated so keenly, such reformation was itself premised on the prison's function as a technique of subject formation and social control, materially and ideologically hewed to the emergent ontologies of citizenship, individualism, and the market within the new republic. The prison emerged in service to a transforming industrial capitalist economy not simply as a humane alternative to beatings and executions, but through its very production of docile, individuated, and disciplined subjects. Changes in the penitentiary's form and function have since kept apace with the changing imperatives of the capitalist state. So, while the earliest ideals of the nineteenth-century prison architects fused seamlessly with proto-industrial ideas about the laboring self, the American prison's heyday of rehabilitation would correspond, in the mid-twentieth century, to the full maturation of the Fordist economy and Keynesian state. As Angela Davis puts it, "the process through which imprisonment developed into the primary mode of state-inflicted punishment was very much related to the rise of capitalism and to the appearance of a new set of ideological conditions" (2003, 43). Its apogee, under the mantle of what is now known widely as mass incarceration, has been reached alongside the ascendance and entrenchment of neoliberal capitalist restructuring over the past four decades of American life.

It is precisely in its deep imbrication with the emergent capitalist state over two centuries that Davis, Ruth Wilson Gilmore, and other prison activists and scholars urge us to think of the prison not as simply an edifice, as a place made up of walls and cells and mess halls, but to conceive it as a *set of relationships*. It is this characterization of the prison that this book takes up and elaborates in its case studies. *Prison Land* offers a geographic investigation—a journey across place and space—into the functions and consequences of the social relations that constitute the prison. These relations include property, work, gender, and race, enacted and expressed across various landscapes in American economic and political life. It is the ways in which these relationships organize everyday existence in the United States that make the prison possible, but not inevitable.

This book thus attempts to *displace* the prison in two senses. First, it proposes an array of places and spaces outside the penitentiary's walls that help disclose the functions and consequences of the contemporary prison regime. Second, it demonstrates how the frameworks tradition-ally used to think about the prison and its functions (the place of the prison in our imaginaries) are inadequate to the task of comprehending the prison's role in American society, and thus to *unthinking* its necessity in our lives.

Each of the book's central case studies asks what it means to consider the prison not merely as a building or a place indexed to the ostensibly closed circuit of crime and punishment, but rather as a structure of power whose influence is spatialized across the uneven geographies of the nation. In each, I ask how the prison intersects with and upholds other structures of power and to what end it does so for the current neo-liberal social order. By geographically excavating the relationships that render the prison system productive for neoliberalism in particular, the book attempts to deconstruct the very function and necessity of the prison in our lives. It is, in other words, an attempt to rethink the very *place* of the prison in the American political and economic landscape, precisely so that we can begin thinking of life beyond it.

To this end, *Prison Land* reconsiders what constitutes carceral space and how it functions to both produce and manage social inequities in late-capitalist American life. Carceral space is explored as a complex ge-ography, one that inscribes the production of racialized poverty, social control, and devalued life into its everyday sociospatial relations. The book investigates the production of carceral power at various sites, from long-distance buses to rural coalfields and from cities in decline to finan-cial urban hubs, in order to demonstrate how the organization of carceral space is ideologically and materially grounded in the neoliberal restruc-turings of racial capitalism. In so doing, it challenges both the "common sense"[2] idea of prisons as simply responses to the problem of crime and affective attachments to *punishment* as the relevant measure of a trans-formed criminal-justice system. The different cases studied all demon-strate that the production of disposability and surplus life is an active process, racially coded through the shifting category of the criminal and spatialized in a range of mutable and contested places and forms.

Incarceration is certainly made possible in part because some lives have been rendered systematically superfluous to the formal labor mar-ket (Peck and Theodore 2008; Wacquant 2009a) and ungrievable within the public imagination (Butler 2004). Yet carceral space, I argue, also *contributes* to the construction of disposable people in our social worlds.

The production of the "criminal" as a racialized category of so-called indisputable depravity provides powerful legitimizing cover for the making of surplus populations and socially differentiating them. This occurs even while carceral spaces do all kinds of work that bears little actual relation to so-called crime or its resolution.

Today, criminal status consigns some people to informal and hyperexploited labor markets and marks some bodies as legitimate targets of state and vigilante violence, abandonment, and dispossession, while it also categorically divides the poorest and most oppressed people against each other (Linebaugh 2004). It further serves as a powerful vehicle of ongoing racialization in the ostensibly "postracial" era, enshrining racialized disentitlement as *natural* and *legitimate* insofar as individuals can be seen to have brought it upon themselves by their own ostensibly deviant actions, behaviors, or choices. The criminal is a paradigmatic category of disposability in capitalist democracies precisely because the ideology of neoliberalism makes it so hard to divest from the economy of individualized responsibility and accountability. This may be why the category of innocence has such purchase within liberal reform movements: it is a way of rescuing some, and thus attenuating aggregate harm, without actually challenging the underlying premise of responsibilized and individualized subjecthood.

At its broadest, this book is about the production and operation of carceral spaces as landscapes of power, but it is also about the work of carceral space in managing the social fragmentation of those at the lowest echelons of the neoliberal social order. The demolition of racialized sociality is one important part of this story and is intimately related to the historical production of black "criminality" (Muhammad 2011). The ideology of black criminality finds reinforcement in analytic frameworks that treat the criminal-justice system as a kind of closed circuit of laws and policies within which tautological claims and logics (for example, that the prison is a response to crime and that crime is performed by individuals) tend to circulate unchallenged. Examining the prison not as a *place* but as a set of relations, in contrast, serves to upend the crime-and-punishment dialectic as the putative centerpiece of the penal order. In this way, the book attempts to offer a new framework for understanding the work that prisons do and then for imagining how things might be otherwise.

What Is the Work That Prisons Do?
Neoliberalism and the Spatial Turn

The scene from which this book emerges is the scene of penal space in the late-capitalist era of mass incarceration. This period runs from about 1973 onward in the United States and is characterized broadly by the roll-back of the Keynesian welfare functions of the state, deindustrialization, deregulation of the labor market and the stagnation of workers' wages, revanchist restructuring of urban space, and the unprecedented expansion in the number of prisons and of prisoners.

The U.S. prison population began climbing in 1973 and rose dramatically over the next forty years. By 1985, the number of people behind bars had doubled to 740,000. Over the course of the 1990s, America saw an unprecedented average annual growth of nearly 8 percent, leading it to surpass the 2 million mark in 2000 (Wacquant 2009a, 60). Today, the number of people imprisoned in the country's jails and prisons hovers around 2.2 million. The United States has the highest rate of incarceration in the world, and its rush to incarcerate has progressed along profoundly racialized contours. No other country in the world imprisons so many of its racial or ethnic minorities.

The past half century of spectacular prison expansion is also the period of neoliberalism's ascendance and entrenchment across the industrialized West. The term neoliberalism describes a particular set of transformations in the organization of free-market capitalism, and as a project, it bundles a variety of policies and practices. Forged as an attack on the Keynesian welfarist state, and flourishing in its wreckage from the 1970s onward, neoliberalism heralded the construction of new institutional forms and regulatory conventions designed to secure and extend "market rule" into all realms of life (Peck 2003, 224). Neoliberalism also constitutes an active zone of experimentation, spatial restructuring, and ritualization of "individual responsibility" in all spheres. The buildup of the state's criminalization and incarceration mechanisms over the period of neoliberalism's advancement has been essential to securing such experiments and to managing their social costs and damages (McNally 2011).

Scholars have by now well demonstrated that the phenomenon of exploding incarceration rates and the ascendance of neoliberal policies and rationalities in American life are correlative rather than coincidental. As techniques of state dominance have shifted decisively in the neoliberal era, the period has given birth to what Bernard Harcourt (2010) terms "neoliberal penality": a particular mode of crisis abatement wherein market deregulation and the delegitimation of state entitlements are secured through the expanded deployment of carceral interventions and institutions. Noah De Lissovoy similarly posits the "carceral turn" of the past four decades as a central expression of neoliberal culture: "Networks of solidarity and obligations to the vulnerable are replaced by a culture of blame and externalization . . . . In this process, structural crises and contradictions are reinterpreted in moralistic terms, as the proper neoliberal subject recognizes itself through its exclusions of the pathologized other" (2012, 740).

The institutions of prisons and policing of course have a long history of managing the poor and disciplining waged labor under the sign of the market. Criminalization has been actively deployed as a mechanism for both capital accumulation and the production of social differentiation along axes of race, class, and gender since at least the nineteenth century (Linebaugh 2004; Muhammad 2011). In the neoliberal period, however, such work has intensified and become even more central to the state's facilitation of market rule. Criminalization functions to absorb the social wreckage wrought by neoliberal policies by displacing state violence onto responsibilized and disciplined individuals while simultaneously serving to uphold the neoliberal myth of state retreat. Everywhere in the world that economic inequality has increased, prison space has expanded, and this is especially true in the United States. And there is less sympathy for the homeless mother who steals food or the poor teen who runs drugs within a worldview that upholds the individual's ultimate responsibility for their own material well-being rather than assigning this role to the state or to society.

Attempts to explain mass incarceration in the United States are by now numerous, spanning multiple disciplines and analytical approaches (see, for example: Garland 2001; Simon 2003; Gottschalk 2006). In recent years, however, geographers and other spatial theorists grounded in historical-materialist research methods have made some of the most insightful connections between prisons and capitalism generally, and between mass incarceration and neoliberalism in particular. Characterizing prisons as "partial geographic solutions to political economic crisis, organized by the state, which itself is in crisis," Gilmore's *Golden Gulag* heralded an emerging field of carceral geography (2007, 26), out of which we have seen increasing attention paid to the spatialities of prison siting (Bonds 2009; Norton 2016), state restructuring and labor market management (Peck and Theodore 2008), and urban social control (Parenti 1999; Camp 2016). These scholars have generated important insights into the work that prisons do by couching their inquiries in increasingly geographic terms. It turns out that asking questions about *where* yields remarkably insightful answers to the question of *why*.

When one asks, for example, *where* the majority of the nation's prisoners come from, most roads lead back to the metropolis. Indeed, one place to begin an investigation into mass incarceration is the city and the structural homologies between urban redevelopment and prison expansion over at least the past forty years. Beginning in the late 1960s and early 1970s, states and cities across the United States were hit by dual economic and social crises: a series of economic recessions that rocked the country, on the one hand, and increased social and racial unrest, most dramatically manifest in urban rebellions, on the other. Emerging out of this period, President Nixon's 1970 "war on crime" focused explicitly on the poor, racialized populations of the nation's major cities, constructing them as a social problem by conflating black men in particular with criminality. Urban restructuring and prison expansion from this era onward constituted duel spatial strategies for addressing these intersecting urban crises (Parenti 1999; Gilmore 2007; Camp 2016).

With the decline of Fordist manufacturing economies in many American cities, the reconfiguration of industrial capitalism through what Harvey (1990) calls "flexible accumulation" and the uneven ascendance of urban economies organized primarily around finance, real estate, and the service sector, large segments of the workforce historically contained in the "black belts" of major metropoles were rendered economically redundant (Wacquant 2002, 48). Expanded prison space in the neoliberal period, the sociologist Loïc Wacquant argues, served "to warehouse the precarious and deproletarianized fractions of the black working class, be it that they cannot find employment or are underemployed" (2002, 53). Wacquant thus suggests that the urban ghetto and the prison constitute a "carceral continuum" with shared functions vis-à-vis surplus labor and the production of race. Relatedly, Jamie Peck and Nik Theodore (2008) have analyzed the labor-market impacts of mass incarceration in the more recent period, arguing that the twenty-first-century prison functions institutionally not only to manage but also to *produce* systemic unemployability across a criminalized class of African American men in particular.

As cities in the neoliberal period have restructured increasingly along revanchist terms (Smith 1996), the emergence of interurban competition for corporate investment, real-estate speculation, and luxury consumption has ushered in a flurry of new punitive ordinances and spatial exclusions in U.S. cities across the country. The rise of new forms of urban sociospatial exclusion, strategies of urban policing, and tactics for criminalizing "undesirable" urban populations (Davis 1990; Harcourt 2001; Beckett and Herbert 2008) mark the emergence of what has been termed the "punitive neo-liberal city" (Herbert and Brown 2006). Beginning in the 1990s, for example, "broken windows policing" and civility laws were introduced as part of the broader coercive project of eliminating hindrances to downtown revitalization efforts. These new legal tools and techniques have increased the criminalization and social control of poor, often black and brown individuals and communities across urban space.

Within this picture of urban restructuring and the coercive management of urban poverty, the state has been ever-present, even while elided by the neoliberal myth of the state's retreat. While prison privatization has figured as a popular bogeyman of left critique, the overwhelming majority of prisons and jails in the United States are actually *public* institutions financially underwritten and organized by the state. To ask why, then, the state undertook such an expansion of its organizational and financial capacity to arrest, forcibly remove, and then immobilize mass numbers of people from the early 1970s onward, one must ask how the state itself was transforming during this period. This was the period in which neoliberalism began to ascend as the dominant mode and rationality governing social relations.

The state, in the formulation of Stuart Hall and his collaborators, building on the work of Antonio Gramsci, "is not so much an entity, or even a particular complex of institutions, so much as it is a particular site or level of the social formation" (1978, 205). They make the case that the state should be conceived less as a *thing* and more as an *organizer*. It organizes capacity in the sense that it puts capacity—financial, political, ideological, and logistical—into force. In terms of the state's relationship to capitalism and class power, Hall et al. argue: "[The state is] the key instrument which enlarged the narrow *rule* of a particular class into a 'universal' class leadership and authority over the whole social formation. Its 'task' is to secure this broadening and generalizing of class power, while ensuring also the stability and cohesion of the social *ensemble*" (1978, 204; emphasis in original).

This conception of the state helps us bring into focus the character and condition of something that scholars of the prison system have come to call the "carceral state" (Gottschalk 2015) or the "penal state" (Peck 2003). Simply put, the carceral state is a state restructured and expanded through its punishment and criminalization functions. The expansion of prisons and the criminalization mechanisms that lead to imprisonment are politically organized as well as underwritten by the state, which is itself in the process of radical restructuring. The concept of the carceral state thus refers to the state as it has *remade itself* using the newly vast prison system's coercive powers (Gilmore and Gilmore 2008).

The upward march of incarceration rates in America beginning in 1973 maps onto a period in which the state began to shed its role as welfare provider and employment broker. As a consequence of this withdrawal, the post-Keynesian state faced a growing crisis of legitimacy for which a buildup of its military and punishment infrastructures (themselves premised on the claim of new threats from which the public required state protection) became the favored solution. The mission of the state became redefined: its social welfare functions were diminished while its coercive and penal capacities were expanded and intensified. In Peck's words, "in terms of the regulation of poverty and poor subjects, this is not less government but *different* government" (2003, 224). As the state's resources have been redistributed toward its policing and incarceration apparatuses, its legitimacy has been purchased through its promise to punish.

Rather than constituting a state in retreat, the neoliberal state might be better characterized as an "anti-state state:" a state that *grows* on the *promise* of shrinking (Gilmore and Gilmore 2008). Indeed, the myth of the state in retreat is belied by the money alone: in the United States, state expenditure at all scales (federal, state, and local) has increased as a percentage of GDP by approximately 10 percent (from about 30 percent of GDP to about 33 percent) since the beginning of the nation's prison-building boom in the early 1970s (Gilmore and Gilmore 2008, 146). According to a 2008 study by the Pew Center on the States, prison spending by the nation has outpaced all other comparable spending budgets except Medicaid, based on federal and state data (Harcourt 2010, 85).

As Ruth Wilson Gilmore and Craig Gilmore write, "prisons are symptomatic and emblematic of anti-state state-building" (2008, 142). They are the product of increased state power under the mythology of a downsized state apparatus. To this end, anti-state state-building might be itself characterized as emblematic of globalized capitalism and the crises and instabilities endemic to an economic system constantly in search of new terrain for growth and profitability. Under capitalism, if money doesn't circulate, it creates a crisis for the system as a whole. And when it does circulate, exploitation of the earth and its people intensifies, straining both and creating new conditions for instability and unrest.

Carceral spaces, including prisons, signal the function of spatial restructuring as a mechanism of crisis abatement and neoliberal experimentation. The economic concepts of surplus, crisis, and spatial fix are particularly salient to this discussion, and their connection to the carceral state has been most prominently invoked and elaborated in Gilmore's work. As she demonstrates in her study of California's prison boom in *Golden Gulag,* surplus labor, surplus land, surplus state capacity, and surplus capital geographically distributed along the poles of urban and rural space all threaten to produce crisis in a capitalist system, either economically, through over-accumulation, or socially, as political unrest. Prison expansion offered not just a fix, but a specifically *spatial* fix to the multiple manifestations of capitalist crisis experienced in California and many other states from the early 1970s onward. Prison infrastructure helps absorb over-accumulated capital and puts idled or surplus land back into productive use, partially and temporarily resolving some of the contradictions inherent to capital circulation (Marx 1976).

The social production of race also constitutes an important component of how the prison system serves the accumulation of capital. As Cedric Robinson (1983) has demonstrated, capitalism, even in its earliest Western European formations, has always been *racial,* even while processes of racialization have themselves shifted over time and across bodies. As a system and mode of production that necessitates inequality to function, capitalism, and perhaps especially within liberal democracies, requires race as an ideology and racism as a hierarchical system to enshrine that inequality as legitimate, even natural. Insofar as prisoners themselves have come to constitute a kind of class (Gilmore 2007, 7), and are themselves overwhelmingly racialized before incarceration and *through* incarceration (Goodman 2008), the prison has come to play a central role in the production of race and the reproduction of racial capitalism. Indeed, the prison can be considered, among other things, a race-making institution (Goodman 2008; Alexander 2010).

In sum, the phenomenal rise in the rate of incarceration from the 1970s onward in the United States can at least partly be explained by the various kinds of productive work that prisons do, even while they destroy communities (Clear 2007), shorten life spans (Patterson 2013), and bear little relationship to fluctuations in crime (Travis and Western 2014, 3). The achievements of this work, in service primarily of the capitalist social order, can be found primarily in the external geographies of the prison regime. Indeed, spatial inquiry has been instrumental in explaining the prison system's productive functions, alerting us to how most of those functions fall outside the narrow parameters of crime and punishment or "law and order" within which the prison is most often scrutinized. Prisons offer legitimacy to the neoliberal state, while also constituting an active zone of state-building. They absorb the labor and land rendered surplus by deindustrialization and the globalization of capital. They also operate as a new kind of labor-market institution, one that, as Gretchen Purser writes, "has shown to conceal unemployment in the short run, by absorbing many who would assuredly otherwise be jobless, but exacerbate it in the long run, by dramatically increasing joblessness among inmates after they are released" (2012, 399). Prisons and (I will argue) carceral space more broadly, further shore up the racialization of crime and the ontology of the criminal, adding new ideological cover to the production and racialization of disposable bodies, exploitable labor, and ungrievable lives.[3]

In the survey of carceral sites that follows, I critically investigate the processes by which these spaces threaten to be harnessed, generated, or transformed to extend the work that prisons do *even in a political context of prison downsizing.* Such work has new urgency in the era of bipartisan prison reform and a conservative-led "right on crime" movement. Framing the prison as a set of relations, rather than as a place hewed to crime rates and punishment imperatives, allows us to ask about the production of new carceral forms and correlative carceral places across the landscape of contemporary reform efforts. And it allows us to build toward a world in which the social relationships for which prisons operate, or seem to operate, as the solution are themselves transformed in terms that are life-building rather than life-destroying.

Prison Reform and Its Discontents

Two centuries after the penitentiary's introduction as an institution of discipline and state making at the margin of the new republic, the scale and associated fiscal burden of the U.S. prison system have provoked bipartisan calls for prison reform. Under the aegis of the conservative right-on-crime movement and other coalitions critiquing mass incarceration, politicians of all stripes and parties are jockeying to position themselves, and in some cases reinvent themselves, as "prison reformers," forging common cause on sentencing reform and the fiscal downsizing of the U.S. prison system.

Coupled with mass incarceration's legitimacy crisis, the fiscal burden of the U.S. prison system has proven to be a lightning rod in recent years for bipartisan penal reform efforts. Since the 2008 onset of the "great recession," liberals and conservatives have joined in a chorus of criticism faulting mass incarceration for failing to generate projected social returns and exacting too high a cost for cash-strapped states. While Donald Trump claimed the mantle of the "law and order" presidential candidate during the lead up to the 2016 election, others vying for the nomination in both major parties spoke of sentencing reform, mass incarceration, and even "the New Jim Crow." The Koch brothers, Tea Party stalwarts otherwise famous for their aggressive union-busting campaigns (Teal and Lessin, 2014), have organized major meetings around penal reform, including a recent three-day conference in New Orleans that included critical scholars and activists from Black Lives Matter among its participants. "Strange bedfellows" is almost an understatement for the unlikely alliances that form a part of today's prison-reform movement, as intellectual architects of tough-on-crime policies claim they have simply been misunderstood, dismantlers of the welfare state like Newt Gingrich join liberals like Van Jones in calling for change, and private prison companies jostle with charitable nonprofits for a share of the reentry market.[4]

This rhetorical attention accompanies some gestures toward legislative and judicial change, at least before the 2016 election of Trump: The Department of Justice (DOJ) announced, to great fanfare, the end of its use of private prisons; more than half the nation's states have passed some kind of sentencing reform, including scaling back mandatory minimums; the federal government passed the Fair Sentencing Act, reducing, although not eliminating, the violent disparity between powder and crack cocaine sentences; and a handful of jurisdictions, including the federal government, have tried to ban employers from querying job applicants about their criminal records in an attempt to lower the barriers former prisoners face during reentry and during their return to the workforce.

Many of these changes, however, are quite narrow in scope or largely symbolic. The DOJ's 2016 announcement that it would not renew contracts for privately owned and operated prisons, for example, does not come with any commensurate prisoner releases or plans for actual prison closures (Bello 2016). Meanwhile, freedom for what Marie Gottschalk (2015) calls the "non-non-non's," meaning those "redeemable" prisoners incarcerated for nonviolent, nonserious, and nonsexual offenses, has been purchased only through the hardening of punishment regimes against many others. As Gilmore (2015) notes about the privilege accorded to the "relatively" innocent within many reform initiatives, "most campaigns to decrease sentences for nonviolent convictions simultaneously decrease pressure to revise—indeed often explicitly promise never to change—sentences for serious, violent, or sexual felonies."

Groups like the Council of State Governments and the DOJ have channeled the financial discontent of today's right-on-crime movement into a firmly neoliberal approach to penal reform, focusing on what Gottschalk calls "the three R's" of reform: reentry, justice reinvestment, and recidivism (2015, 3). Fiscally oriented prison reform has subsequently been operationalized through a set of initiatives and interventions that take place outside of prison walls and, as James Kilgore (2014a) and Maya Schenwar (2015) have pointed out and I discuss further in chapter 5, risk widening the carceral net through the rise of electronic monitoring and other postcustodial forms of social control.

Finally, despite a handful of prison closures and legislative changes, new or expanded prisons and other carceral institutions continue to appear, albeit through notably different justifying logics than we are used to seeing. Indeed, a fuller vantage of the carceral state affirms Gottschalk's recent observations: "A tenacious carceral state has sprouted in the shadows of mass imprisonment and has been extending its reach far beyond the prison gate. It includes not only the country's vast archipelago of jails and prisons but also the far-reaching and growing range of penal punishments and controls that lie in the never-never land between the gate of the prison and full citizenship" (2015, 3).

With the story of mass incarceration's legitimacy crisis still unfolding, it remains to be seen whether the emerging mainstream critique leads to anything other than a repackaging of the carceral state and an exercise in the recapture of corrections budgets. In the meantime, this book attempts to anticipate the character of a decarcerated future by critically excavating the carceral state's investments in the broader political and economic landscape. This landscape includes "deep structural changes in the job market, growing income and other inequalities, the escalating political assault on the public sector and organized labor, and the economic decline of wide swaths of urban and rural America" (Gottschalk 2015, 7). If we are indeed witnessing what Michael Hallett calls "the unfolding failure of America's hyper-incarceration security state" (2012, 223), a question still remains: what *is* the future of mass incarceration? And might there be a postprison landscape in which the work that prisons do is continued through new institutional, juridical, and spatial arrangements?

This book raises crucial questions about this particular moment of bipartisan prison reform and attempts to anticipate some of the ways in which recent reform initiatives might portend a widening and repackaging of the carceral net across social space. Reform efforts that treat the prison as merely a place, narrowly indexed to the metrics of crime and punishment, offer little insight into or promise for a truly decarcerated future. For a better view, it is worth considering the prison *out of* place, dislodged from the literal spaces of courts and detention facilities, disarticulated from law-and-order frameworks, and anchored instead to the transformative politics and dialectic analysis of the prison-abolition movement.

Abolitionist Mappings

This book emerges out of and seeks to contribute to a movement of radical prison critique that calls itself "penal abolition." A politics of prison abolition aims at changing the relationships that produce the kinds of events, interests, crises, and behaviors for which prisons and other carceral formations operate as surrogate solutions. Such a politics reminds us that at stake in the excavation of carceral space are the social relationships through and for which those spaces make sense and do productive work. An abolitionist politic is, at its core, transformative, seeking to remake the social relations and power inequities that give rise to the prison system and for which the prison system does work. Rather than beginning from the premise that the prison system is broken, and thus in need of reform, it invites us to ask to what ends and in whose interests the prison system *succeeds,* an invitation that requires a remapping of carceral power as connections are necessarily forged between racial capitalist forms and sites of exploitation and the criminalization and confinement of ever-growing numbers of people.[5] Prison abolition, in other words, necessarily encompasses antiracism *and* class struggle, just as the freedom of prisoners is fundamental to any truly emancipatory anticapitalist politics and social justice.

Prison Land offers a set of concrete case studies investigating how carceral space produces and manages social disposability in late-capitalist American life. Together, they demonstrate that the production of disposability is an active process, spatialized in a range of places and forms that are politically mutable, highly contested, and differentially experienced. Throughout my case studies, geographies of capital accumulation are seen functioning alongside the neoliberal logic of individual responsibility to undermine black sociality and counterpower at every turn. I approach these investigations from the position that race, crime, and space are all social and political constructions. This does not make them not "real" (Fields 1990; Hacking 2002; Muhammad 2011). Indeed, a central ambition of *Prison Land* is to demonstrate, through an interrogation of diverse carceral landscapes, the intimacy with which ideological and spatial productions inform and reinforce each other as social realities, with serious implications for the state-sanctioned production of surplus life and premature death.

Each of the book's chapters examines the imperatives, logics, and crises that produce carceral space, including but not limited to the prison edifice. Its central case studies traverse a diverse set of geographies across the United States in which criminalization and incarceration are both a condition and consequence of contemporary social relations within late capitalism. They are, in effect, investigations into the work carceral space does for racial capitalism and the production of disposable life to those ends. The themes of crisis and neoliberalism, isolation and individuation, and sociality and racialization appear prominently throughout, anchoring each chapter's inquiry and its analysis and underscoring the stakes of investigating the functions and consequences of the carceral state.

In the book's first two chapters, the coproduction of urban transformation and mass incarceration is explored through the lens of the property relation, specifically real estate. Here I investigate transformations in urban space and carceral control by critically tracking the role of police and security within urban revitalization strategies in both Detroit and New York. Through these case studies, I link historical carceral practices such as broken-windows policing to contemporary urban interventions posed as alternatives to incarceration, finding shared logics and underlying commitments to urban real-estate markets and property rights.

The first of these chapters takes place in Detroit, where approximately 2.2 square miles of downtown make up ground zero for multibillionaire Dan Gilbert's current urban investment ventures. In Gilbert's billion-dollar downtown, a Rock Ventures security force patrols the streets twenty-four hours per day, reinforcing the unflinching gaze of the hundreds of high-tech security cameras fixed to the buildings. If the revitalization of downtown Detroit is underwritten by Gilbert's mortgage and real estate empires, those investments are themselves buttressed by a vast infrastructure of surveillance technology and network of private security companies working in collaboration with the Detroit Police Department. I investigate the 2013 introduction of broken-windows policing in Detroit and increased securitization of downtown as part of the city's revitalization efforts, suggesting that property, specifically the real-estate economy, continues to drive carceral power and its racialized operation in urban space.

In chapter 2, I explore the predominantly working-class African American neighborhood of Brownsville, Brooklyn, home to the largest concentration of public housing towers in the nation and high numbers of criminalized and incarcerated residents. The neighborhood is also a frequently cited example of community-based efforts to interrupt the cycle of mass incarceration. Such reformist efforts are examined against the broader context of real-estate pressures and generalized gentrification in Brooklyn as a whole. I offer insights from a study of two alternative-to-incarceration initiatives in Brownsville to argue that their overall effect has been to extend the power of the neoliberal carceral state in the service of real-estate demands in one of New York City's last remaining "frontiers" of gentrification.

In chapter 3, "Rural Extractions," the wage relation is examined as an animating ideological pillar of continued rural prison expansion in the Appalachian coalfields of eastern Kentucky. Here I ask how unemployment, poverty, and the ideology of work structure the desirability and logic of prison siting as an economic development strategy. In the post-coal communities of eastern Kentucky, prison construction has proliferated over the past decade, despite state legislative commitments to the reformist politics of "justice reinvestment." Coal mining has been in decline in the region for close to half a century, and local coal jobs have plummeted dramatically over the past two decades. By mapping the salience of work and waged labor to the spatial politics of rural prison development in the region, the chapter suggests that the unemployment of poor Appalachians cannot be seamlessly disentangled from the structural poverty and joblessness that conditions both the preincarceration and postincarceration lives of prisoners across the country.

The increased geographic fragmentation of rural communities, where prisons are built, and urban neighborhoods, where prisoners come from, has generated new corollary carceral spaces that both bridge and circulate between the geographically segregated lives of prisoners and their loved ones. Chapter 4, "The Prison In-between," considers one such liminal field—the prison bus—as a carceral space within which the loved ones of immobilized prisoners experience the slow violence endemic to both incarceration and neoliberal austerity. The prison bus is investigated as a gendered "in-between" space and a site of secondary prisonization, structuring and circumscribing the socially reproductive labor of caregiving across the isolating geographies and economic margins of the prison system.

Every Friday and Saturday night, hundreds of visitors, mostly working-class women of color and their children, gather on specific street corners across New York City to wait for the buses that will travel all night to take them to prisons dispersed across the state. As well as constituting itself a carceral space, the prison bus is also explored as a scene of ordinary crisis, neoliberal subjectivity, and fragile solidarity for its riders. I argue that riding the bus constitutes, among other things, a means of reproducing life in a context proven to diminish life. As such, it offers at least a partial basis of opposition to the fragmentation and isolation of the prison regime.

In chapter 5, "Community Confinements," I survey the extension of the prison's functions of racialized containment and banishment into community spaces, encompassing neighborhoods, homes, and public space. I examine three specific carceral tactics that extend and outsource the reach of the carceral system into communities: spatial restrictions and the rise of pocket parks and other banishment mechanisms for registered sex offenders; neighborhood-based gang injunctions and the introduction of "safety zones"; and the rise of electronic monitoring devices like ankle bracelets and their transformations of home space. I consider the ways in which these tactics continue the functions of the prison proper, including by controlling movement and dispossessing subjects of access to public resources, while simultaneously *absorbing* family, friends, and neighbors into the coercive roles conventionally occupied by police, guards, and parole officers.

The book's concluding chapter brings the insights produced by my case studies to bear upon the current conjuncture, taking stock of how the multiple crises of this moment are producing struggles for power both at the elite level and on the streets. A primary challenge for penal abolitionists is to rehistoricize prisons as social, rather than natural, constructions, hewed to a set of mutable social relations and contestable political imperatives. I describe how the sites visited within the course of the book's journey help us deconstruct the ideologies and ontologies that naturalize the abusive force of the prison regime as both ahistorical and asocial. I conclude with an investigation into new carceral futures by critically assessing the prison-reform strategies that have emerged or been augmented by the most recent economic recession, as well as the revanchist law-and-order politics heralded by the Trump presidency. *Prison Land* ends by pointing to some of the ways in which the capacities of the carceral state are seemingly being retrofitted for the current political–economic conjuncture, but also to new liberation struggles, like the Black Lives Matter movement, that aim not just at dismantling prisons, but at interrupting the very capitalist social relations that produce penal institutions and disposable lives in the first place.

Together, these spatial investigations demonstrate how a variety of seemingly nonpenal ideologies and ontologies, including property, labor, and race, work powerfully to animate and legitimate the penal regime. At the same time, the prison and other carceral spaces work to mystify those underlying relations by ideologically reproducing the current era's most paradigmatic figure of racialized disposability: the criminal. So long as the actual social relations for which the carceral state is put to work remain unchallenged, the spatial organization of oppression and disposable life remains a pressing and pernicious threat. It is in this sense that a radical deconstruction of carceral space serves not only to demystify the prison itself as a social construction but also to erect an alternative analytical framework that disarticulates crime from punishment, disposable life from danger, and carceral space from collective life-building.

Perhaps most important, this remapping of carcerality serves to connect spaces, and in connecting spaces, to connect people and their struggles. The spaces documented throughout this book are contiguous rather than self-enclosed, as are the sufferings experienced by their inhabitants. The degradations of low-wage work and unemployment, of unaffordable rent and housing foreclosure, and of illness and vulnerability to violence are certainly unevenly distributed along lines of race, class, and gender, among other axes. They are at the same time all expressions of a capitalist economic system that functions through exploitation, creates perverse levels of inequality, and then legitimates that inequality though various tools of social division. If abolition politics is about rebuilding the relationships that have been severed by the machineries of the carceral system—severed in some cases by cell walls and arrest warrants and in other cases by remote distances or no-trespass zones—it is also necessarily about facilitating connection and coalition among the exploited and the oppressed. Just as sailors joined port workers and former slaves in eighteenth-century movements of "excarceration" (Linebaugh 2004, 372), today's liberation struggles will require alliances between workers, the unemployed, welfare recipients, land defenders, prisoners, and the many others with shared stakes in a world that is as free of poverty and racism as it is free of cages.

1
The Prison in the City
Securitizing Property
in Bankrupt Detroit

It is July 2014. Home water shut-offs have begun in parts of Detroit and I am staring down at a man-made beach from the window of a tenth-story office tower. The beach sits mostly empty, the cocktail bar set up on one side of it quiet, for now; a few brightly colored beach chairs strewn across the sandy square; a nearby office building casting shadows. This vista of urban leisure is one stop on a three-hour publicity tour of what is potentially the most ambitious experiment in privately financed urban reclamation in the nation. Approximately 2.2 square miles of downtown Detroit, including Campus Martius Park and Capital Park, are ground zero for multibillionaire Dan Gilbert's current urban investment ventures. Everything I'm told to look at from the heights of Gilbert's corporate headquarters is underwritten by his fortune.

Gilbert has purchased approximately ninety-five buildings in Detroit's downtown core since 2007. Even while fully capitalist in their motivations and ambitions, Gilbert's investments in Detroit have been publicly hailed as a civically oriented recoupment project by the benevolent patron of a dying city. As one *New York Times* profile puts it: "Opportunity Detroit, as Mr. Gilbert has branded it, is both a rescue mission and a business venture that, if successful, will yield him a fortune" (Segal 2013). In just the past three and a half years, under the corporate umbrellas of Rock Ventures, Quicken Loans, and Bedrock Real Estate, Gilbert has invested over $1.5 billion in Detroit real estate. He has also moved 3,600 of his employees (referred to as "team members") downtown from a nearby suburb and now boasts almost 10,000 employees who work in the city's central business district (Sorge 2013). Gilbert is buying up, at fire-sale prices, a city whose 2013 $18-billion bankruptcy declaration remains the largest in municipal history. Detroit is the nation's poster child for industrial decline. Once a thriving capital of auto manufacturing, the city has been devastated by almost seven decades of factory closures and job losses. Since 1990, its municipal workforce has been cut in half, and since 1992, more than three-fifths of its public schools have closed. Its predominantly African American population, already hit hard by the loss of good union wages and public sector jobs in the post-Fordist period, experienced a new round of plunder and abandonment in the wake of the 2008 housing crisis, when a wave of foreclosures and evictions decimated black home ownership across the city's east and west ends. By the time the city was declared bankrupt and an emergency manager called in to impose a savage regime of austerity measures, Detroit had the highest rates of unemployment and child poverty of any major U.S. city. In the past decade, one-third of all residential properties entered into foreclosure, many of them still occupied at the time of being seized. The bailiffs who have overseen these evictions frequently bring backup in the form of armed law enforcement, and elsewhere, police harassment and arrest rates have escalated (Jay 2017).

The prison and the city have long held an intimate relationship, going as far back as the early industrial period and the concomitant production of new classifications of urban crime (Linebaugh 2004). The governance of cities on behalf of capital, the policing of the urban poor, and the swelling of prison and jail spaces are interrelated processes, bound especially over the past four decades in the United States by the shared vicissitudes of neoliberal restructuring, deindustrialization, wage stagnation, shifting racial inequities, and the decline of the welfare state. The structural codependence between urban restructuring and expansion of the carceral state has only deepened over the neoliberal period. Geographer Neil Smith's description of urban transformations in Manhattan in the 1980s and 1990s would prove prescient: "Largely abandoned to the working class amid postwar suburban expansion, relinquished to the poor and unemployed as reservations for racial and ethnic minorities, the terrain of the inner city is suddenly valuable again, perversely profitable" (1996,

6). Smith noted how, in service of that profitability, then-Mayor Giuliani instructed New York police officers to remove homeless people from public spaces and to criminalize a broad swath of activities deemed inimical to "the quality of life" in city neighborhoods. The quality-of-life rubric offered a kind of blank check to the New York City Police Department, whose officers marshaled their unprecedented powers to forcibly move homeless people and poor people from certain streets and from certain neighborhoods.

While the criminalization of acts of poverty, including sleeping on sidewalks and public benches, has long fallen within the purview of gentrifying cities across the United States, a new and growing wave of cities are adopting laws that effectively criminalize homelessness and indigence in urban space. In June 2017, the *New York Times* reported on measures the city of Honolulu was taking to drive out the homeless, considered a scourge against the tourism industry so central to the state's economy. The governor had just declared a state of emergency, passing tough new criminal ordinances aimed at ridding the city's public spaces of homeless people and poverty activities such as panhandling. The tourism industry chipped in as well, offering to cover airfare for homeless people who agreed to return to the mainland (Nagourney 2016). According to a survey of 187 major American cities by the National Law Center on Homelessness and Poverty, by the end of 2014, 100 urban municipalities had made it a crime to sit on a sidewalk, a 43 percent increase over 2011. Laws outlawing panhandling and sleeping in cars and authorizing the removal of tent cities have also increased across the country.

Detroit is part of this trend, undergoing a top-down urban transformation so dramatic it has been likened to the structural adjustment policies brutally imposed on countries of the global south in the 1980s and 1990s. After decades of economic decline that led to depression-era levels of unemployment, the city is being remade as a mecca of real estate and tech finance. As municipal assets are privatized and real-estate speculators cash in on rock-bottom property prices, those excluded from the city's economic revival are being managed in other ways. This chapter examines the Detroit Police Department's (DPD) 2013 introduction of broken-windows policing and the criminalization of its majority-working-class African American residents in the context of the city's privatization and revitalization efforts, in particular of Dan Gilbert's multimillion dollar buy-up of Detroit's downtown core. To secure the profit of downtown development for the wealthy few, real-estate developers like Gilbert are working hand-in-glove with city managers and municipal and state law enforcement to build up Detroit's policing and security apparatus. In the Motor City, like elsewhere, police power is in thrall to the profit margin while carceral space is conjured out of the exclusions of the property relation on which that profit is hinged.

"We Eat Our Own Dog Food"

My tour begins when the guide, Bruce Schwartz, the Detroit Relocation Ambassador for Quicken Loans, beckons me to a window here on the tenth-story of the Quicken Loans headquarters. He quickly points out highlights of the landscape below, including the "publicly organized, privately financed" man-made beach in the center of the square. Like Kublai Khan surveying his empire in Italo Calvino's *Invisible Cities*, Schwartz rattles off a quick list of figures and acquisitions: "We bought that building, which was one of our first acquisitions, and in four months we gutted it and we Quickenized it and we moved 2,500 people in there. It's now 100 percent occupied. And then we bought the building to the left—First National Building. That building we paid about 8 million dollars for. And we put a lot of money into it." Every so often Schwartz stops to reiterate Gilbert's instrumental role in the city's "revival": "He is doing amazing things and he has a great mission and great leaders that are working together as a team to bring this city back. And there's a lot of momentum. If you want to live down here right now, good luck finding a place."

Indeed, Schwartz is right. With the influx of Gilbert's capital and the corollary investments of another local billionaire, Mike Ilitch, the downtown of Detroit has become a significantly more exclusive place to live. As developers snatch up low-income apartments and transform them into luxury complexes, the downtown rents have soared, nearly doubling since 2010. Displacement of poor and low-wage residents has accelerated in turn. Housing in general is a major crisis in Detroit, though less so for the population of tech workers who concern Schwartz than for the predominantly poor and working-class African American residents who have lived in the city for generations. Just a couple of miles away from the urban square where young professionals are encouraged to play volley-ball on their lunch breaks, neighborhoods have been destroyed by a fore-closure and eviction crisis. Since 2006, more than 150,000 Detroit resi-dents have lost their homes due to foreclosure, the majority of them in the east and west peripheries of the city (Jay 2017, 24). For the majority, the foreclosure crisis has been disastrous. For land speculators, however, the crisis offers a financial boon. Local researchers have found that more than 20 percent of property in the city of Detroit is currently held by land speculators. Much of this surge in speculation has occurred since the housing market crash of 2008, which hit Detroit particularly hard. After the eviction of foreclosed homeowners and the seizure of their build-ings, property speculators and financial firms have been able to buy these single-family homes at rock-bottom prices and quickly transform them into far more expensive rental properties (Akers 2017). The result is a property pipeline from those individuals and families with modest means to the wealthy corporate elite.

Gilbert made his fortune after founding Quicken Loans, the second-largest home mortgage lender in the country and the largest online lender. His personal net worth, according to *Forbes* magazine, is over $6 billion, up from $3.8 billion in 2013, and in 2018 *Forbes* ranked him the 71st-richest American. Quicken Loans closed a total of $96 billion in loans in 2016, a company record buttressed in no small part by its profiting from the foreclosure crisis. Gilbert began purchasing buildings in down-town Detroit in 2011, exploiting the "skyscraper sale" that followed the 2008 financial crisis, which intensified the city's economic decline almost a generation after shuttered factories and real-estate speculation began pushing prices down and vacancies up (Akers 2013). Among Gilbert's first acquisitions was a twenty-three-story neoclassical wonder built in 1912 called the Dime Building. Bedrock bought its full 330,000 square feet in August 2011 for the reported steal of $15 million (Segal 2013). Gilbert's real-estate company, Rock Ventures, now owns or controls more than thirty properties (including buildings and store fronts) in down-town Detroit, totaling nearly 7.5 million square feet. His stated ambition is to turn downtown into a high-tech hub, and indeed, Schwartz referred to a number of the offices we toured as tech incubators. Roughly eighty small companies have moved into buildings owned by Bedrock, many of them start-ups founded by Detroit Venture Partners, a venture capital firm co-owned by Gilbert. They include a branch of Uber, the controversial taxi-hailing service, and Twitter. Venture capital is quickly eclipsing auto manufacturing and the public sector in the Motor City, but with no commensurate provision of unionized, permanent jobs, especially not for the city's majority-black working class.

Halfway into our tour of Gilbert's Detroit-based holdings, Schwartz pulls out the bible of Gilbert's corporate empire, "The Book of Isms," which contains such plucky maxims as: "The inches we need are everywhere around us"; "We are the 'they'"; "A penny saved is a penny"; and "We eat our own dog food."[1] The book is a playbook of sorts for the cultural branding to which Gilbert's sprawling urban empire aspires, like tech mammoths Google and Facebook before it. By now, its tropes are familiar hallmarks of "creative capitalism," especially in the tech field: communal workspaces, integration of "fun" in the form of Nerf guns and ping pong, and an expanding office landscape populated predominantly by young, tech-savvy white men. Of a similar tour only months before mine, *New York Times* writer David Segal described a walk through the third floor of the Chase Building (home to some 300 of Quicken Loans's approximately 2,500 mortgage bankers) as analogous to "a visit to a frat party at a telemarketing firm" (2013). It is unclear whether the footballs we both happened to see thrown across an office space are a site-specific performance staged to exemplify the culture Schwartz was so keen to show off or a fully integrated part of the average workday.

It is fitting that Schwartz is dressed like a nineteenth-century captain of industry and that one of our tour stops is a refurbished but aesthetically fossilized gold vault once belonging to the Federal Reserve. The tour as a whole feels like a throwback to the boosterism of the late 1800s, when the leaders and owners of small towns in the expanding American and Canadian West made extravagant claims about the future of their settlements with the aim of attracting residents and inflating the prices of local real estate. Schwartz gushes more than once about the "amazing things" Gilbert's "vision" has accomplished in Detroit, referring to Gilbert's downtown investment initiatives as a "magic dust," a property assumedly analogous to King Midas's golden touch. Meanwhile, at a large table under the basement gold vault's glass chandelier, two "team members" host a Skype conversation with their boss to discuss the pros and cons of outfitting the entire office with bean bag chairs.

Schwartz's optimistic claims have a great deal of heavy lifting to do to counter the pervasive and seemingly self-evident narrative of Detroit as a dying city, a city in decline, or a "postapocalyptic'" city. Indeed, Americans have perhaps become so inundated with the stock images of Detroit's unceremonious urban decline, such as the towering Grand Central Station with its shuttered windows, that the actual flow of capital through such spaces has been obscured. As Detroit scholar Josh Akers argues (2013), drawing on Smith (1984), abandonment and vacancy are actually *productive* strategies of capital accumulation, part of the seesaw of uneven development necessary to capitalist growth. The state, moreover, is often a committed, rather than absent, partner in the production and exploitation of such abandonment. Akers explains:

> Local governments are actively involved in the mitigation of vacancy and abandonment through a variety of approaches, many of which are centered on economic development and growth. The use of state policy to privilege private markets and ownership allows for the expansion and deepening of devalorization cycles. It buttresses a market for the exchange of vacant and abandoned property that is removed from the physical conditions of the actual structures and is reliant on the speculative possibilities of urban entrepreneurialism and grant coalitions targeting redevelopment. (2013, 26)

In other words, the "skyscraper sale" through which Gilbert's Detroit real-estate empire has expanded in just three years was made possible by the same rent gap that facilitates gentrification in global cities like New York: a long-term widening in the ratio of land values to property that render it profitable for developers to reinvest in undervalued urban space (Smith 1996; Rousseau 2009, 770). The very conditions that lure investors like Gilbert to a city like Detroit (low prices, high vacancy, government tax subsidies, and accelerated access for those who can pay in cash) are the conditions that, in recent decades, attracted capitalist developers to some of the most expensive urban real estate in the country, including in Los Angeles, San Francisco, and New York, preceding their generalized gentrification (Smith 2002). While those wealthy cities differ from Detroit in various ways, investors saw and continue to see spectacular profit margins at the expense of low-income residents living in neighborhoods divested of adequate infrastructure and state resources. When investment inevitably arrives there too in search of profit, residents face eviction and displacement rather than the benefits of state-subsidized private capital. Often, those state subsidies even aid in that eviction and displacement, as in Detroit, where three-quarters of the $188 million sent to Michigan from the federal government as part of the Helping Hardest Hit Homeowners program went to "blight removal," including the razing of vacant and foreclosed homes (Jay 2017, 24).

Real estate acquisition is only one part of the profit-making equation, however. For value to be recuperated from that real estate and the corporate labor subsidized within it, space itself needs to be socially "activated": people from elsewhere need reasons to want to be there. The social and cultural cachet associated with that real estate, or the urban space in which it is embedded, must also be cultivated. Gilbert's strategies for activating the downtown core include constructing a skateboard park and an urban beach, commissioning international art stars to adorn a multitiered parking lot with urban graffiti, and dotting street corners with gimmicky creative-capital emblems, such as a human-sized novelty Jenga game.

The sheer volume and presence of security guards and police officers who line the urban core make clear that these resources are not intended for the city's 20,000 homeless people, many of whom also populate the downtown core. According to the local American Civil Liberties Union (2013), the police have made a point of targeting the downtown's homeless population, often picking them up only to drop them off late at night in far away neighborhoods.

In Gilbert's billion-dollar downtown, a Rock Ventures security force patrols the streets twenty-four hours per day, reinforcing the unflinching gaze of hundreds of high-tech security cameras affixed to the buildings purchased by his companies. Meanwhile, a model of downtown Detroit in miniature sits in the boardroom of the Quicken Loans headquarters, with Gilbert's properties illuminated in a bright orange glow once he acquires them. Situated in one of those buildings, the Bedrock-owned Chase Tower, is a command center where dozens of computer screens

A model of downtown Detroit in miniature sits in a boardroom of the Quicken Loans Headquarters. Buildings light up once they have been purchased. Photograph by Maya Bankovic.

monitored by security guards link to live feeds from the arsenal of video cameras planted downtown. The monitors connect to approximately 1,000 different cameras in the streets and sidewalks surrounding Rock Ventures properties in seven different states, with over 300 of those cameras located in metro Detroit alone (Davies 2013). The camera program is a collaborative effort that includes most of the big downtown property owners, including General Motors, Ilitch Holdings, and Compuware. Once a month, the representatives of those companies meet in a boardroom at the Compuware headquarters, the same building that hosts Quicken Loans, along with members of the DPD, Wayne County Sheriff, Wayne State University Police and representatives of the numerously deployed private security forces (Davies 2013).

While the scale and speed of Detroit's security build-up in support of Gilbert's reinvestment schemes has been dramatic, the deployment of police and security technology in the service of urban revitalization is not itself anomalous. Capital invested in property has always required the coercive scaffolding of enclosure and securitization in order to generate profit (Davis 1990; Linebaugh 2004). The most familiar form of that scaffolding is extensive surveillance technology, along with increased urban policing and the proliferation of mechanisms for criminalizing undesirable bodies and behaviors (Beckett and Herbert 2010). If the re-vitalization of downtown Detroit is underwritten by Gilbert's mortgage and real estate empires, that financial investment is itself buttressed by a vast infrastructure of surveillance technology and a network of private se-curity companies working in collaboration with the DPD. The private-public security partnership is insidious not only because it indicates the privileging of corporate property over ordinary residents but also because the limits of public law enforcement are offset by the private security guards, and vice versa. For example, the Guardsmark Inc. security guards Gilbert employs are under no legal obligation to read detainees their Miranda rights, but they do have the power to use force. They tag team with Detroit police forces when removing unwanted people from the downtown, com-municating via radio and sharing video feed from the multimillion-dollar surveillance system. That system is even put to use monitoring social dis-sent, such as when it was used to scrutinize activists from Black Lives Matter who gathered downtown in the summer of 2016 (Jay 2017, 33).

While various levels of Detroit and Wayne County police have been absorbed into an expanded multimillion-dollar, high-tech private-public security and surveillance apparatus, reconfigured police tactics even within the municipal police department itself suggest intensified securi-tization and criminalization of select swaths of Detroit's urban space. The DPD strategy in the gentrifying downtown core has concentrated around quality-of-life offenses and the criminalization of homelessness through security technology and police powers deployed to displace those deemed inimical to the corporate investment and luxury consumption for which the area is being cordoned off. The tactics deployed in Detroit's deeply impoverished east and west ends, however, where the majority of the city's poor and working-class African American population reside, have been even more aggressive. What this suggests is that police harassment, criminalization, and arrest are all carceral tactics that serve capital inter-ests insofar as they help securitize property values and gentrify neigh-borhoods, but they also play a significant role in the management of racialized urban poverty as a whole.

Broken Windows Redux

In November 2013, at least 150 federal, state, and local law-enforcement personnel raided an apartment complex called Colony Arms on Detroit's east side. Residents' names were run through the system and every violation, no matter how minimal or how dated, was treated with "zero tolerance," meaning that police action was taken (Gross 2014). Dubbed "Operation Clean Sweep," the raid resulted in at least thirty arrests. Less than a month later, forty-two people were arrested in a DPD raid of another public housing complex, and two weeks after that, on December 17, some 300 officers and law-enforcement agencies conducted what was considered at the time to be the biggest sweep in the department's history, flooding a one-square-mile area of the city's west side. Monthly policing assaults have since been launched under the umbrella of an operation called "Operation Restore Order," a series of seventeen SWAT-assisted paramilitary operations that the DPD waged between 2013 and 2015 in some of the city's poorest neighborhoods (Gross 2014).

The raids are just one manifestation of the department's new zero-tolerance policing agenda, a component of the DPD's recent prioritization of quality-of-life issues, such as graffiti elimination, drug enforcement, and the general problem of "vice." Assistant Chief James E. White is quoted in one recent news report explaining the department's approach: "We go out and do drug raids—that's a quality of life issue. But then we go out to the local party stores in the area and if they are selling loose cigarettes or the store is dirty then they are cited for that as well" (quoted in Gross 2014). White continues in the same report:

> You have to approach crime almost as a holistic approach, where you have to look at every aspect of the community and what's happening in the community. Some people would laugh and say, what difference does it make if the store is clean? Well, if the store is dirty and there is no investment by that storeowner to have a clean store that is welcoming to regular, everyday, working class people, then you're going to draw only the people who may be looking to what's not necessarily a good thing.

It is worth noting that the areas targeted for quality-of-life policing in Detroit are all predominantly black. In the Colony Arms complex, for example, 90 percent of the residents are African American (Gross 2014).

The theory of policing that White describes has a name, one familiar to many residents of large cities and theorists of urban policing and mass incarceration: "broken-windows theory." Under the watch of Mayor

Rudolph Giuliani and Police Commissioner William Bratton in the 1990s, New York City implemented an expanded network of policing, surveillance, and civil ordinances under the complementary security rubrics of "zero tolerance" and broken-windows theory. The latter idea, coined and popularized in the 1980s by conservative scholars George Kelling and the late James Q. Wilson, suggested that the aggressive policing and criminalization of "undesirable" behaviors related to designated quality-of-life issues such as vandalism and trespassing, as well as drug use and panhandling, could be an effective way to stymie a putative escalation of criminal activities in the urban core. In practice, broken-windows policing in New York (and elsewhere) meant the aggressive criminalization of poor and mostly racialized urban residents, functionally displacing to the urban peripheries mostly victimless and survivalist activities related to extreme poverty, especially those deemed damaging to property or speculation on property. As Jordan T. Camp and Christina Heatherton explain, broken-windows policing emerged out of the urban crises of the 1960s and the 1970s to become "the political expression of neoliberalism at the urban scale" (2016, 2). Its most lasting achievement has been the wholesale displacement of the multiracial poor and working class from urban spaces around the globe.

Broken-windows policing is popularly associated with major cities like New York, but in a seeming throwback to the 1990s (a period, significantly, also associated with the widespread revalorization of real estate in the country's major cities), it is Detroit that is witnessing a resurrection of these controversial practices. In the summer of 2012 and winter of 2013, the conservative think tank the Manhattan Institute "loaned" George Kelling to the city of Detroit to help implement, in collaboration with the DPD, broken-windows pilot programs in two of the city's high-poverty areas, one in the northwest neighborhood of Grandmont-Rosedale and the other in the northeast neighborhood of East English Village. The strategy was to flood the neighborhoods with police and specifically identify and target what they call "the neighborhood's most at risk offenders" (Manhattan Institute n.d.). Detroit's government paid $600,000 to the Manhattan Institute and an undisclosed amount to the Bratton Group for their support facilitating the DPD's adoption of broken-windows policing, even while it was itself, as a city, on the verge of the largest municipal bankruptcy in U.S. history.

It is noteworthy that Detroit's broken-windows experiments are being championed for the same reasons and by the same interests as Gilbert's downtown property investment and securitization efforts. In one laudatory opinion piece in the local media, the author introduces himself as a collaborator of Kelling's in the implementation of "community-policing" programs informed by broken-windows theory. He is worth quoting at length:

> Downtown and Midtown have become remarkably safer places because of outside influences. A visionary chief executive, Dan Gilbert, has purchased dozens of buildings, created a high-tech surveillance-camera system, and founded an outdoor oasis called Campus Martius Park. An enterprising university, Wayne State, has developed a strong police department to provide public safety around its ever-growing campus. And entrepreneurs have leveraged low interest rates and government incentives to open up shops in the area. These largely top-down economic activities have allowed for a vibrant civic life to develop in the urban core, and [as] a result the place has become safer. But these sorts of activities cannot be expected to occur all across the 130 remaining square miles. For the "neighborhoods," a bottom-up and targeted approach is required . . . Just as New York began to reclaim its quality of life by cracking down on subway-fare cheats and squeegee men, Detroit has had to begin with a crackdown on home invasions. In Grandmont and Rosedale, this has meant organizing citizens to report suspicious behavior, having police take reports seriously, having probation officers serve outstanding warrants, and having prosecutors do their part. (Allegretti 2013)

One of the primary discursive contributions made by the Manhattan Institute over the past decade has been to popularize the myth that quality-of-life policing and broken-windows theory were responsible for New York's decline in crime rates, despite overwhelming evidence to the contrary (Harcourt 2001). In this passage, the author reproduces this myth and extends it, claiming not only that New York "reclaimed its quality of life" through broken-windows policing tactics, but that Detroit's putative crime problem would require the same and more, aggressive and oppressive action from all arms of the carceral dragnet, including parole officers, law enforcement, prosecutors, and even those residents convinced or coerced to collaborate with police. The question of safety for whom is never addressed, even while classist and racist assumptions about who poses danger and whose quality of life matters remain implicit.

In 2013, Detroit appointed a new police chief, James Craig, who had worked under "broken windows" Police Commissioner Bratton in Los Angeles when the latter was head of the Los Angeles Police Department in the 2000s. Bratton had himself hired Kelling as a consultant during this time (Hackman 2014). As he had directly observed Bratton's implementation of broken-windows policing in Los Angeles, the local media lauded Craig's appointment, considering the city's so-called crime problem to be out of control. Detroit's Emergency Manager, Kevyn Orr, also appointed in 2013 by Michigan's Governor Rick Snyder to oversee Detroit's bankruptcy, is on record as saying that crime was the city's number one impediment to economic development (Jay and Conklin 2017, 27). In other words, crime is considered a problem by local powers insofar as it threatens an economic bottom line. Those deemed as threatening to the revitalization of the profit rate tied to private property in Detroit's urban core are cast as criminals in order to render their systematic exclusion, dispossession, and containment legitimate. Meanwhile, of the thirty arrests made during the Colony Arms police offensive, twenty-one were related to parking violations, and not one person was ultimately convicted of any wrongdoing (Jay 2017, 21).

Policing, privatization, and the securitization of real estate markets are thus intertwined processes in Detroit, as elsewhere. They are also thoroughly racialized processes whose most dire consequences, including arrest and imprisonment, are borne predominantly by its poorest residents, who are also mostly African American. Detroit is a city that is 84 percent black. It is also reportedly the most segregated metropolitan region in the nation (Logan and Stults 2011; Vanhemert 2013). Nearly 40 percent of residents live below the poverty line and approximately 50 percent of the population is unemployed. Nearly 60 percent of the area's black population lives within the Detroit city limits. Akers writes: "The material segregation of the city and suburbs is explicit in both the suburb-city boundary, but it is also implicit in the struggles over control of regional services and the reluctance of suburban communities to participate in regional approaches to regional issues" (2013, 6). In such a context, the politics of municipal service provision and the aggressive privatization of such services in the wake of Detroit's bankruptcy are inextricable from the ongoing revanchist politics of race and class immiseration.

Water Wars and the Property Relation

At the same time as Schwartz was showing me Madonna's favorite life-sized horse lamp in the basement office of a tech start-up, hundreds of Detroiters were facing an acute resource emergency. That summer, the city's Water and Sewerage Department (WSD) had begun aggressively turning off the water supply of select families who had been late in paying their recent water bills. Upward of 10 percent of Detroiters were subject to water shutoffs (Jay and Conklin 2017: 41). The shutoffs began in March 2014, when the WSD announced it would begin ending water service for 1,500 to 3,000 customers per week, claiming it was facing a financial crisis that left it "no choice" but to begin cutting off residents. In truth, starting in 2011, the Detroit government had actively *disinvested* the Water and Sewage Department by hundreds of millions of dollars and re-allocated that money to repay Wall Street creditors. Local news investigations quickly poked holes in the city's crisis plea, pointing out that large-scale customers such as Ford Field, home of the Detroit Lions football team, Joe Louis Arena, where the Red Wings play hockey, and numerous city golf courses had also amassed huge unpaid water bills but were not being cut off.

Resource scarcity is neither natural nor inevitable. In Detroit, as elsewhere, it is a product of social processes and political decision making. Like housing foreclosures and job layoffs, municipal disinvestment is also increasingly what carceral space is made out of. Detroit sits on the edge of the largest group of freshwater lakes on the planet, and yet residents have seen water rates rise by 119 percent within the last decade, making them among the highest rates in the country. The official unemployment rate of the city, widely considered understated, is at a record high, and the official poverty rate, also understated, sits at about 40 percent (Detroit People's Water Board et al. 2014, 3). When the City of

Detroit declared bankruptcy in the summer of 2013, the well-paid bankruptcy lawyer who was named its emergency manager declared Detroit "for sale." To lure buyers, he imposed a savage austerity regime of severe cuts to public services across the board. Water service was among the public utilities currently being considered for regionalization, sale, lease, and/or public-private partnership. Unpaid water bills operate as the utility company's "bad debt" and depress its potential resale value. The Detroit WSD was a candidate for privatization as part of Detroit's bankruptcy, and was therefore actively seeking to make itself more attractive to private investors. Removing poor black customers from the entity's resource rolls can thus be seen as one part of the broader tactic of accumulation by dispossession (Harvey 2004).

The Michigan Welfare Rights Organization (MWRO), a union of public assistance recipients and low-income workers, has been on the frontlines of the battle against Detroit's water privatization and resource expropriation. A chapter of the National Welfare Rights Union, its leadership is predominantly made up of African American and Latina women, such as Maureen Taylor, Mariam Kramer, and Sylvia Orduño, with historical roots in radical, anticapitalist and antiracist struggles. These activists played central roles in historically pivotal Detroit-based organizations such as the Dodge Revolutionary Union Movement and the League of Revolutionary Black Workers. Through their work with MWRO, they continue to demonstrate how welfare rights such as the right to water and shelter might be a cornerstone of organizing the poor and working class against those who seek to exclude them from the social surplus.

In their *Submission to the Special Rapporteur on the Human Right to Safe Drinking Water and Sanitation,* for example, the MWRO (in concert with the Detroit People's Water Board and others) made it clear how Detroit's water cutoffs constitute a continued gentrification strategy in a city already deeply segregated by class and race:

> These water cut-offs to poor Detroit households need to be understood within a broader context of Detroit's appeal in the real estate market. With its proximity to the Great Lakes and the Canadian border, the city is considered prime real estate, and is available at fire sale prices. People's overdue water bills are being transferred to their property taxes and people are losing their homes as a result.

Given the utility's lack of interest in cutting costs or generating revenues by collecting on the arrears of business users, fixing leaking
pipes, and cutting off services to abandoned homes, the organization sees the crackdown as a ploy to drive poor people of color out
of the city to facilitate gentrification—what the Michigan Welfare
Rights Organization refers to as a 'land-grab.' (Detroit People's Water
Board et al. 2014, 4)

Reports from the MWRO indicate that some families had been living
without water for over a year, eventually becoming homeless as a result.
As many as two-thirds of the water cutoffs are happening in homes with
children, moreover, increasing residents' fears about speaking out. Many
of them know through experience that child-welfare authorities may remove children from such homes in accordance with a state policy man-
dating working utilities in all residences with children (5). Meanwhile,
there are reports of people being charged as much as $500 per month
for water. The average water bill is about $150–$200 for a family of four.

The recent story of Detroit's water cutoffs, the broken-windows policing strategy, and the accumulation of downtown real estate by Gilbert,
taken together, recall Peter Linebaugh's "history of the neck" in *The
London Hanged,* which he describes as "a history of the eighteenth century class struggle that includes both the expropriation of the poor from
the means of producing (resulting in 'urbanization') and the appropriation by the poor of the means of living (resulting in 'urban crime')" (2004,
xxiii). In this history of eighteenth-century penalty and its political economy, Linebaugh demonstrates that crime and capital operate in dialectic
relation; so too do the spaces of capital and the carceral. The property
relation is a central bridge between the two, insofar as it prescribes a set
of political imperatives and practices of power while simultaneously
transforming the social landscape into a fixed set of structural arrangements and ideological commitments (Blomley 2004, 5). The investment,
boosterism, and racialized securitization of Detroit's downtown core by
Gilbert and his companies emerge out of a political economy that itself
produces the dispossession and criminalization of Detroit's impoverished black residents. Indeed, the profit margins of real-estate investment and speculation are made *possible* by dispossession and criminalization. In restructured urban cores like Detroit across the country,

the property relation motivates the enactment of police power, while penal tactics of dispossession and containment are deployed to produce class-fortified enclaves of carceral space.

In using the term "property relation," I mean to distinguish the relation from property as such, or from merely the *objects* of ownership. Rather, "property" as it is used here points to an organized set of relations, primarily between people, in regard to a valued resource. As a relation, then, property organizes much of the world, legally and socially. It assigns resources to owners, it allocates rights and duties, and it serves as the grounding for a great deal of contestation and protest. As Nick Blomley reminds us, property provides both a rationale for dispossession and a ground for its opposition (2004). Property is an expression of social relationships, insofar as it organizes the way in which people relate to and exercise power over each other and their material environment. Calling into question the secure "thingness" and individualized ownership of property not only brings to light the socially determined nature of *who gets to own what* in our society, as Shiri Pasternak points out, but also provokes important questions about *who gets to divest, police, govern and incapacitate whom,* on the basis of one's ownership status. "By 'social relations,'" Pasternak writes, "I mean the legal and political institutions that create, protect and enforce property laws, which in reciprocal ways, socialize us to understand and accept the particular distribution of ownership in our society" (2010, 10). Property as a social relation thus organizes and legitimates state and private practices of securitization, livelihood dispossession, and criminalization, intertwined processes whose political geographies, as I have demonstrated, connect city neighborhoods to the jail and prison cells overcrowded primarily by the urban poor and under-resourced.

Akers argues that Detroit provides an opportunity to examine this dynamic in action within spaces of decline: "Rather than inert places left behind or struggling to keep up, spaces of decline incubate reconfigurations of state power and capital. It is in these reconfigurations—the shifting accumulation strategies of capital to feed off disinvestment and government interventions in the making of markets and privatization of space" that decline is produced (2013, 263). Such activity must also be seen to include the state production of prisons and prisoners. In asking how capital is being *deployed* in spaces of decline and to what ends, rather than simply assuming its singularly outward flow, we are able to better grasp the intricate relationship between capital and the carceral as it plays out in urban space. Downtown Detroit constitutes a carceral space, insofar as the production of prisons and prisoners emerges from both the abandonment of the urban core and the activities of the state there on behalf of investment capital. This occurs through technical innovations in securitization and policing as required by the restructured privileging of urban markets and the privatization of urban property, including real estate. It also occurs through the production of "crime" itself (for example, defining as "theft" the continued use of water in situations of nonpayment), the creation of scarcity through propertization, and the uneven dispossession of residents of the means of their own survival: most recently, in the case of Detroit, that of water and of shelter.

"Abandonment," "blight," and "vacancy" thus constitute the material terrain of capital accumulation and the ideological fodder for its coercive infrastructure. It is significant that the Detroit imaginary invoked by Schwartz during our tour of Gilbert's revitalization efforts is replete with metaphors of frontier and settlement. These imaginaries have a long history not only in the reconstruction of urban land markets (Smith 1996) but also, of course, in the colonization and theft of Indigenous lands. As Akers points out, "the apparent disuse or non-use of land and the array of policies deployed to put land back into productive use raise questions about fundamental claims to property in settler colonial societies based on Locke's notion of use and productivity" (2013, 267). The frontier ideology deployed to secure property rights throughout the ongoing settler colonial history of the Americas is also put to work today in the making of urban real-estate markets, in part by rationalizing social differentiation and exclusion as natural, even inevitable.[2] The work of Detroit's frontline activists, however, like Taylor and Kramer, has long been to demonstrate that it is neither.

In the early hours of the hot summer morning of July 23, 1967, a rebellion erupted on Detroit's 12th Street. Over four days, it would become the largest urban uprising in U.S. history. In his address to the nation on July 27, President Lyndon B. Johnson drew a straight and unequivocal

line between protest and crime: "First—let there be no mistake about it—
the looting, arson, plunder and pillage which have occurred are not part
of the civil rights protest. . . . That is crime—and crime must be dealt with
forcefully, and swiftly, and certainly" (U.S. National Advisory Commission on Civil Disorders 1968, 297). Dealt with forcefully it was, as some
7,000 National Guard and U.S. Army troops were deployed alongside
thousands of police officers to quell the protests. By the time the rebellion was over, forty-three people were dead and hundreds injured and
nearly 1,400 buildings had been burned.[3]

Sparked by the police harassment of a homecoming party for two
black soldiers, the Detroit rebellion was fundamentally an expression of
deep-seated discontent with chronic state disinvestment, police brutality,
and urban renewal policies whose destructive consequences were born
most heavily by the city's working and wageless communities of color. The
revolt, meanwhile, was just one in a wave of large-scale protests that
swept urban downtowns across the country in the late 1960s and early
1970s, many of them led by African Americans in multiracial, predominantly working-class coalitions. "These cycles of rebellion," Camp writes,
"articulated demands for dignity and freedom among aggrieved and insurgent people who had been displaced and dispossessed by joblessness,
housing segregation, militarism, and aggressive policing throughout the
postwar area" (2016, 1). Indeed, urban life during this period was deeply
marked by racialized uneven development: white flight to the suburbs,
accompanied by capital investment in suburban housing and infrastructure, produced wealthy outer rings, while deindustrialization, state *disinvestment,* and intensified assaults on trade unionism coalesced to undermine the quality of life of the predominantly African American and
Latinx working classes left residing in the nation's inner cities.

Forged out of the urban ferment and racial rebellions of this period,
including the Detroit uprising, President Johnson's Safe Streets Act of
1968 exemplifies the profound and long-standing imbrication of the carceral system with urban structures of capitalization and governance. A
massive piece of crime-control legislation, the Safe Streets Act expanded
police powers at the municipal level in order to quell the uprisings rock-
ing cities across the country. The close relationship between this extension of state power to arrest and incarcerate and the urban crises of

racialized unemployment, public disinvestment, and ongoing racial discrimination fuelling the rebellions was clear to urban activists of the period. Community-based African American and Puerto Rican organizations such as the Black Panthers and the Young Lords drew a chain of equivalence in their analysis between the underdevelopment of ghetto spaces in the nation's largest cities and the criminalization and imprisonment of their racialized urban residents. The Black Panthers' dictum to organize the "brothers on the block" was thus understood to apply simultaneously to both the cell block and the city block (Berger 2010, 59).

Detroit's black-led, multiracial, working-class rebellion expressed a collective awareness that a few were being made rich at the expense of the survival and well-being of the majority. Politicized by imperialist war in Southeast Asia and systemic racism and inequality at home and then emboldened by the power they found in collective action, participants in the uprising, in the eyes of the state, had to be put down. For their actions in the name of freedom and equality, Detroit's rebels were cast as a threat, transformed from protestors with legitimate grievances to criminals who posed danger to the average citizen. Their threat, in fact, was to the social order. The dispossessed and unemployed working-class African Americans of today's Detroit are similarly cast as security threats, begging the question: what, exactly, is being secured? In this case, it continues to be the profit rate, here invested in urban real estate. The practice of protecting property values, existing and projected, is fundamentally connected to practices of policing and the carceral management of urban space (Bonds 2018). As in the municipalities of St. Louis County, poor people of color are being systematically excluded from the new residential and commercial property markets of Detroit. The property relation organizes the strategy of the police state, while disinvestment and dispossession condition the production of carceral space. Whole neighborhoods are divested of water, amenities, schools, and jobs and then cast as dangerous enclaves requiring massive police repression.

An excavation of the carceral spaces of contemporary Detroit demonstrates that it is the property relation, and specifically the valorization of real estate as a central engine of urban revitalization strategies and their attendant displacement of poor, mostly black residents, that underpin and reproduce the carceral order. Thinking about the city and the prison as dialectical spaces whose transformations are structurally bound by shared imperatives and relations of power not only reveals the prison as an expression of the property relation and its centrality to contemporary urban economies but also simultaneously invites us to consider the prison as an urban exostructure. Its dismantling will require no less than a transformation of the structures of profitability that currently organize urban space—a lesson we see further demonstrated in the neoliberal prison reform initiatives being enacted in cities like Brooklyn, New York.

2
Neighborhood Watch
Reform and Real Estate
in Gentrifying Brooklyn

New York was once described much the way Detroit is now. Empty buildings competed with mysterious arsons as code for urban blight. Postwar downtown neighborhoods were largely abandoned to the poor and
working-class, including large African American and Puerto Rican communities. Capitalist speculators viewed the city as a hostile landscape,
replete with busted infrastructure, social drop-outs, and sunken property values. With the restructuring of the global economy and the turn
toward service, recreation, and consumption in urban centers across the
West in the 1970s, however, money started to come back to New York
City. Gentrification, that urban process characterized by the forced residential displacement of those without resources by those with means,
and the recoupment of profit via rising real estate values, transformed
neighborhoods like the Lower East Side and Brooklyn Heights into enclaves of wealth and whiteness. Since the late 1980s, even the far limits
of downtown squalor have been colonized by prosperity, with capital
showing no sign of abandoning its domination of the city. Today, the
children of privilege circle the blocks below Houston Street admiring
the architecture and every neighborhood in Manhattan—and increasingly Brooklyn—takes its turn as the subject of a lifestyle piece in a glossy
magazine.

The seminal economic geographer of gentrification, Neil Smith, argues that gentrification has long ceased to be a marginal urban process,
relegated to one or two areas of major metropolis (Smith 2002). Rather,

gentrification has become so generalized that, in some cities, like New York, there are few neighborhoods left that have withstood the encroachment of speculative real-estate development. One partial bulwark against such encroachment is crime, or rather fear of crime, a central trope in folklore about New York in the 1970s and 1980s. "Crime surpasses healthcare and 'the economy' as current public anxiety number one," suggests Ruth Wilson Gilmore, "even though it is well reported that in recent years average crime rates have gone down" (Gilmore 1994, quoted in Smith 1996, 209). In Brooklyn, the borough of New York today witnessing the most rapid transformations in wealth and race composition, perceptions of crime continue to organize property speculation. This is true, perhaps, nowhere as palpably as in the majority-poor, majority–African American, and intensively policed Brooklyn neighborhood of Brownsville.

Brownsville is also, more recently, a frequently cited example of neighborhood-based efforts to *interrupt* the cycle of mass incarceration, specifically through so-called alternatives to incarceration programming such as the Brownsville Anti-Violence Project (BAVP) and the Brownsville Youth Court (BYC), on which much of this chapter focuses. In September 2012, the U.S. Department of Justice (DOJ) announced that it would be allocating $599,000 in funding toward the BAVP. This was just one bundle out of $11 million in grants the DOJ distributed throughout fifteen neighborhoods across the United States. Denise O'Donnell, Bureau of Justice Assistance Director, said at the time: "This program is not about the federal government changing neighborhoods. It's about community members and stakeholders working together to identify priorities and solutions to persistent crime problems" (quoted in Center for Court Innovation 2012). The program is one of many initiatives taken in the wake of the 2008 fiscal crisis and attendant penal reform efforts, which have so far tended less toward downsizing corrections spending and more toward the allocation of increased funds into private-public initiatives launched in the names of justice reinvestment, antirecidivism, and reentry.

Justice reinvestment, originally conceived as a financial accountability mechanism, has proven to be a particularly popular policy mantle for fiscally oriented prison reform initiatives focused on reducing and reorganizing state correctional expenditure (Cadora 2014, 280). Formally institutionalized as the Justice Reinvestment Initiative (JRI) and adopted as a project of the Council of State Governments, the national association of state legislators and executive branch government leaders, justice reinvestment offers a policy canopy under which states can ostensibly downsize their spending on prisons under the guise of criminal-justice reform. In 2011, Congress passed the Criminal Justice Reinvestment Act, which essentially authorizes the Bureau of Justice Assistance to provide monies for states to reduce their correctional expenditures and manage their correctional populations and then *reinvest* that money in neighborhood-based crime and recidivism-reducing efforts such as the BAVP and BYC.

Indeed, the current period has witnessed a proliferation of state initiatives, usually underwritten by the criminal-justice apparatus in partnership with a variety of private agencies and civil society organizations, that target particular urban neighborhoods as key sites of intervention in the name of prison reform. This agenda has accelerated in the wake of the 2008 fiscal crisis and subsequent pressures to stem massive prison-cost overruns. Both the BYC and the BAVP are emblematic of this increased allocation of state funding for private-public partnerships sited in prisoners' home communities and represented as carceral alternatives. This is a phenomenon, I argue, that must be examined within the broader context of the borough's real-estate pressures and generalized gentrification across the financially booming urban terrain of New York City. So examined, the BAVP and BYC demonstrate how neoliberal prison-reform strategies can serve to reproduce, rather than upend, the dynamics of criminalization, economic displacement, and racialized social control in urban space. They also demonstrate how even so-called incarceration alternatives can be impelled by the property relation and the search for profit in urban real-estate markets.

Brownsville and Its Discontents

Encompassing approximately two square miles, Brownsville is a majority-poor and predominantly African American neighborhood of 86,000 people in central Brooklyn. With 39 percent of residents living below the federal poverty line and a median household income of $23,000, Brownsville is nearly twice as poor as the city as a whole. Unemployment rates stand in a similar proportion: 17 percent of its residents (twice that of New York's average) are unemployed (Bellafante 2013). Brownsville also hosts the largest concentration of public housing in the United States. The New York City Housing Authority (NYCHA) runs eighteen separate buildings in the neighborhood, and almost one-third of the neighborhood's residents live in public housing (Smith 2013). As one journalist in a recent magazine profile of the neighborhood put it, bleakly, "according to nearly every metric of social malady, Brownsville is ranked among the most imperiled places in the city. Brownsville has the highest incidence of infant mortality, for instance, as well as the highest percentage of pre-pregnancy obesity among mothers" (Smith 2013). Meanwhile, one out of every ten males aged sixteen to twenty-five is incarcerated (Winsa 2008).

Brownsville is the source of so many of the state's prisoners that it has been designated home to multiple "million-dollar blocks" and multi-million-dollar blocks. The million-dollar block is a carceral and carto-graphic phenomenon first mapped in the United States in the early 2000s. Originally designed as a progressive instrument for advocating for prison downsizing, the million dollar block refers to the spatially concentrated urban origins of the nation's 2.2 million prisoners, a disproportionate number of whom come from just a handful of neighborhoods in the country's biggest cities. In many places the concentration is so dense that states are spending in excess of a million dollars a year to incarcerate the residents of single city blocks (Cadora and Kurgan 2006).

Brownsville's impoverishment stands in particular contrast to sur-rounding Brooklyn neighborhoods, which, while also historically poor and black, have seen soaring rents and transformed race and class com-positions in recent years. Its closest demographic counterpart, nearby Bedford-Stuyvesant, was hailed in the *New York Times* as "Brooklyn's newest investment region" (Hall 2000) back in 2000, a promise that the neighborhood has since made good on. In the decade following that proclamation, Bedford-Stuyvesant's white population soared 633 percent (Roberts 2011). Meanwhile, laments and speculations abound on Browns-ville's own fate amid the rising tide of Brooklyn's generalized economic pressures, with some arguing that Brownsville remains "immune to gen-trification" (Bellafante 2013) because of its association with public hous-ing and high crime.

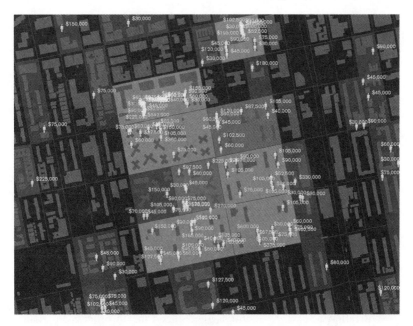

It cost $17 million to imprison 109 people from these seventeen blocks in Brownsville, Brooklyn, in 2003. They have been called "million dollar blocks." Source: Columbia Center for Spatial Research, "Million Dollar Blocks" (c4sr.columbia.edu/projects/million -dollar-blocks).

There are, however, indications that the pressures of real-estate development will soon overwhelm even Brownsville. In an online architecture blog called *Untapped Cities,* Julia Vitullo-Martin, a senior fellow at the Regional Plan Association and director of the Center for Urban Innovation, asks rhetorically: "Is Brownsville Brooklyn ready for its Jane Jacobsian comeback?" (2013). The answer, she suggests, is a resounding yes, and as she makes clear, "Jane Jacobsian comeback" is a euphemism for the gentrification elsewhere electrifying developers' profit margins. Among the hopeful signs she lists for Brownsville's real-estate class are: a revitalized Pitkin Avenue Business Improvement District (BID), new condominiums, and a charter school that shares ground-floor real estate with retail stores. As Vitullo-Martin puts it: "Geographically, Brownsville is the next in line to receive the youngsters and members of the creative class (to use Richard Florida's term) that helped pull Bushwick up from the economic devastation wrought by the arson and riots of 1977. If

Bushwick, Brooklyn (despite high crime) can attract investment and in-come diversity then so, surely, can Brownsville" (2013).

In the real-estate section of the *New York Observer*, Stephen Jacob Smith notes brightly: "If trends in nearby neighborhoods are any indication, it won't be long before Brownsville—a byword for blight, home to the largest concentration of public housing towers in the city and to this day a place that some mail carriers fear to tread—is selling something artisanal besides stamp bags" (2013). Smith here goes on to describe the inevitable economic encroachment as developers buy up real estate closer and closer to Brownsville's edges: "Developers struck out as far as Halsey Street, only three L stops away from Broadway Junction, the gateway to Brownsville, during the height of the last boom, and 'East Bushwick,' which bumps up against Brownsville's northern border, is again heating up." The far eastern edge of nearby Crown Heights, which butts up against Brownsville's western front, has also experienced rising residential rents and a real-estate boom, substantiating arguments that gentrification has now become a generalized urban process for major global cities such as New York (N. Smith 2002). In the *Observer*, Stephen Jacob Smith notes that "residential demand continues to far outstrip supply in the five boroughs and we expect that the gentrification bubble will continue growing at more or less the same pace it has been for the past few decades" (2013).

The headline of Stephen Jacob Smith's 2013 article, "Closing in on Brownsville: Brooklyn Gentrification Nears the Final Frontier," cannot but recall the title of Neil Smith's 1996 work *The New Urban Frontier*. In the book's introduction, the latter describes a "frontier ideology" put to work in the service of the class and race recomposition of poor urban neighborhoods. He defines gentrification as "the process by which poor and working class neighborhoods in the inner city are refurbished via an influx of private capital and middle-class exodus" (1996, 32). While structurally driven by the agents and imperatives of capital in search of profit, the gentrifiable neighborhood is often constituted ideologically as an "urban frontier" whose class conquest is hung either on the myth of "wasted" or "empty" space to be pioneered or on its perceived occupation by an "'uncivil class' whose behavior and attitudes reflect no acceptance of norms beyond those imperfectly specified by civil and criminal law"

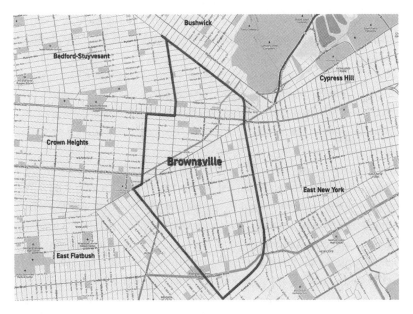

Map of Brownsville in relation to the rest of the borough of Brooklyn. Source: NYC Department of City Planning.

(N. Smith 1996, 17). In other words, if there are people already living in the urban frontier at all, they must be constituted as both undesirable and disposable for their displacement to be justified. The "criminal," as a socially constructed category, has long operated as cover for both those undesirable and disposable.

The problem of "crime" has thus been a consistent trope in the rendering of certain urban landscapes as hostile to capital, both affectively and ideologically. Aggressive state tactics to combat crime have similarly been rationalized by the myth of a frontier in need of taming. In Brownsville, crime is named outright as the single biggest barrier to gentrification. One *New York Times* article, titled "As Brooklyn Gentrifies, Some Neighborhoods Are Being Left Behind," does this by quoting a Brownsville resident asking, rhetorically: "Here, how can you have a cafe where people eat in the sun if they're concerned about gangs shooting each other?" (quoted in Berger 2012). Meanwhile, the media has also reported on how "postmen are too scared to deliver letters and packages" to Brownsville, characterizing the area as "one of Brooklyn's most crime-ravaged neighborhoods," with one postal worker described as "terrified" and quoted telling the reporter: "The neighborhood is bad. . . . I wouldn't want to go inside those buildings" (Bain and Gartland 2013).

While crime statistics would at first seem to lend some legitimacy to this fear, many accounts use *arrest records* as the evidentiary index, even while rates of actual criminalized acts remain unknown or contested. For example, one report begins by claiming: "Crime rates have been rising in Brownsville while falling elsewhere in the city." It then goes on, however, to cite arrests, not crimes: "Many of the offenders arrested are in their teens. In 2009, police made almost 4,500 arrests of youth aged 8 to 24 in a neighborhood with a total youth population of almost 13,000" (Newman 2011). High rates of arrest and incarceration do in fact plague Brownsville. In 2010, one out of every twelve males aged sixteen to twenty-four years served time in jail or prison, compared to one out of every twenty-five males borough-wide (Newman 2011). This, however, does not mean that criminal acts actually occur in Brownsville at a higher rate than anywhere else, only that there are more police performing more arrests here.

Indeed, while arrest and incarceration statistics are used to back up perceptions of high crime, little is said of the role of policing strategies in producing such numbers. Police are highly visible in Brownsville, especially around the housing projects. The local police precinct, the 73rd, is among the biggest in the city and possibly the largest. Designated a "high impact" zone, Brownsville has long been flooded with novice police officers fresh out of the police academy. The NYPD's highly controversial stop-and-frisk program, deemed unconstitutional in 2013, was enforced with exceptional vigor in the neighborhood. In the small portion of the 73rd Precinct that covers Brownsville's public housing towers and overlaps with its high-incarceration blocks, 3,020 stops were recorded in the first three months of 2013. This is compared to 751 stops for the rest of the precinct (Brice 2014).

The years leading up to and immediately following the constitutional challenge of New York's stop-and-frisk program were increasingly tumultuous ones for law enforcement in many urban centers, including New York. The increased visibility of and public attention to the deaths of young people of color at the hands of law enforcement during these years, including the high-profile choking of Eric Garner in Staten Island by NYPD officers in 2014, has provoked a new wave of public protest and unrest in urban and suburban neighborhoods. Stop-and-frisk policing is viewed by many as just one symptom of the wider problem of law enforcement's biased targeting of young people of color and the neighborhoods they live in, a perception backed up by the data. According to the New York Civil Liberties Union, 87 percent of those stopped and frisked in 2011 were black or Latinx (New York Civil Liberties Union 2018). Faced with a public relations fiasco, the NYPD shifted tactics.

In September 2013, New York police adopted a new strategy in Brownsville, ostensibly shifting away from the controversial stop-and-frisk tactic and toward a targeted focus on "youth gangs." Under the banner "Operation Crew Cut," the police department has redoubled its policing efforts specifically against local "crews": informally grouped neighborhood youth who "are organized geographically, around a housing project, a block or a single building" (Goldstein and Goodman 2013). Members of crews, police acknowledge, are rarely involved in the larger illegal enterprises usually attributed to gangs, such as drug dealing. Rather, their conflicts, according to police, are mostly geographic, having to do with rivalries over neighborhood turf (Goldstein and Goodman 2013). As a local resident and antiviolence activist in Brownsville explained to me, the crews are as much area-delineated groups of allies as they are anything else and their primary function is to offer a social support network: "It's kinda like—I don't want to call it survival—but it's like, I live here, if I'm going to continue to walk through the neighborhood, I better have people around me" (Erica Mateo, interview with author, 2013).

Police have been quick to declare Operation Crew Cut a success, telling the *New York Times* that the operation has helped drive murders down to new lows over the past year. Police Commissioner Raymond W. Kelly is quoted as boasting: "If I had to point to one reason why the murders and the shootings are down, it is this program" (Goldstein and Goodman 2013). About 500 officers have been assigned to the department's anticrew efforts. That number includes a division devoted entirely to gangs that has seen its numbers doubled, to 300 officers, and about 75 officers in precincts across the city whose responsibility is primarily to track and pursue crews. To this effect, social media like Twitter,

Facebook, and Instagram have become important tracking infrastructures. Police also keep old-fashioned lists of teens believed to be affiliated with crews; in Brownsville, that list contains 178 names by last count. "On the street, the officers might pick them up for truancy or issue summonses for biking on the sidewalk, to reinforce the notion that the police are watching" (Goldstein and Goodman 2013). Indeed, through social media, minor incidents that would be considered outside the purview of law enforcement, such as arguing in the classroom, become, under this strategy, fodder for further police intervention.

What must be underscored is that strategies of geographically uneven policing and tactics of criminalization are as responsible, if not more so, for high arrest and incarceration rates as are any actual particularly nefarious or harmful activity on the part of residents. Yet it is precisely at the level of *individual behavior* and neighborhood-based *social relationships* that even the most seemingly progressive of Brownsville's prison-reform initiatives seek to intervene. Two such examples are the BAVP and the BYC.

Deconstructing the Alternatives

The BAVP and the BYC are two alternative-to-incarceration projects of the Center for Court Innovation (CCI), an organization founded as a public-private partnership between the New York State Unified Court System and the Fund for the City of New York. The CCI runs community justice centers in two other low income, predominantly nonwhite areas of the city, Red Hook and Harlem, and a total of five youth courts in New York and New Jersey. While the CCI positions itself as an incubator of prison-reform strategies aimed at creating "a more effective and humane justice system," a close study of both the BAVP and BYC helps reveal some of the limitations and contradictions of prison reform executed through neoliberal logics and imperatives. Their operations illustrate how perceptions of crime and high incarceration rates in Brownsville have been constructed, problematically, as "neighborhood effects"[1] in need of redress, thus facilitating continued and refashioned carceral state intervention within the space of the racialized and newly prospected urban neighborhood. A close reading of these two programs illustrates some of the problematic program and policy effects of contemporary prison-

reform efforts in the broader context of neoliberal entrenchment, gentrification and the crisis of the carceral state.

Established in 2011, the BYC operates as both a diversion program
and a leadership training program for young people. Youth aged ten to
eighteen years are referred by local schools, community organizations,
courts, and police for offenses ranging from assault to truancy. Located
in a multiuse building just meters away from both the 73rd Precinct of
the NYPD and the Crossroads Juvenile Detention Center (one of two such
facilities in New York City), the BYC trains area teenagers aged fourteen
to eighteen to serve as jurors, judges, and "youth advocates" and "community advocates" (the last two being the court's terms for the defense
and prosecution, respectively). These teens spend six months hearing
real cases of other youths (aged ten to eighteen) accused of committing
low-level offenses who have been referred to the BYC by outside partners. Those referees include New York City Department of Probation,
the NYPD in Brownsville (73rd Precinct), the NYC Law Department,
family and criminal courts, the Kings County District Attorney's office,
local school officials, and even family members.

Every two weeks, the youths hear up to two referred cases. The referred youth meets with his or her youth advocate and then, during the
hearing, is questioned by members of the youth jury. After considering
the information presented, the jury decides on a particular set of sanctions. There is no option for finding the defendant *not* responsible. Sanctions might include mandatory workshops such as "Better Decisions,
Better Choices," "Motivation 101," and "Youth Anger Management," or
they might involve writing an essay in which one is asked to take responsibility for one's actions and describe the harm one thinks those actions
have caused. If the young person does not comply with the sanctions
meted out, his or her file can be returned to the original referring
agency (usually an institution of the juvenile justice system or the police
precinct) to be processed according to the agency's discretion. In effect, this means that the entire diversion process is underwritten by the
threat of arrest and prosecution by either the juvenile- or criminal-justice
systems.

The BAVP is similarly presented as a decarceration strategy, but it
targets adults in the neighborhood who have been "justice-involved,"

mostly those on probation or parole. It "seeks to improve public safety in Brownsville and enhance local perceptions of justice" (Brownsville Community Justice Center n.d.). The program describes its activities in these terms:

> The Brownsville Anti-Violence Project convenes monthly "call-in" forums where parolees returning to the neighborhood meet with representatives of law enforcement, social service providers, and ex-offenders who have gotten their lives back on track. Participants in the meetings receive a targeted, three-pronged message: that future violent behavior will be rigorously prosecuted at both the state and federal levels; that many ex-offenders have successfully re-entered the community; and that individuals seeking help will be supported by the community and its service providers. (Brownsville Community Justice Center n.d.)

The BAVP is touted as operating "in partnership with a range of agencies and community-based organizations" (Brownsville Community Justice Center n.d.). To date, its partners include the Kings County District Attorney's Office, the NYPD, the New York State Department of Corrections and Community Supervision (i.e., parole), the New York State Division of Criminal Justice Services, the U.S. Attorney's Office of the Eastern District of New York, the Pitkin Avenue BID, and the Brownsville Partnership. It is important to underscore that, despite the emphasis on "community-based" organizations, all but *two* of the actual partner agencies are institutions of the criminal-justice system. Of the remaining two, one is a business improvement organization and the other is a well-financed not-for-profit, the Brownsville Partnership.

I spent time with staff and participants from both the BYC and the BAVP conducting interviews and observing some of their programs, including numerous iterations of the youth court proceedings. Four themes emerged that revealed a *continuation* of carceral logics and recourse to state intervention, despite their positioning as alternatives-to-incarceration: (1) the reification of the categories of crime as a problem to be solved and the "criminal" subject as the cause of that problem; (2) collaboration with law enforcement and the reparation of police–community relations as an animating goal; (3) the centrality of Brownsville's branding crisis and the programs' emphasis on combating negative public perceptions of the neighborhood; and (4) the deployment of neoliberal frameworks, in particular the dominating trope of individual responsibility, to explain and support the type and character of intervention being deployed.

At their foundations, both the BYC and the BAVP accept and reproduce normative ideas about what constitutes crime and the criminal subject as the cause of crime and legitimate target of state attention. As interventionist strategies, these initiatives extend the logic of the prison system in taking for granted the centrality of crime as the neighborhood's foremost problem to be resolved. Their programming initiatives seek to resolve that problem by directing their efforts at its presumed cause: the individual criminal subject. This, for example, is how James Brodick, project director of the Brownsville Community Justice Center, characterized the goals of the BAVP during our interview in 2013: "There's a few different goals. Obviously everyone's going to want to talk about the main one, right? You want to reduce crime. So one goal of our policy is to kind of reduce crime in the community."

The BYC, meanwhile, reifies the categories of crime and the criminal by precluding from its organizational premise anything other than admission of responsibility (and by association, guilt) on the part of the subjected youth. So, while the youth court is voluntary and presented as an alternative that families opt into, it is an option available only to those who forego their right to contest responsibility and do not seek to *justify* their actions in some way. During an interview I conducted with her, project director Sharese Crouther explained: "Youth court is voluntary. It's an option that the families opt into. They can either accept the adjustment, or they can say this adjustment is essentially admitting like they did something wrong and . . . they can take their chances in family court and try to [find the youth] not responsible."

The very structure of the youth court, therefore, takes as a given the responsibility of individual "offenders" and proceeds on those terms, with the youth jury listening to the details of a given case *only* for the purpose of deciding on the most appropriate sanctions, rather than possibly clearing the subject of responsibility for said deeds or learning more about the broad social context in which they occurred. Its very organizational conceit, therefore, would seem to contain the same coercive pressures that lead most defendants within the criminal-justice system to "plead out." Faced with the choice between the greater prison terms and potentially harsher punishment threatened by a trial, the vast majority of criminal defendants agree to plead guilty in return for lesser prison terms, *even when innocent or believing themselves innocent of the charges.* In 2013, for example, more than 97 percent of federal criminal charges that were not dismissed were resolved through plea bargains, meaning fewer than 3 percent actually went to trial. By imitating this process, the youth court plays a central role in extending the responsibilization of young neighborhood subjects, foreclosing even the possibility of innocence, let alone any appreciation for the structural and social relations that cause, condition, or construct the problem of "crime."

A second theme of these programs is a commitment to cooperation and even collaboration with law enforcement. This prerogative is echoed in the descriptions by staff and management of a felt imperative to repair police–community relations in the neighborhood. Indeed, at numerous points during my interviews, it was openly suggested that the programs served a key public relations role for the police department and related criminal-justice agencies. Brodick named this goal explicitly, returning time and again to the problem of negative perceptions of the police among neighborhood residents and the necessity of counteracting those perceptions and "repairing relations" between law enforcement and the neighborhood:

> We want to work as a justice center to have police and community have better relations. . . . I don't want you to leave here thinking that a justice center is like a hug-a-thug kind of place, where people get out easy. I actually think it's the opposite—I think people are held accountable, but it doesn't mean it's held against them for the rest of their lives. . . . We constantly try to find a balance between good policing and good public safety, good community relations, working with both to bring them together. (Interview with author 2013)

Later in the interview, Brodick returned to the theme of neighborhood perceptions of police and suggested that:

> It really is about police being perceived in a different way. . . . I think it's that kind of moment where, as good a job as the NYPD thinks they've done and the crime stats say they've done, from their per-

spective, they also understand that there's a public relations piece of this, and a perception piece of this, that they need to address.

When pushed about law-enforcement officials' role in the antiviolence program, Brodick described them as partners of the justice center: "They're at the table. The deputy inspector at the local precinct will talk about his role in keeping this community safe and keeping you safe, but also if you're not going to do the right thing, then his job is to come down on you."

This description of the program's mandate stood in some tension with a counternarrative offered by Erica Mateo, a young woman who was born and raised in one of Brownsville's public housing towers and who now runs the BAVP. She was much more willing to suggest that police have historically been a problem in the neighborhood and that race and racism are intertwined with the feeling on the ground that the neighborhood was and continues to be *over*-policed. "The only people that were white in Brownsville in the 90s were the police," she told me in our interview, suggesting that, while more white people are now beginning to live and work in Brownsville due to encroaching gentrification, police still overwhelm the neighborhood. "And then the other thing is that, if you put a lot of police officers in one place, you're going to find things! And that's what it is; there's so many arrests for so many minor things, like 'general violations of local law.'"

Brodick and Mateo were being interviewed together, and at this point in the interview, Brodick cut in to quickly praise the efforts of police. "To the NYPD's credit, I think they are using their resources as best they can," he said. The real problem, he suggested, was not the police, but rather "the public relations outcry," including resentment among residents about the aggression of local policing activities. A central task, then, as Brodick sees it, is to help ameliorate that public relations crisis in support of policing efforts. The BAVP has thus included a community-wide public education campaign promoting non-violence and "maintaining relationships with . . . law enforcement" (Center for Court Innovation and New York State Senate 2012).

Similarly, the Brownsville Youth Court's mandate was described in terms not only of serving as an alternative *to* the criminal and juvenile justice systems, but also of better *ingratiating* the criminal-justice system with community residents. This work is especially emphasized within the internship part of the program, in which youth from the neighborhood are recruited and trained to play all the roles of the court, including the judge, jury, prosecutors, defense attorney, and bailiff. In a supervised interview I conducted in 2013 with two of the youth interns,[2] both sources exalted the hard work of law enforcement and criminal-justice agents and suggested they would be interested in careers in those fields. One of them had an aunt who was a prison guard and said that she had heard volumes about how challenged correctional officers are by the violence and irresponsibility exhibited by prisoners. One of the advantages of the youth court, another interviewee told me, was that it showed that a justice system can be "less bad" than some local youth think it is.

The degree to which rehabilitating the police in the eyes of local youth seems to be a central goal of the court is worth underscoring. As the communities most affected by police harassment and violence, African American– and Latinx-majority neighborhoods such as Brownsville have historically viewed law enforcement with apprehension. The National Institute of Justice, for example, reports that "research consistently shows that minorities are more likely than whites to view law enforcement with suspicion and distrust" (National Institute of Justice 2016). Black and brown urban neighborhoods across the United States have also been the most likely to take to the streets to protest police violence. This was as true in 1967 when Detroit residents rebelled in mass as it was in 2014 when residents of Baltimore, Ferguson, and other major urban and suburban areas took to the streets to demand justice for black lives. A major effect of these protests has been to erode police legitimacy more generally, at least in urban centers, where increased attention to racial profiling and the militarization of policing methods has provoked something of a public relations crisis for law enforcement. This crisis, rather than the crisis of police harassment of local youth, is the focus of BYC's efforts.

The BYC's and BAVP's concerns about the legitimacy of law enforcement and the criminal-justice system relate closely to a third thematic present in my study of these two initiatives: the centrality of the public perceptions of Brownsville and the necessity of better "marketing" the neighborhood to the broader urban community. The problem of perception of crime and a public conception of Brownsville as a neighborhood riddled with crime came up much more often in my interviews with program staff than do actual harm and violence. Brodick said explicitly at one point: "As far as the pathway we're taking here in Brownsville, there was as much a kind of marketing thing, where we wanted to show. . . . folks who weren't always identified as doing the most positive things, [and instead] to say, 'Look! They are doing really good stuff.'"

Mateo chimed in to describe a public education campaign the project had planned:

> I get really excited about this because it's about creating messaging and images to kind of highlight the strengths of the community, instead of doing an antiviolence project that's just about putting an image of a gun with a "no" mark on it. Of really taking a stance of just highlighting the positive of everything that's here in Brownsville. . . . I think that's going toward changing the perception that Brownsville is only violent, that everyone here is violent.

Attempts to flip the script about a neighborhood conventionally represented in negative terms is not a problem by itself, and it may indeed constitute an important facet of building community power and resources. However, the programmatic emphasis placed on the public *optics* of Brownsville's incarceration problem cannot be disentangled from the real-estate pressures and perceived obstructions to gentrification described earlier. The fact that incarceration itself and its effects on individuals and social networks is secondary in importance to negative perceptions of the neighborhood should alert us to the conflicting agendas underlying and perhaps underwriting these interventions on the ground.

Finally, the interviews revealed the pervasiveness of a neoliberal rationality in the orientation, operation, and legitimation of both programs. The tropes of "flexibility," better "outcomes and returns," and the perceived advantages of private-public partnerships are all hallmarks of neoliberal discourse and policy and all permeate the mandate and operation of both the BAVP and the BYC. Highlighting the advantages of the programs offered by the Brownsville Community Justice Center and the BAVP particularly, Brodick boasts: "More information allows you to come up with a better outcomes. And that's what the criminal-justice system misses." Brodick thus likens the project of the Justice Center to the growing leverage of social-impact bonds, suggesting that inefficiencies in the public model of criminal-justice enforcement might be offset by greater involvement of private actors: "I think it's interesting to get public and private monies to come in [to] try to solve these issues, by holding them to systems savings."

One of the most persistent findings of my fieldwork in Brownsville was the way in which the solutions offered by these programs are deployed almost entirely through the neoliberal tropes of individual responsibility, accountability, and choice, rather than policy change, public investment, or institutional restructuring. Indeed, it is in their consistent orientation around the premise of individual responsibility and rational, entrepreneurial action that the BYC and the BAVP most resemble mainstream reentry services. Reentry programming, alongside justice reinvestment, has become one of the most popular trends within penological discourse and practice. Since the late 1990s, but especially after the passage of the Second Chance Act of 2007, major reentry initiatives have been developed across the United States. The act appropriated funds for community-based prisoner reentry programming and signaled the ascendance of prisoner reentry as a major component of contemporary state policy. Reentry services, handled mainly through probation offices and a slew of privatized reentry organizations, saw a spike in their funding from 2007 until 2013 (Byrd 2013). Every state has now established a reentry taskforce and created reentry service units across its correctional departments at both the municipal and county levels (Travis 2007).

Critical studies of reentry programming reveal important insights that parallel the issues raised by the community interventions being enacted in Brownsville. These insights bear usefully on the broader panorama of community-based criminal-justice-related programming forged under the auspices of corrections-budget-recapture strategies, especially those that, like the reentry movement, are deployed under the guise of augmenting the increasingly tenuous state project of mass incarceration. For example, Renee Byrd describes how the "responsibilizing" discourse of the reentry programs she studies frames both the horizon of accountability and possibility for the lives of formerly imprisoned people, thus precluding the social or the political as domains through which circumstances might be changed: "The notions of personal responsibility circulating within reentry discourse posit transformation as a process through which the state intervenes with the soul of the offender as opposed to a collective process of political struggle" (2013, 76). What these programs emphasize is change in people's habits and choices, rather than in structures, institutions, or power relations. The vision of change they propose is thus limited to individual rather than collective action.

The central initiative of the BAVP is a monthly call-in or forum in which a panel constituted of law enforcement, former prisoners, and service providers "speak to people who are being paroled and who have a history of violent crime or of gun possession" (Community Justice Center n.d.). Mateo describes how the call-in is organized in partnership with the local police precinct, the district attorney's office, and the Department of Corrections and Community Supervision. "The message that's given to the panel," she tells me in the interview, "is a message about choices and responsibility and accountability." She continues:

> And they talk about the consequences of parolees' actions if they're caught with a gun. They talk about a choice and the precinct's role as a guardian of the neighborhood, to keep everyone safe, even including the people around the table. And then the discussion starts to shift. Then we get to the ex-offender who says "I've sat in your shoes before, and I was able to make a difference." The person that we had speaking most recently is from Brownsville. He did seventeen years . . . So he sits on the panel and he actually gives a really powerful talk, about the choices he made to change his life.

These initiatives thus posit the behavior of the individual being criminalized and the neighborhood as spatial incubator for that behavior as the primary terrain for transforming both mass imprisonment and the community. Reuben Jonathan Miller (2013), an ethnographer who has charted the proliferation of reentry programs across urban communities, advances the term "carceral devolution" to describe what he sees as a kind of "double movement" of hyperlocal intervention targeted at former prisoners' home communities, on the one hand, and inside former prisoners' heads, on the other. Miller describes how the reentry programs he's examined focus their interventions almost entirely on the *character* and *behavior* of prisoners returning home, rather than the infrastructures, institutions, and economies of home communities or the structural conditions of their lives. Thus, he notes how a programming emphasis on "work-readiness" preparation has almost entirely supplanted concern with (let alone support for) actual employment. He describes the dominance of such mandatory treatment groups as "the ethics of self-sufficiency" and the "maintenance of 'pro-social' relationships." In their emphasis on personal transformation, job readiness, and individual responsibility, Miller argues, reentry programs occlude the structural processes that go into undermining secure employment while offering little in the way of material redress for the marginalization particular populations face within the formal labor market. What such programs do, however, is further expand the surveillance and control functions of the criminal-justice system within urban neighborhoods while simultaneously recasting "the role, force, and consequence of the state" (37).

The programs and sanctions offered by the BYC are similarly couched in entirely individualized, behaviorist terms, almost totally eclipsing the material- and resource-related challenges, including structures of racism and poverty, faced by their subjects. Sanctions dealt out by the court include workshops like "Youth Anger Management," "Drug and Alcohol Information," and "Better Decisions, Better Choices," the latter of which "focuses heavily on decision making, goal setting, how to handle pressures from media, social media, peers, etc.," according to Crouther, who describes the BYC job-readiness course thus:

> What we focus on is how to really get someone ready for an interview, for someone who may just be coming out of prison or had dropped out of school, has issues with authority or whatever the case may be, just has had a hard time with anyone giving them a chance, period. How to walk into a room confidently, look someone in the eye when you're speaking to them, or not to get upset, or upset with receiving a task to do that you don't feel like you should have to do—"Dress for Success," "Resume Writing," all of those things. So that when they do go for that interview, they're prepared to handle it. (Interview with author, 2013)

Like much prisoner reentry programming, both of these Brownsville programs assume and reproduce an individualization of responsibility for crime and its associated harms while also using techniques for governing populations. So, even while Crouther emphasizes the social-service side of the youth court, its programming is geared entirely toward changing "offender" behavior: "Here are the things that we can offer you to help you not recidivate, and not fall back into the same patterns that led you into prison." The problematic event or action is interpreted through the individualized neoliberal frameworks of responsibility, accountability, choice, and consequence. Prison ethnographer Lorna Rhodes argues that the strong attribution of individual choice to prisoners—and therefore to would-be prisoners—is not only central to the contemporary politics of incarceration, but remains thoroughly embedded in a larger discourse of economic and social autonomy (2004, 10). In prisons, however, "choice is the currency that negotiates the resulting dynamic of domination and abjection" (66). Self-generated action is assumed to be the terrain upon which these programs do their work, just like prisons. The proper site of intervention, it follows, is that individual, including the neighborhood that incubates him/her as a choice-making subject.

Insofar as the BYC and the BAVP share with mainstream reentry programs an emphasis on responsibilization and psychosocial behaviorist conditioning, they perpetuate one powerful guiding myth about incarceration and the prison system writ large: that its origin lies in individual fault. The pseudosocialization of that fault to encompass the space of the neighborhood must be read as critically as we now read the "culture of poverty" thesis[3] popularized in the 1960s, as a strategic and instrumental frame threaded through with racist and classist assumptions and deployed, in this most contemporary instance, to make the urban neighborhood available for capitalist recoupment by ideologically effacing its already existing social value and legitimizing oppressive state intervention in the lives of its residents.

The emphasis on individual responsibility also serves to obscure the structural dynamics and social relations at play in the lives and neighborhoods of high-incarceration communities, including racism, poverty, and chronic disinvestment. This mystification is particularly problematic when considered in light of today's contingent labor opportunities for former prisoners. Rather than poor choices or neighborhood effects, it is chronic unemployment that characterizes and conditions their chances of reimprisonment, as does their systematic relegation to the lower echelons of the poverty-wage structure. In Brownsville, one in six adults has no employment whatsoever, while many others work part-time and/or minimal-wage jobs (New York City Department of Health and Mental Hygiene 2015). These numbers do not include the community residents who happen to be jailed and incarcerated (in fact, all conventional unemployment rates are deceptively lowered by concealing joblessness among the many able-bodied, working-age men and women in prisons and jails). For those with a criminal record, the chances of finding any employment at all, let alone work that pays a living wage, are formidable (Pager 2003; Western and Beckett 1999).

The Brownsville alternative-to-incarceration initiatives also widen the scope of police intervention while posing as opportunities for contracting it. For example, a feature of the BYC is the way it allows community and family members to refer children and youth to the court for a wide variety of behaviors deemed undesirable. Breaking an actual criminal or civil statute is not a requirement for referral and processing. This means that a parent whose child *has not* been arrested but who wants to, as Crouther puts it, "be proactive" and who feels as though it would be useful to go through some kind of court experience can also refer the case to the youth court. As Crouther explained: "It could be anything from a kid punches a hole in the wall, or destruction of property, or is exhibiting violent behavior. . . . We could have it fall under an offense. We would explain to the parents and child what they can expect to see . . . so they know that it's not a real offense, but if they keep doing things, this is what it could eventually be and what they could expect."

The resemblance of this aspect of the BYC operating model to the broken-windows theory of policing is instructive. Both operate under the assumption that crime is a sliding scale in which interventions in low-impact behaviors deemed undesirable, even if not actually harmful to others or even necessarily illegal, are a productive use of state and community resources in order to prevent more "serious" offenses. Broken-windows theory has by now been thoroughly debunked; its greatest legacy has been the escalation of low-level arrests and confinement of youth of color (Herbert and Brown 2006). Its echo in Crouther's description of the BYC, however, is telling. The real productive work of broken windows, as an ideology of criminogenic risk operationalized as policing strategy, is to securitize real-estate investment capital searching for profit through the gentrification of systematically disinvested neighborhoods.

Byrd places the dominant reentry movement squarely in line with the neoliberal project of statecraft, insofar as it "expands the punishment system, shores up its legitimacy, and renders the system more flexible and cost effective" (2013, 67). Likewise, a powerful consequence of alternative interventions such as the BYC and the BAVP is to blur the borders between the space of the prison and that of the city. Despite representing themselves as critics of mass incarceration, their effect is to extend the power and influence of the neoliberal carceral state, its rationalities as well as its technologies, into communities and neighborhoods outside the prison gates.

It is well established that the massive buildup of the U.S. prison population known as mass incarceration did not develop as a result of rising crime rates or new trends in the so-called criminality of individual offenders. Rather, it has its roots in changing dynamics in the economy, state formation, and racialization processes, and it at least partly constitutes an expression of shifting state strategy in the management of racialized urban poverty (Simon 1993; Beckett and Western 2001; Gilmore 2007). The fact that it is urban, poor communities of color that bear the majority consequences of reentry programs and other state interventions positioned as alternatives to or ameliorations of incarceration must therefore be similarly analyzed within the broader framework of neoliberal state-building and urban restructuring.

Miller's definition of carceral devolution can be applied to Brownsville's alternatives to and interventions against incarceration: "A reformist shift in criminal justice and social welfare policy and practice where the state's capacities to rehabilitate prisoners have been offloaded onto community based actors and organizations" (2013, 34). The offload is only a partial one, and indeed, the notion of carceral devolution aligns with other terms scholars have deployed to describe how the carceral state is restructuring itself in the face of its own legitimacy crisis. James

Kilgore (2014a), for example, delineates what he calls "non-alternative alternatives" to incarceration, a category that, for him, encompasses such community-based initiatives as drug courts, day reporting centers, and electronic monitoring schemes. He considers these non-alternative alternatives to be a form of "repackaging" mass incarceration and suggests that, however well-intentioned they might be and however much they purport to change existing penal practices, they ultimately serve to perpetuate the culture of punishment. Such programs constitute "non-alternatives" because, as he puts it, they "typically involve heavy monitoring of a person's behavior including frequent drug testing, limitations on movement and association, [and] a whole range of involuntary but supposedly therapeutic programs of dubious value and very little margin of error to avoid reincarceration" (Kilgore 2014a). Given where these programs tend to be located and who they are targeted at, their aggregate effect is often to reinforce, rather than mitigate, punitive state intervention in the lives of poor black and brown urban residents. Their effect may also be to ameliorate investment anxieties and calm would-be property buyers whose fears of crime and racialized poverty serve as some of the final remaining challenges to full-bore gentrification and the exploitation of real-estate profits in Brooklyn's central core.

While much of Detroit's downtown real-estate conquest is underwritten by an individual billionaire, his private security forces in tandem with local police, and neocolonial narratives of vacated land free for the plunder, the discourse accompanying very similar efforts in Brooklyn can be seen as accommodating, even appropriating, growing criticism of the NYPD and the criminal-justice system more broadly. At stake in both instances is the reproduction and proliferation of carceral state power in the lives and neighborhoods of, in particular, poor and working-class communities of color. Simply relocating new forms of state intervention out of the prison and into the community, then, does not in itself mark a transformation of the carceral system, its dominant logics, its harms, and its productions of disposable life; indeed, it might even reproduce and reinforce a *remade* carceral state via the material of its own critique.

Kilgore's criticism of community-based initiatives finds resonance with the forewarning offered almost four decades previous by the scholar Stanley Cohen in his essay "The Punitive City: Notes on the Dispersal of

Social Control" (1979). Writing from another period in which the legitimacy of the prison system seemed to be waning and calls for alternatives to incarceration had reached seemingly hegemonic status, Cohen surveyed such alternatives in order to problematize the ideology of community control itself:

> The major results of the new movements towards "community" and "diversion" have been to increase rather than decrease the *amount* of intervention directed at many groups of deviants in the system and, probably, to increase rather than decrease the total *number* who get into the system in the first place. In other words: "alternatives" become not alternatives at all but new programs which supplement the existing system or else expand it by attracting new populations. (347)

Foucault's 1977 genealogy of the prison system, *Discipline and Punish*, similarly reminds us that the circulation and dispersion of penal tactics is not new. Well before the period known as mass incarceration in the United States, Foucault described how massive, institutionalized sites of discipline "are broken down into flexible methods of control, which may be transferred and adapted" (1977, 113). The imperatives and capacities of the neoliberal era only intensify such flexibilization of carceral forms. This means that strategies forged in a particular era or set of places, like broken-windows policing, might be resuscitated to fit new spatial and political conjunctures, as witnessed today in Detroit. Or it might mean the invention of new policies and tactics to resolve emergent crises and contradictions, such as the legitimacy crisis of mass incarceration or the state fiscal crisis of 2008. The question to ask of these initiatives is not how they purport themselves discursively, but what relations of power they serve to either augment or reproduce, and thus what they portend materially for the lives of those subject to them. In the cases of both Detroit and New York, the imperatives of private property and profit margins of urban real estate underwrite much of the state intervention in low-income neighborhoods of color, continuing and extending carceral power and police violence in the lives of the urban poor.

Over the neoliberal period, the city has figured as a key site for experiments in new strategies for capital accumulation, one consequence

of which has been the rise of the urban real-estate economy and attendant processes of gentrification and intensified urban policing. Insofar as
such restructurings have deepened rather than abated, the lasting effect
of alternatives-to-incarceration initiatives forged under the fiscal logics
and imperatives of neoliberal prison reform—and organized under the
sign of real estate—will be only the blurring of the borders between the
space of the city and the space of the prison. They do so by extending
the power and influence of the carceral system into neighborhoods, further absorbing the family, the school, and various community agencies
into the carceral work of responsibilization, individuation, dispossession,
economic abandonment, and social control.

Mark Mauer, executive director of the Sentencing Project, notes
that, almost a decade after its introduction, "most of the justice reinvestment movement has focused on shifting resources within the criminal
justice system, particularly reducing prison funding while *increasing* resources for community-based supervision and services" (2011, 36; italics
added). Indeed, much of the prison savings afforded under the mantle of
the JRI have been simply reallocated to other, often noncustodial departments of the criminal-justice system. These include, on the one hand,
increased investment in law enforcement and policing infrastructure, but
also increased spending on reentry programming and other facets of postcustodial state supervision. As prison-reform advocates James Austin
and Eric Cadora and their coauthors have noted, with some disappointment, "among many lawmakers, the 'justice reinvestment' label has come
to stand for any correctional reform effort that is expected to save states
money and improve public safety, but without concomitant reinvestment
in community and, it turns out, without significantly reducing correctional populations" (Austin, Cadora, et al. 2013, 4).

We continue to see a neoliberal approach to state formation for
which the prison system has for many decades now served as its epi-
center. My suggestion is that the prison may prove to be neither the only,
nor even the most necessary, penal space through which neoliberalism,
racial capitalism, and the carceral state reinforce each other. The urban
landscape and neoliberal transformations therein constitute a significant
site for the transformation, adaptation, and contestation of state carceral
power, but they also suggest to us the importance of the city itself as a

critical focus of abolitionist struggle. As Neil Smith noted about Manhattan in the 1980s: "The new urban frontier is a frontier of profitability. Whatever else is revitalized, the profit rate in gentrifying neighborhoods is revitalized" (1996, 22). Insofar as the prison is an expression of the property relation and its centrality to contemporary urban economies, its dismantling will require no less than a transformation of the structures of profitability that currently organize urban space. Antigentrification campaigns can also thus be considered abolitionist projects, insofar as they simultaneously contest the rule of real estate, the law of private property, and the power of police in the determination of who gets to live where, and under what conditions.

3
Rural Extractions
Work and Wages in the Appalachian Coalfields

Rondell Meade is a former coal miner who has lived in Letcher County, Kentucky, his entire life. Three decades ago, he applied his skills strip-mining mountaintops to a 200-acre plot of land that he and his wife, Sharon, had acquired in the 1970s to live on with their family. He mined the land and removed the mountaintop, outfitted it with water, gas, and sewage infrastructure and a few small shelters, and then invited the community to share in its open space. Since the 1980s, the Meades' land has hosted wild mushroom pickers, weddings, model-airplane clubs, and even bluegrass shows. The famed musicians Bill Monroe and Ralph Stanley once played on the Meades' field for more than 6,000 people.

Flat land is scarce in eastern Kentucky, especially flat land that has water and gas infrastructure already built in. This might be why, in 2006, the U.S. Bureau of Prisons (BOP) approached the Meades and told them it wanted to survey their property for consideration as the site for a new federal prison facility. The Meades were told that, if their land was chosen and it passed the requisite environmental-impact study, the BOP would purchase it from them. Further communication on the matter was sparing, and the potential land acquisition was presented as a statement of fact, rather than a choice. The Meades' land had a lot of things going for it in the eyes of the feds. While the BOP had several sites under consideration, all of the other plots they were looking at would still have to undergo mountaintop removal in order to accommodate the sprawling horizontal architecture required of a penitentiary. They would also all need extensive infrastructural development. Judah Schept, a Kentucky-based scholar who has studied Appalachian prison siting and conducted extensive fieldwork in the area, notes: "Without knowing it, the Meades did most of the work for the Bureau" (correspondence with author, 2014).

If built, United States Penitentiary (USP) Letcher will be the fourth new federal prison to come to eastern Kentucky, and the fifth federal prison built in central Appalachia since 1992, with two of the previous four built just since 2000: USP Big Sandy in Martin County in 2003 and USP McCreary in McCreary County in 2004. Central Appalachia is home to sixteen prisons in total. Many of them were built on much less hospitable terrain, several literally on top of coalmines. When I asked him why he thinks the BOP picked his property, Rondell pointed out that "it's the only piece of property in this county that's not been under-mined." In other words, his land, unlike most of the extensively mined hills whose open coal seams still scar the landscape, is structurally sound, bearing little risk of cracking or breaking, or, indeed, swallowing up the floor of a heavy penal facility into its hollowed center.

Prison growth in central Appalachia is part of a dramatic trend in rural prison siting across the United States. Since the onset of systematic economic deindustrialization, an increasing number of struggling rural regions, including parts of Arkansas (Eason 2016), California (Gilmore 2007), New York (Huling 2002; Norton 2016), and areas in several other states in the West including Oregon, Washington, and Idaho (Bonds 2013, 2012, and 2009, respectively), have sought to suture their economies to the promise of prison development. In communities where industrial decline and soaring poverty rates render land cheap and residents eager for new forms of employment, detention spaces are commonly pitched as economic development projects and job creation strategies. Ruth Wilson Gilmore describes these regions as spaces of abandonment, or "forgotten places," pointing to the economic continuities between the disinvested urban neighborhoods from which so many prisoners come and the impoverished rural communities in which the prisons are built. "Forgotten places are not outside of history," she writes; "rather, they are places that have experienced the abandonment of contemporary capitalist and neoliberal state reorganization" (2007, 31). In these places, disinvestment of capital, declining wages and work opportunities, and a retrenchment of public amenities coalesce to produce the systemic poverty and deprivation that prison boosters target and exploit.

In eastern Kentucky, the symbolism of new prisons built on top of former coal mines is clear. These facilities infuse local imaginaries with the promise of being the next great form of economic development. Perched atop mountains artificially flattened by industrial dynamite, penitentiaries fill both *literal* spatial cavities and the economic and affective voids left by coal and the extraction process known as Mountain Top Removal (MTR). Like elsewhere across the country, prison development has been used in this region to respond to various crises at once, particularly those crises of material well-being arising out of deindustrialization, structural joblessness, and low wages. Poor people with little economic future are asked to support carceral expansion on the grounds that prisons will bring self-worth and prosperity back to Appalachian families and communities.

In the putatively postcoal era, the racialized vagaries of uneven economic development and attendant social anxieties about work and wages have coalesced to repurpose the impoverished Appalachian coalfields into carceral landscapes. Drawing from fieldwork conducted in the working-class counties of eastern Kentucky, where a spate of new prison construction dots the scenery, I explore how the growth of the carceral state in this part of the country is underwritten by the ravages of economic divestment and systemic unemployment. This is an argument that requires jettisoning a popular narrative about prison expansion in which *punitiveness* is positioned as the guiding emotional logic of the carceral state. I find instead that ideological and emotional attachments to punishment actually prove quite brittle when compared to attachments to work and wages, at least in the rural communities increasingly asked to host such facilities. The coalfields-turned-prison-grounds in Appalachia thus provide a useful place from which to decenter the narrative of crime and punishment in favor of a renewed focus on the materiality of poverty and waged labor within critical analysis of (and antiprison organizing against) the carceral state.

One Dirty Industry Atop Another

USP Big Sandy is eastern Kentucky's newest federal prison. A high-security federal facility for male prisoners perched on a mountaintop-removal site and finally opened in 2003, Big Sandy is also on record as the most expensive federal prison ever built, largely due to the extra $40 million needed for site remediation to address the sinking of the prison's foundation into the abandoned deep mine beneath even before completion. The incident was a major security threat and high-profile embarrassment to the BOP and earned the institution the unfortunate, albeit clever, local nickname "Sink-Sink," which it has yet to shake (Lockwood 2002).

The USP Big Sandy is located around the corner from a pivotal site in American history, the town of Inez, Kentucky. In 1964, U.S. President Lyndon B. Johnson chose Inez, a community of fewer than 500 people, as the location from which to declare his "War on Poverty." From the front porch of an unemployed coalminer and father of eight, President Johnson promised to eliminate poverty once and for all, announcing a slew of federal programs and legislative initiatives meant to ameliorate the hardships faced by the poorest Americans. Johnson reportedly chose Inez because it was the poorest all-white county in the country. The poverty rate in this coal-mining area was then more than 60 percent, and over two-thirds of the population faced chronic unemployment.

If Inez was a face of rural poverty in 1964, it is even more strikingly so fifty years later. Appalachia is now host to the largest concentration of white impoverishment in North America. Industrial coal extraction bears much of the blame. Over the past century, local residents have made a living by growing tobacco and corn or logging and carrying timber, but mostly by working for the coal industry, either mining or moving that once widely revered staple of the industrial revolution. Central Appalachia, a region that encompasses counties across eastern Kentucky, southwest Virginia, eastern Tennessee, and West Virginia in particular, is now synonymous in the national imagination with coal mining, mountainous landscapes, and white poverty (even while parts of the region are actually quite racially diverse).

Central Appalachia has been alternately described as an internal colony, an internal periphery of the world capitalist system, and as a "national sacrifice zone" (Scott 2010), characterizations that all point to the capitalist exploitation inherent to the extractive industries of timber and coal. The charge of national sacrifice zone is particularly hard to deny upon close examination of the area's history of resource extraction, environmental pollution, and state abandonment. Martin County, where Inez sits and where USP Big Sandy now houses prisoners from as far as Hawaii and Alaska, is today ranked the eleventh poorest county in the nation by median household income.

In 1980, the Appalachian Land Ownership Task Force documented that absentee coal corporations owned approximately 57 percent of the surface area of Martin County (1982, 35). Today, over a quarter of that surface area, roughly 37,760 acres, has been surface-mined, giving the county the highest percentage of surface-mined land of any county in the state of Kentucky. As surface mining's most extreme form, MTR characterizes much of the coal extraction in the region, particularly in Kentucky, and has done so over the last several decades. MTR refers to the aggressive process of dynamiting and destroying mountains to access the coal within them. MTR transforms peaks to plateaus, and in the process produces the flat, seemingly empty land that prisons are then constructed upon. MTR coal mining is also a deeply toxic industrial practice whose ecological consequences have already been borne out in the region in the form of a massive 306-million-gallon coal-sludge spill in 2002. Surpassing the amount of the Exxon Valdez oil spill over thirtyfold, the flood of toxic waste contaminated the public water supply for 27,000 people and killed all aquatic life in the local waterways. Martin County is also now currently in the midst of a clean water crisis, one reminiscent of that faced by the residents of Detroit, albeit rooted in its own distinct, though parallel, history of resource appropriation, economic exploitation, and state abandonment.

Capitalist underdevelopment of Appalachia, of course, precedes the discovery and large-scale extraction of coal in the region. A set of colonial forces and historical contingencies made it possible for mineral rights to be sold to speculators in the first place, and for those rights to enable the industrial-scale resource extraction that would define the region for much of the twentieth century (Schept 2017). Vast territories of southern Appalachia were expropriated in the eighteenth century from the Native American groups that lived and hunted there. Between 1763 and 1773 alone, more than 4.5 million acres of Appalachian frontier were taken from indigenous groups as southern planters and eastern capitalists expanded their speculative endeavors and transformed land previously held as a common resource into a privately possessed commodity (Dunaway 1995; Billings and Blee 2000). Capitalism entered the region not through industrialization, but through colonialism, whereby the commons were enclosed, the land expropriated, and the indigenous inhabitants ethnically cleansed and dispersed.

These early settlers observed coal seams and other mineral deposits, and by the middle of the nineteenth century, speculation had proliferated. Mineral rights and mass acreage were bought up by speculators representing northern capitalist interests, both through direct sales from local farmers and through land grants provided to them by the state of Kentucky (Dunaway 1995, 61). By privileging absentee monopoly landowners over local residents, the state paved the way for private industrial development, and thus the rise of deep mining. Another tool that abetted this rise was the "broad form deed," a trick of paperwork that "effectively transferred to the land agents all of the mineral wealth and the right to remove it by whatever means necessary, while leaving the farmer and his descendants with the semblance of land ownership, that is until the industries penetrated the region through railroads and exercised their claims to both land and what lied beneath" (Eller 1982, 55). Millions of acres of land and vast quantities of timber and mineral rights were transferred this way, and the broad form deeds would be put to later use by industry to authorize ever more mechanized, labor-free, and destructive extraction methods (Schept 2017).

For over a century, coal dominated the region as its singular economic industry. The foundational study of land ownership in Appalachia concluded in 1982 that "the dominant single industry development is highly dependent upon the control of a few, primarily corporate hands, who control the land and resources" and that companies active in the region "are taking their money out of the state and leaving nothing behind but wages: no roads, no recreation, nothing" (Appalachian Land Ownership Task Force 1982, 67). While large amounts of wealth were produced, much of it left the region, and even the wealth that stayed was unevenly distributed.

After over a century of extractive activity, the coal industry's most lasting legacy has been to produce a place with "rich land and poor people" (Eller 2008). One recent study found that every single Appalachian county in Kentucky qualified for distressed status, meaning that they are in the bottom 10 percent of all U.S. counties in terms of economic status. Kentucky's Fifth Congressional District, meanwhile, covering all of Appalachian Kentucky, was ranked second to last out of 436 districts on the Gallup-Healthways Well-Being Index, which includes physical health and basic access.

Coal mining has now been in decline in the region for close to half a century, with the number of local coal jobs plummeting precipitously. Between 1979 and 2006, the number of people working in the mining industry in Kentucky declined from 47,190 laborers to 17,959, a decrease of over 60 percent (Kentucky Office of Energy Policy n.d.). The combined structural forces of increased mechanization within the industry, the outsourcing of manufacturing jobs to Asia and Latin America, and the migration of domestic coal production to lower-cost mines in the American West culminated in the 1980s in an Appalachian recession that has only deepened in subsequent decades (Eller 2008). According to local reporting from 2013, the region had lost nearly 6,000 coal jobs over the previous two-year period (Estep 2013). In just the first quarter of 2016, the industry lost over 1,500 jobs, bringing the total number in the industry down to 6,900 for the state, which marks its lowest total since 1898 (Kentucky Energy and Environment Cabinet 2016).

For the impoverished region, one devastated by high unemployment rates and limited by a rolling topography ostensibly inhospitable to a more varied industrial future, the promise of new prison construction is an enticing development strategy. It is also in keeping with a broader geographic trend that has seen local prison siting pitched as economic relief for similarly idled and devastated rural areas across the country (Huling 2002; Gilmore 2007; Bonds 2009, 2012; Williams 2011). Between 1990 and 1999, approximately a third of all new rural prison development across the United States occurred in four of the most economically depressed regions in the nation: the West Texas Plains, south-central Georgia, the Mississippi delta, and the coalfields of central Appalachia (Ryerson 2013).

Between 2000 and 2010, Kentucky's prison population grew by 45 percent, compared to 13 percent for the U.S. state-prison system overall. Total state spending on carceral facilities in the fiscal year 2009 reached

$513 million, up from $117 million in 1989 (Schept 2014a, 204). Schept describes how coal and prisons have been cast as the past and future, respectively, of eastern Kentucky. He characterizes the overlap in their land bases, workforces, and animating logics as the spatial exchange of one dirty industry for another (204). This shift, however, has occurred despite the *dearth* of evidence that this is actually an effective economic strategy (Hooks et al. 2010; Huling 2002; Ryerson 2013). Once the coal is gone and the land devalued, prison construction is introduced as a "socio-spatial fix," a geographic solution to an economic crisis, able to reinvest capital into the landscape (Gilmore 2007). Prison siting is pitched by state actors and corporate leaders as a way to "reclaim" sites of mountaintop removal otherwise destroyed by some of the most powerful coal companies in their world and their increasingly automated mining methods.

If land is one material basis for the cultivation of a local prison imaginary, then labor is the other. Supporters argue for the prison not only as a source of crucial waged labor lost in the departure of coal jobs but also as a kind of Keynesian development tool, providing construction jobs, spreading gas and water to remote areas, and extending other infrastructure. Thus, fifty years after the "war on poverty," the nation's most expensive federal space of confinement, USP Big Sandy, was built in one of the poorest places in the nation in the name of economic revival and job creation. Central Appalachia has been failed not only by its coal companies in their scramble to automate the industry and depress wages but also by the state's promise to eliminate poverty once and for all. Today, organized abandonment is indicated by rising rates of poverty and opiate addiction, plummeting median mortality and other indexes of well-being, and a fast-rising "sea of white, working class despair" (Achenbach and Keating 2017). This abandonment might be the most defining feature of rural eastern Kentucky, even while many residents continue to receive the last dregs of the welfare state in the form of Medicaid and disability benefits.[1] The imperative of work—understood as both waged labor and the ethic of self-determination—retains powerful purchase within such a landscape and is worth considering as a central driving force in the production of carceral space.

Rondell Meade's mountain-top-removed land, the potential site for USP Letcher County in Kentucky. Photograph by Maya Bankovic.

The Prison at Work

Letcher County is a rural area of about 25,000 people located in the heart of the Appalachian coalfields of eastern Kentucky. Like many of its neighbors, including Martin County, where USP Big Sandy is housed, Letcher County is not in great shape. In 2016, Fox News described its largest town as "the poster child for the war on coal"—the conservative cable news network's way of pointing to the deleterious impacts of the decline of the coal economy. Today, the county has the second-lowest rate of labor-force participation in the country, as well as the second lowest median household income (Becker 2016). While three other federal penitentiaries have already been built in the district, the proposed USP Letcher, to be built on the reclaimed surface mine currently owned and occupied by Rondell Meade and his wife, has been in the works for a long time. Early plans for USP Letcher started in 2003, and the local planning commission has put fifteen years of work into paving the way for what was at one time an anticipated 2018 opening.

Multiple hurdles still loom for USP Letcher, and the prison is by no means a done deal. Even the Meades, who have a front-row seat to the development process, remain uncertain as to whether the prison will actually be built. There are, however, other indicators that the county is betting its economic future on the opening of a new penitentiary. Reports from the county's newspaper suggest that it is reorganizing its educational priorities in anticipation of the labor force the prison will require. Starting in the fall of 2013, students at a vocational institution next to Letcher County Central High School were offered the possibility of applying to a new law-enforcement and criminal-justice program designed to prepare local youth for prison jobs. The Letcher County Board of Education and the Letcher County Area Technology Center formed a partnership to create the new curriculum, which is partly funded by a $40,000 gift from Kentucky River Properties, LLC, a mineral-rights holding company. The *Mountain Eagle*, a local newspaper, quotes the assistant superintendent for the county noting that the new program, which includes a mock courtroom and a firing range, is necessary because "2,559 criminal justice related positions now exist within a 40-mile radius, and . . . more positions are expected to be created with the opening of [the new] federal prison" (*Mountain Eagle* Staff 2012). The tone of the article is decidedly anticipatory: "If indeed a new federal prison were built in Letcher County, nearly all of the 350 workers who would be hired there initially would need to bring some skills with them." The article goes on to describe the creation of a law-enforcement and criminal-justice program "in order to meet the demand for skilled workers" (*Mountain Eagle* Staff 2012). These reports suggest that actual educational curricula are being reorganized around a future forged through prison expansion. A similar expansion and restructuring of the criminal-justice system within the Big Sandy Community and Technical College system preceded the development of the federal penitentiary in Martin County (Ryerson 2010, 187).

Representative Hal Rogers, a long-time champion of prison construction, has promised between 300 and 450 new jobs for the area in the new prison economy. Rogers is the longest-serving Kentucky Republican in a federal office. First elected to Congress in 1980, his enduring popularity hews closely to his commitment to securing federal funding for the region, particularly in the form of projects that might revive the economic fortunes of his district. To that end, he has been a consistent champion of federal penitentiary proposals, trumpeting the benefits of hosting penal facilities in central Appalachia. In a report Rogers wrote in 1998 to the people of his district called "Creating Jobs and Opportunity for the People of Southern and Eastern Kentucky" and published in local newspapers, Rogers stated:

> If there is one thing the people of southern and eastern Kentucky appreciate it's the value of a good paying job. For generations, too many of our people have packed their bags to find a job to support themselves and their families. But time and effort are reversing that sad tradition. We are now creating new jobs at home, restoking an economy that can change the face of our region for generations to come.

The revival strategy he then goes on to outline centers around plans to build two more prison facilities in partnership with the BOP, in addition to a penitentiary already secured nearby in 1991.

For those keeping a close eye on trends in law and order, national crime rates, and even Kentucky's particular legislative policies on criminal-justice matters, it might seem something of a surprise that the state is continuing its corrections building spree. The U.S. prison population has recently seen its first decline in almost forty years, and polls show that the majority of Americans believe it ought to keep shrinking. Meanwhile, crime rates have remained stable in Kentucky over the past few decades, as they have elsewhere in the country. Kentucky legislatures have embraced at least the rhetoric of prison reform by enacting a series of justice-reinvestment measures, symbolizing a turn away from the tough-on-crime policies associated with mass incarceration. Yet prison and jail expansion continues in the region, suggesting that, just as increases in crime cannot explain Kentucky's prison growth, neither can *perceptions* of crime or an upsurge in "punitive feeling" among the region's voters. Instead, the discourse among prison boosters, local politicians, and residents alike is decidedly focused on one central and glaring local crisis: chronic unemployment.

Schept asks how "the carceral state animates a particular future" (2014b, 215). The postcoal towns of eastern Kentucky suggest that it does so, at least partly, by harnessing prisons ideologically to the drive to labor and all the complex material, psychic, and affective needs and aspirations that drive encompasses, especially among the working class. Taken to include people who work as well as people who are expected to work, the category of the working class as it is used here encompasses, importantly, the unemployed and the unwaged. The *ideology* of work must be thus considered, in tandem with the wage-relation, as itself a structuring and coercive force in the production of the carceral state.

Both the stagnation of working-class wages and the consolidation of government programs around the ethic of work are hallmarks of the neoliberal state and its transformation of the welfare system into a workfare system. Indeed, neoliberal restructuring encompasses ideological as well as material processes. One consequence of the ideological force of neoliberalism has been the reduction of all social aspirations for well-being to the narrow field of individual struggle and privatized responsibility. Neoliberal policies and rationalities thus organize the horizon of possibilities at all scales. So, while economic despair animates carceral growth in eastern Kentucky, ameliorations to its injuries are imagined primarily through the frameworks of individual responsibility and self-improvement, and employment is considered the primary vehicle for both. These frameworks obscure the social production of scarcity in regions underdeveloped by capital disinvestment and austerity measures. As geographer Anne Bonds points out, for example, in the case of Idaho and Montana, "as neoliberal rural restructuring leads communities to pursue development strategies that put places in direct competition with one another for scarce resources (e.g. community block grants, industrial development) and employment opportunities, poverty is denied and invisibilized by community officials seeking to remain competitive for investment" (2009, 433). Insofar as neoliberalism's purchase on individualism structures us affectively as fragmented subjects, all socially, economically, and politically produced problems are themselves converted into consumer items. The improvisation of a viable existence emerges as the ongoing crisis and privatized burden of people's lives.

Appeals to the job needs of local residents, meanwhile, continue to misrepresent the material realities of their actual chances of employment. So while the various prisons built in eastern Kentucky over the past dozen years have been proposed and marketed as *de facto* federal jobs creation programs, this has been done without any guarantee of actual work or economic improvement. Research into the economic impact of existing facilities proves how hollow such promises often are. For example, in Elliot County, where Little Sandy Correctional Complex was built in 2001, the civilian-labor-force participation hovers around 39 percent, the median household income is $29,700, and the poverty rate remains at 31 percent (Letcher Governance Project).

Indeed, the *un*likelihood of being hired in the new institutions often becomes clear only late in the process, once construction has begun and the conditions for employment in them are finally released to the public (Ryerson 2010). In the case of USP McCreary, the qualifications were laid out at the first job-information seminar held at the local high school after prison construction had commenced:

> All applicants would be drug-tested and put through an extensive background check that would go back seven years or to their 16th birthday. All new hires would need a clean credit history and no criminal record. All new hires would have to be younger than 38 years of age. There would be a rigorous physical exam and interview process. County residents would be given no preference in the hiring process, and a four-year college degree and previous institutional experience were "highly recommended." (Ryerson 2013)

As Sylvia Ryerson notes, these requirements eliminated most of the county's unemployed and underemployed population. In my own interviews with residents of Martin and Letcher Counties, even those who knew about the low local hiring rates of nearby penitentiaries were still hopeful that prisons would continue to be built. One person said to me about USP Big Sandy, "when that prison was first built, from the way I understand it, about 60 percent of the jobs were filled by people transferring in from other prisons," yet he was adamant that it still offered the possibility of "a good job" (Dan, interview with author, 2014).

North of Letcher County in Wheelwright, Kentucky, Sam Little, head of the Wheelwright Historical Society, noted in conversation with Schept the rumored plans to reopen a decommissioned private prison in the community. "I don't care if they put in a donut factory, as long as it brings us jobs!" Little said to Schept. Little's sentiment, reiterated in some form by many others, conveys how central the hope for jobs is to local support for prison development. It also, however, reveals an incipient politics of a possible alternative future unmoored from the prison industrial complex. While a donut factory specifically might not be the most promising or transformative economic alternative, the point is that job-creation strategies other than prison construction do exist and *can* be imagined.

When we consider carceral politics through the framework of work, wages, and uneven development, alternatives to prison building and prison filling become newly and, perhaps, even more easily imaginable. If local people were offered alternate economic strategies or policies that made possible survival and prosperity while staying in their communities and living well there, then the promises of the prison boosters would lose their psychic hold. Prison expansion, in other words, makes sense only when it at least appears to fill a need that indexes to actual experience. Fill the need through other means, and the prison as a social and spatial fix becomes redundant. The politics of abolition, within this view, fuses necessarily with the politics of economic justice. The struggle to create a society free of cages *is* the struggle to create a society free of poverty and class oppression.

The town of Wheelwright is a proper company town, established in 1916 by the Elk Horn Coal Company. Inland Steel provided the bulk of the town's jobs and funded much of its infrastructure until the late 1960s, just shortly before the local coal mine was finally closed. In more recent years, Wheelwright also had its own penitentiary, a private prison owned and operated by Corrections Corporation of America (CCA) called the Otter Creek Correctional Facility. CCA closed Otter Creek in 2012, making 180 workers redundant immediately. The economic conditions in the community were already abysmal, and the closure only worsened them. In 2011, census data showed that 27 percent of the population of the county lived below the poverty line, with per capita income hovering around $16,000. Compared to the rest of the county, Wheelwright's situation is even worse, with 42.3 percent of people living below the poverty line and a $7,447 per capita income (U.S. Bureau of the Census 2010).

The town's history demonstrates the work of uneven development, the theory that observes that capital investment in one place necessitates divestment elsewhere, because capital must remain in constant motion in order to avoid crisis. Neil Smith calls this the "see-saw" movement of capital (1984). Observing this see-saw in Wheelwright, Schept notes that the land went from a mountain to a coalmine, from a coalmine to a trash dump, from the dump to the prison, and from the prison to the empty facility (2017). The constant movement of capital in search of new ground for increased profit margins, dating back more than a century and a half, continues today to structure Wheelwright's poverty and dependence on new investment. In the absence of alternatives, even investment that proves bad for labor is welcomed. While many in the area conflate prison construction with progress, much as industrial coal mining also long signaled economic improvement, several other residents, all former coal miners and former corrections officers, spoke to Schept of adjusting to consistently lowering wages, a trend against which they felt powerless. One, for example, noted the relatively high starting wages available to miners, compared with the diminished wage of a beginning CCA guard, which was around $8.50 an hour. Wheelwright residents long for the prison to reopen, even though they realize they are not in a position to negotiate for wages or better living standards (Schept 2017; Story and Schept 2018).

As these examples illustrate, prisons are being actively marketed in the coal towns of eastern Kentucky as the future of postindustrial economic development and the only real hope for reliable jobs. Prison boosters have exploited real and well-founded fears of unyielding destitution among the residents of Appalachia in order to sell a narrative of prison growth as the solution to the region's economic woes. The material and ideological scaffolding for that narrative is the dire situation of hemorrhaging mining jobs and rising poverty rates. Especially notable in the narrative is the near total *absence* of concerns about crime or particular feelings about penalty as such. The affective infrastructure of "law and order" here, it turns out, is not so much the punishment imperative as it is the work ethic.

In more than two dozen interviews conducted with residents of prison-hosting or would-be communities across Letcher, Floyd, and Martin Counties in eastern Kentucky, not a single person spoke of crime, criminals, safety, or punishment in their reflections about existing or forecast prison facilities (Story and Schept 2018). The terms in which people spoke about prisons in their counties were almost entirely contained within the frameworks of work and economic development. Gary Cox, a former coal worker who now manages a small airport that shares a resurfaced mountaintop with USP Big Sandy in Martin County, explained: "The prison is a good paying job. And it's recession proof. You close a factory down, and you ship the jobs overseas. You can't do that to a federal prison." Even Meade, who admitted he couldn't imagine leaving his land, was fairly un-equivocal on the issue of USP Letcher's necessity to the region: "If the prison brings jobs then of course I'll welcome it here."

Ryerson's exhaustive study of the process and debates surrounding the construction of new prisons in eastern Kentucky over the past fifteen years discovers a similar sentiment. With a few minor exceptions, she writes, "The fate of those to be held within did not enter the public dis-course at all" (2010, 118). Instead, authorities and media tended to frame both the function and promise of new prisons entirely in terms of em-ployment, whether directly through prison jobs or indirectly through the goods and services putatively required by workers and visiting family members. On the opening day of USP McCreary in 2004, for example, Jim Johnson, chairman of the local steering committee, stated: "From the very beginning, the prison has been a symbol of hope and opportunity for McCreary County. . . . The best is yet to come as more citizens are hired and our businesses are able to sell more goods." At the same event, Congressman Rogers remarked: "A lot of communities don't want a prison but obviously there was interest [here], this community and this county were hungry for jobs. . . . For the first time in around 100 years, we're gaining population. . . . We're keeping young people here. We're seeing a whole new middle class develop where one has been absent" (both Johnson and Rogers quoted in Slaven 2004).

The near absence of punishment rhetoric or concerns about crime in his comments suggests the carceral state's adaptability to multiple le-gitimating narratives. While Kentucky has been among the fastest grow-ing carceral states over the past fifteen years, and one that has seen an expansion of its incarceration rate during the recent period of prison downsizing elsewhere (Vera Institute 2018), it is poverty rather than pu-nitiveness that supports its carceral logic. The chronology of prison development in the region bears repeating. First, it is concern about rural work, rather than crime rates or sentencing policy, that animates local support for new prison development. Second, the drive to punish so-called offenders follows from, rather than produces, the prison's place in the community.

Against Punishment: Work as Ideology

Within criminal-justice scholarship, there is a long history of analysis that lays the rise of mass incarceration at the feet of what has been called the "punitive turn," the "culture of control" (Garland 2001), the "punishment imperative" (Clear and Frost 2014), and the "get tough" or "tough on crime" movement. These works make some variation of the same argument: the rise of the carceral state is largely or exclusively due to changes in sentencing policies and a broader law and order politics characterized by hardened attitudes toward crime. Such analysis makes valuable contributions to an understanding of such an unprecedented rise in imprisonment, accurately noting the harsher and broader scope of sentences that are constitutive of our national reliance on incarceration. But as Jordan Camp (2016) argues, the carceral state arose as the central political expression of neoliberal racial capitalism concerned with challenges to its legitimacy. Camp notes that prison and police power became the predominant—and, crucially, the "common sense"—way for the state to respond to freedom struggles and social movements and a way to fix the social wreckage wrought by neoliberal policies and state disinvestments from the 1970s onward. That wreckage includes rising and systematic rates of unemployment, underemployment, and stagnant wages.

The prison is used as a political tool to resolve numerous crises of the neoliberal moment, particularly those arising out of structural joblessness and chronic poverty. Evidence from current developments in the carceral state would seem to confirm this analysis. First, recent work on the continuation of carceral practices under the guise of criminal-justice reform demonstrates that incarceration and forms of custodial control do not necessarily need to rely on discourses of punishment for legitimacy (Kilgore 2014a; Schept 2015). Furthermore, the emergence of newly branded spaces of detention across the United States over the past two decades, often cloaked behind euphemisms that cast them as more humane or somehow socially progressive, indicates the mutability of confinement architectures, or at least their labels. Some of these prisons and jails are now called "reflection cottages," "justice campuses," "gender-responsive prisons," and "mental health jails," thus suggesting the carceral state's adaptability to reformist critique and its autonomy from neo-conservative law-and-order politics (Citizens United for a Responsible Budget 2007; Cullors-Brignac and Zuñiga 2014; Parks 2013; Schept 2015). While it must be acknowledged that changing discourses of punishment can have real consequences for incarcerated people's lives and that distinctions in confinement conditions and conceptual mantles do matter for those inside,[2] such distinctions in general do little to change the monopoly of detention spaces as the state's go-to fix for social problems. More to the point, however, the logic of punishment and punitive feeling inadequately explains the stability and even extension of the carceral state in these instances when the expansion of carceral institutions (jails, prisons, juvenile detention centers, work release, etc.) have been justified *precisely through* a set of logics that mimic a critique of punishment-oriented penal policy. In other words, the discourse of punishment can itself operate ideologically to mystify the actual animating forces of police and carceral power.

The problem with the language of punishment, as a guiding concept for critique, is that it is indexed to a deviant act. Its very invocation alludes to the existence of a thing to be punished. That thing (which, in the case of prisons, we call "crime") is bracketed off as self-evident and beyond debate. The concept of punishment thus succeeds in framing any contestation over particular practices deemed punitive in terms of degree and of type: how much punishment is enough or too much and what should be its proper character and form. The fact that crime itself has been demonstrated historically to be both a relative and mutable socio-legal category and one that, as Linebaugh argues, belongs to capitalism and its vicissitudes (2004), is allowed little space within the characterization of incarceration as a regime of punishment. The same necessarily goes with the category of the criminal, which, as Gilmore points out, "has long been on the rise in the lexicon of putatively transparent or self-explanatory terms—like race or gender—used to designate fundamental (whether fixed or mutable) differences between kinds of people" (2009,

80). Within the neoliberal logic of personal responsibility, the designation of someone as criminal and the racialization of so-called criminals more often than not as black and brown do a great deal of work to congeal increasingly exclusionary regimes of civic participation and access to public goods. The criminal fuses the "undeserving" and the "dangerous," who become one. Any critique that fails to also challenge the very ontology of the "criminal," let alone its racialized and classist investments, as a placeholder for all things bad and threatening thus only furthers to consolidate the conflation of prisons with safety in the political imaginary.

Indeed, the assumption that it is fear of crime and attachment to punishment that constitute the ideological infrastructure of America's prison regime leaves the logics, relations, and interests that actually produce prisons, prisoners, and the carceral state wholly intact. Dislodging the prison as a "key ingredient of our common sense" (Davis 2003, 18) therefore requires thinking less about punishment and more about the social relations that currently order the social landscape, their ritualization in social space, and their representation in thought. In other words, we must rethink what constitutes the ideology or ideologies that currently uphold America's sprawling prison regime. The historian Barbara Jeanne Fields, in her own investigation of the production of race as ideology, writes, instructively: "A commonplace that few stop to examine holds that people are more readily oppressed when they are already perceived as inferior by nature. The reverse is more to the point. People are more readily perceived as inferior by nature when they are already seen as oppressed" (1990, 106). The challenge for critical prison scholars, reformers and abolitionists alike, then, is not that of *convincing* people that African Americans and other highly incarcerated and criminalized groups are not indeed inferior, for that is not how ideology works anyway. The task is rather to abolish the very institutions and relations that oppress them. Doing so first requires demystifying the prison itself as a system of social relations, including the exploitative relations of waged labor. The prison is an institution that *produces* punishment norms rather than one *produced* by punitive feeling.

While crime-and-punishment remains the dominant framework for theorizing the function and failures of the nation's carceral apparatus, there is a growing body of work that demonstrates how prisons have come to perform a significant function as a labor market institution (Western and Beckett 1999; Wacquant 2009; Purser 2012). The prison's structural relationship to employment has perhaps been analyzed most thoroughly in relation to the idled labor of those incarcerated, a disproportionately urban and African American population rendered increasingly surplus by deindustrialization and the globalization of capital. Indeed, when it is put in the context of the U.S. political economy as a whole, one finds that the expansion of the American prison population from the 1970s onward tracks alongside the deregulation of the U.S. labor market and the stagnation of workers' wages. This surplus population, itself abandoned by capital and the state and residing often in disinvested urban neighborhoods, makes up the greatest share of the nation's prisoners today.

As Jamie Peck and Nik Theodore (2008) have argued in the context of Chicago, the twenty-first-century prison system now functions institutionally to manage but also to *produce* systemic unemployability across a criminalized class. In the restructured urban labor market of the deindustrialized, neoliberal economy, uneducated black and Latinx men and women have been relegated to the lowest echelons of the waged labor system, often as surplus labor. Describing the ways in which incarceration itself functions to structure chronic unemployment, Peck and Theodore describe how African American men are first excluded from the labor market and then locked up in what has become characterized as a warehousing prison system. "So ensnared," they write, "this criminalized class has been almost completely detached from the job market, the segmentations within which have calcified, just as the form of the accompanying regulatory institutions has 'hardened'" (276). They suggest that the contemporary prison system wields significant influence on the social distribution of work and wages, and thus the relative bargaining power of those racially differentiated segments of the working poor. As a labor-market institution, the prison system both absorbs and conceals unemployment, on the one hand, and exacerbates it, on the other, as those released with criminal status find themselves marked and often unable to find full-time work in the formal economy.

The intimate relationship between prisons and the labor market has perhaps only intensified in the neoliberal period, as the enforcement of work, as the flipside to the defense of property rights, solidifies as a particular preoccupation and organizational function of the postwelfare state. Work as an ideology and waged labor as a market institution structure the logic of prison-building as a revival strategy in economically depressed rural regions. Indeed, from the point of view of those nonincarcerated subjects who themselves occupy the lower rungs of what Deborah Cowen and Amy Siciliano (2011) call surplus masculinities in disinvested areas like Appalachia, prisons are first and foremost an employment opportunity, disassociated from normative attachments to punishment.

In the twenty-first-century postcoal prison towns of eastern Kentucky, one encounters something akin to the "aspirational normativity" identified by Lauren Berlant: "The ongoing prospect of low-waged and uninteresting labor" as the horizon of imagined possibility for the project of life-building under capitalism (2007, 275). The social and economic squeeze put on the American working class since the 1970s under the sign of neoliberalism has not only devastated the wages and bargaining power of those in Appalachia who have managed to find employment but has also, for many, reified work *in any form* as the most coveted goal and most significant indicator of a person's value. Even the region's high rates of prescription drug addiction (Potter 2009) are lamented, at least in the interviews I conducted, in terms that position the problem of idled labor more urgently than any other dire consequence. As one local lumber worker I interviewed in 2014 bemoaned: "Drug addicts—they got them state Medicaid cards, and it pays for everything. And they won't work—young, healthy people, who won't work. It's a real shame."

It is in this sense that work, conceived broadly to include both the waged relation and the work ethic, rather than punishment, constitutes the most salient ideological feature and social relation animating Kentucky's carceral state. As political scientist Kathi Weeks theorizes, "the glorification of work as a prototypically human endeavor, as the key both to social belonging and individual achievement, constitutes the fundamental ideological foundation of contemporary capitalism: it was built on the basis of this ethic, which continues to serve the system's interests and rationalize its outcomes" (2011, 109). This ideological bedrock, buttressed by desperate levels of poverty, imbues prison expansion with a logic it might not have otherwise. Which is to suggest, more simply, that the project of rethinking prisons requires a broad rethinking of the very ideology of work and the social relation of waged labor as centerpieces of the political economy.

In eastern Kentucky, like elsewhere, one hears in the testimonies of unemployed and underemployed residents little hope for the future outside of the production of stable waged work, regardless of what that work actually is. Berlant describes such sentiments as "the production as desire of a collective will to imagine oneself as a solitary agent who can and must live the good life promised by capitalist culture" (2007, 278). Citizens of modern capitalism in the United States are exhorted, she argues, "to understand that the 'bottom line' of national life is neither utopia nor freedom but survival, which can be achieved only by a citizenry that eats its anger, makes no unreasonable claims on resources or control over value, and uses its most creative energy to cultivate intimate spheres while scraping a life together feasibly in response to the market-world's caprice" (2000, 127). The drive to work is one very powerful, indeed perhaps central, response to such caprice. If such an observation seems both self-evidently true and natural or immutable, then it is worth revisiting the historical collective struggles once forged around demands that *decentered* or *reimagined* the character, conditions, and affective value of work in social life. These include the fights for governmental guarantees to full employment or income so central to post-Reconstruction black-freedom struggles (see Singh 2003 and Stein 2014b), campaigns for guaranteed basic income (van Parijs 1992), and feminist demands forged under the banner of "wages for housework" (Dalla Costa and James 1973). They also include historical investments by black, brown, and white working people in socialist visions for economic power and the redistribution of the social surplus, including control over industrial processes and universal access to basic goods.

Such aspirational struggles even once had a life in Appalachia. Scholar David Stein recounts that, in the early 1960s, in response to the decline of the coal industry and widespread poverty and unemployment, people in eastern Kentucky formed the Appalachian Committee for Full Employment: "They struggled intensely against mine operators, politicians, the police, and the leadership of the United Mine Workers while pursuing governmental guarantees to a job or income" (2014b). "Full employment" was imagined much more expansively than simply the provision of waged work. The committee's plan included a special education center for children who needed supplemental attention and for adult education, medical clinics, day care centers, and rebuilt homes with adequate plumbing and sewers. Such campaigns underscored that the problem of wagelessness is centrally a political one. People are not rendered surplus in general; they are rendered surplus or disposable from the perspective of the market and the state that serves its needs. Like prisons themselves, the problem of structural unemployment is produced out of a series of competing forces and imperatives endemic to racial capitalism. This suggests that the struggle *against* systemic unemployment, against precarious, low-wage, and uninteresting labor, and against the control of the wageless through a race-making carceral state apparatus, can—and should—be one and the same.

At the summer 2016 gathering of the Saving Our Appalachian Region summit, Rogers, a co-convener of the annual gathering and a central political force behind prison growth in the region, took the stage to discuss the need for economic diversification. While rehearsing a pitch he has now been making for close to twenty years, Rogers was disrupted by activists from the Letcher Governance Project. The protesters stood up and unfurled a banner reading "Prisons are not Innovation" and "Our $444 million," referencing the projected costs of prison construction and implicitly demanding that the money be used in other ways.

These activists are challenging prison siting on the terrain of a just economic transition in Appalachia. They are also deploying a racial justice analysis in their work, insisting that the eastern Kentucky economy not be built on the caging of poor people. What they perceive, which is often lost in sociological and criminological treatments of the prison, is that prison growth is only loosely tethered to punishment regimes. Attachments to *work* (both the wage relation and the work ethic) rather than attachments to punishment constitute the more critical ideological pillar animating Kentucky's carceral state. This reframing is important because it broadens the political horizons of possibility for those arguing for alternatives to incarceration. Focusing too narrowly on the ideology of punishment, so narrowly as to preclude a view of the wider political economy that both hosts and makes desirable the production of carceral space, limits any ensuing debate on questions about the suitability and scale of penalty (how much punishment is too little or too much) rather than questioning the very political and affective economy of the prison itself.

The social project of rethinking the practice of incarceration, and of abolishing prisons and other like structures of captivity and premature death, will fail so long as the terms we use to describe or denounce it hinge on the assumption that prisons emerge *out of* the logic of punishment, rather than vice versa. Such thinking produces a critique of mass incarceration on the grounds that it is a disproportionate, unaffordable, excessively cruel, or racially biased response to the problem of crime and the punitive feeling crime ostensibly generates. Though it may also be those things, the problem is that the prison regime is rendered itself correctable or reformable within such a framework.

Structural unemployment and wagelessness share with prisons a reified status in the modern landscape, but also a historical contingency that tells us, importantly, that the social order could be organized otherwise. This is also to suggest that the joblessness of poor and working-class Appalachians cannot be seamlessly disentangled from the structural underemployment that characterizes both the preincarceration and postincarceration lives of so many prisoners across the country. Activist and scholar Keeanga-Yamahtta Taylor argues: "It is true that Blacks and Latino/as are disproportionately affected by the country's harsh economic order, but this is a reality they share with the majority of white workers. The common experience of oppression and exploitation creates the potential for a united struggle to better the conditions of all" (2016, 214). While high rates of unemployment might be essential for capital to maintain working-class discipline and depressed wages, their disciplinary power works only if struggles and aspirations are also tied to waged labor; one must see jobs as central to one's capacity both to materially survive and to have value in the capitalist economy. Waged labor thus not only offers a site from which to understand the political work of the carceral state beyond punishment but also can serve as an organizing platform across key struggles and disparate geographies, from the impoverished and ecologically devastated coalfields of Appalachia, to the disinvested neighborhood blocks of Brownsville, Brooklyn, to the sites of mass eviction and water privatization in Detroit. In all these spaces, people have been dispossessed of economic power and the resources necessary to survive and to thrive.

The relationship of the prison to the labor market, to the wage relation, and to normative attachments to work must be considered central to any meaningful efforts to devolve, decarcerate, and eventually to abolish the prison as an institution and idea. Recognizing this relationship therefore renders visible the insurmountable contradiction between the so-called prison reform efforts of those, like the billionaire Koch brothers, who simultaneously act to undermine worker power and living wages among both the urban poor and the rural poor. Indeed, this contradiction points to some of the larger problems with contemporary bipartisan reform efforts. While decades of research demonstrate that the growth of the prison system is intimately tied up with the problems of structural joblessness, poverty economies, and stagnation of workers' wages following the economic crises of the early 1970s, mainstream prison reform continues to be propagated as if autonomous from the ongoing issues of labor power and public entitlements.

The carceral state draws its tenacity from diverse political and economic pools, allowing prisons, jails, and other constitutive parts to serve as solutions to very different kinds of communities navigating different elements of capitalist crisis. With both carceral humanism (Kilgore 2014a; Schept 2014b) and rural prison building, the neoliberal state further retracts from the social wage and further cements its political organization around police and carceral power (Camp 2016). The contemporary period's jobless economic growth and contingent labor opportunities for former prisoners coalesce to produce what Michael Hallett calls the "jobless future" as the definitive condition facing those reentering society, a condition that no amount of reentry money or job-readiness training will change (2012). Structural forces work so devastatingly against the income security of the poor and racialized populations that make up the bulk of the U.S. prison population that even the best individual reentry programs offer little chance of offering their participants actual secure employment. Perhaps this is why the wage itself must be defetishized and wage labor decentered from our constructions of alternatives. If a prison job can be so easily sold as the solution to wagelessness, then perhaps we must think not in terms of wagelessness at all, but rather coerced dependence on the labor market and economic justice more broadly.

For sacrifice zones like eastern Kentucky, abolition politics is also, necessarily, class struggle. A sacrifice zone is a geographic area impaired by environmental damage or by economic disinvestment. Eastern Kentucky has been ravaged by both. The devastation brought upon this region and the space it has opened up for prison boosters to pitch carceral infrastructure as the future to which locals must hitch their aspirations tell us that simply disrupting the organizing logics that produce prisons is not enough. Abolitionist scholarship and organizing must also take on the historical patterns and economic relationships that underdeveloped the region and produced systemic unemployment and poverty in the first place. Decarceration strategy and critical scholarship should focus on dispossession, expropriation, the wage relation, and uneven development, since these are the issues that, left unaddressed, underwrite the continued growth of the carceral state, even during periods of so-called reform. It is precisely as a social system that inheres poverty and precarity that waged labor bears so meaningfully, and devastatingly, on the carceral production of surplus life. This is why challenging the very imperative to "just get a job"—for those who are incarcerated as well as for those for whom prisons figure as possible workplaces—constitutes a necessary pillar of abolitionist politics, and liberation struggle more broadly.

4
The Prison In-Between
Caretaking and Crisis on the Visitors' Bus

Prisons isolate, but they also aggregate. They aggregate people on the inside, and they also aggregate people on the outside. People are amassed in courtrooms and in mess halls, in visiting centers and at public defenders' offices. And they are aggregated on the bus. Circulating most often between the poles of the urban neighborhood and the rural penitentiary, a vast network of buses traverse long distances and monotonous highways across the United States, carrying loved ones to and from the prison visiting centers that dot the carceral landscape. The bus riders are caretakers in motion, their route is a holding pattern, and their vehicle is a carceral space suturing the social fragmentations of prison life.

Even for a city that never sleeps, the busy Manhattan intersection where I lean against a window display of brightly colored sneakers feels especially chaotic tonight. There are tourists and businessmen, well-heeled women clutching tiny handbags, and exhausted looking food venders. Illuminated billboards glare brightly over the crush of taxicabs, and I watch more than one elderly man digging through the city's garbage bins. I have arrived early to Columbus Circle in Manhattan, a long-standing pick-up spot for Operation Prison Gap and a small handful of other prison-bus operators. I am waiting to embark on one of the longest bus routes in the state, an eight-hour overnight journey to Attica State Prison, located 350 miles from NYC in the northeast corner of New York. I am among the first to arrive, but within an hour of standing here, I am surrounded by more than two dozen other women.

A New York City prison bus loading passengers headed to upstate New York on the Albion Correctional Facility route. Photograph by Maya Bankovic.

Beginning at about 9 p.m. every Friday and Saturday night at the corner of 58th Street and 7th Avenue in Manhattan, a crowd slowly begins gathering into a loose and shifting line. This group is made up almost entirely of women of color, young and old, some of them accompanied by children. Their presence can be easy to miss amid the bustle of tourists and residents of New York City's hectic midtown area, but their invisibility belies the conspicuousness of shared traits, including the carrying of a small backpack or overnight bag containing a change of clothes and some food. They stand in front of the Chase Bank on this street corner of Manhattan every weekend in all seasons, waiting for the buses and vans that will eventually roll up and take them on the overnight journey to one of the dozens of prison facilities currently affixed to the landscape of upstate New York.

The prison bus is a unique feature of the era of mass incarceration, even while the long-distance bus as a space of working-class life more generally is not. In New York, the buses and vans that carry passengers to visit their loved ones in far away institutions are all run privately, many by individuals or families with their own personal experiences of incarceration. As the state's incarceration rates have ballooned, so too has the bus traffic. There are now more than a dozen different bus and van opera-

tions that service the population of visitors travelling from the city to facilities upstate. A handful of them have been taking passengers to New
York's penitentiaries for almost forty years. These passengers bring notes
and care packages, offer news, comfort, and companionship and, by their
very presence, remind guards that prisoners are not, in fact, unloved and
alone in the world.

Ruth Wilson Gilmore's seminal 2007 book *Golden Gulag* opens and
closes from the space of a prison bus carrying visitors to California's
outer echelons. In bookending her analysis of California's prison system
in this way, Gilmore underscores the importance of the bus and the
people on it as *connectors,* traversing and circumventing a regime that
works by systematizing isolation and segregation. Indeed, the prison bus
is both a carceral space and a scene of gendered and racialized caretaking. As such, it is a space that testifies to the crisis of everyday life that
neoliberal racial capitalism produces for those at the lowest echelons of
the social order, especially those tasked with the work of reproducing life
and maintaining its emotional adhesions. This group tends to be overwhelmingly constituted by women of color, and these women tend overwhelmingly to take the bus: the bus to work, the bus out of town, and the
bus to prison.

The bus to prison can itself be understood as a carceral space, insofar
as its very existence is contingent on the coerced geographic removal of
prisoners from their families, social networks, and communities. It exists
because the prison system exists. The conditions it imposes on its riders
echo the conditions of incarceration. In circulating, over long periods of
time and across vast physical distances, the mothers, sisters, wives, and
girlfriends primarily tasked with the work of caregiving across the deep
fissures produced by the prison regime, the bus functions as a holding
space in which these women serve time in uncomfortable conditions,
enduring the erosion of their bodies, psyches, and resources. In this way,
the bus amounts to a kind of gendered secondary imprisonment for the
predominantly working-class women of color who ride it regularly.

The bus is also a scene of ordinary neoliberal crisis, social reproduction, and fragile solidarity for its riders. To be in crisis, as theorist Lauren
Berlant defines it, is "to bear an extended burden of vulnerability for
an undetermined duration" (2011, 62). This is a crisis, I argue, certainly

intensified by the violence, stress, and social disruption of mass incarceration. But it is also a crisis that both underwrites the carceral state and extends beyond imprisonment, a crisis that the current regime of racial capitalism, intensified under neoliberalism and the most recent financial recession, produces systematically as ordinary, everyday life. A carceral space in character as well as function, then, the bus (much like the prison itself) offers an important vantage from which to investigate the negotiation of life-building and radical sociality within neoliberal capitalism and the social relations it both harbors and fragments.

"Riding the Dog": Organizing on the Public Bus

If there is one machine that symbolizes working class mobility and political possibility in America, it is the bus, and particularly the long-distance bus (Gilmore 2014). "Riding the dog" has long been a familiar expression among working-class Americans, a colloquialism for journeys taken on that most monopolistic of corporate coaches, the Greyhound. Since the postwar explosion of car ownership and the remaking of the American landscape to accommodate automotive travel, intercity bus travel, like intracity public transit, has increasingly become the dominion of low-income people of color. Since the 1970s, coach companies like Greyhound have accepted the flight of most middle-class Americans from their routes and even reoriented their advertising and services accordingly (Walsh 2010). Consequentially, the long-distance bus is now almost entirely considered a plebian mode of travel associated with poverty and the limited options of working-class life.

If the long-distance bus has historically been organized by race and class, so too has been the infrastructure built to carry its weight. The nation's highways have a long and wretched history of violent incursions, constructed to slice like raw concrete wounds through the yards of the poorest and most racialized of U.S. urban neighborhoods. Eric Avila argues that, "race—racial identity and racial ideology—shaped the geography of highway construction in urban America, fuelling new patterns of racial inequality that exacerbated an unfolding 'urban crisis' in postwar America" (2014, 2). The neighborhoods occupied by people of color have been historically coded as blight in planning discourse, paving the way for their targeting by a federal highway program often working hand-in-glove with private redevelopment and public practices like slum clearance and redlining. In this way, the highway is also a classed and racialized space, one that organizes myriad forms of segregation into the built environment. As a key social infrastructure of black working-class life in particular, the long-distance bus and its attendant architectures, including the highway and the bus depot, share defining properties with the prison edifice as another public infrastructure organizing the lives of vast numbers of black, poor, and dispossessed U.S. residents. Sometimes their overlap is more literal than proximate. For example, Gilmore recounts a story about a New Orleans Greyhound bus station transformed into a makeshift jail in the immediate wake of Hurricane Katrina (2009, 80). Spatial repurposing, in this instance, was the objective of the state. But repurposing has also always been a tactic of the dispossessed, whose commoning of the spaces to which they are relegated by force has historically produced movement spaces out of holding spaces. Just as prisons and jails have been transformed into spaces of rebellion for as long as they have existed (Berger 2014), bus infrastructures also generate possibilities for insurgent socialities. Moira Rachel Kenney, for example, describes the emergence of a vibrant gay and lesbian scene in 1940s Los Angeles centered in the bars clustered around the city's downtown Greyhound bus station (2001). These bus-station bars provided spaces where gays and lesbians could both recognize each other and interact without suspicion, a liminal space wherein the shared experiences of abandonment and forced transience also engendered a radical scene of togetherness.

The bus, precisely because of its historical formation as a gendered, classed, and racialized space, has figured importantly in the long history of freedom struggles in the postwar United States. Indeed, there is a long and rich political tradition in which those marginalized populations consigned to the cramped quarters of the long-distance bus have made it into a site for innovative class and race-based organizing. The relationship between buses, race politics, and social struggle is most often underscored by the bus's symbolic distillation of the civil rights era. In 1955, Rosa Parks, a forty-three-year-old working-class black woman in Montgomery, Alabama, refused to give up her bus seat to a white man in an act of political defiance against local Jim Crow laws, sparking the Montgomery Bus Boycott. Two years previous, in 1953, African Americans organized under the auspices of the United Defense League in Baton Rouge, Louisiana, staged the first successful bus boycott in the nation's history. Less than a decade later, in the late summer of 1961, more than four hundred Freedom Riders were arrested for their participation in the struggle against ongoing racial segregation on interstate buses. Defying Jim Crow laws, the Freedom Riders recognized the interstate bus as an infrastructure of racial oppression, but also as a site for collective action.

More recently, the early 1990s saw the unprecedented formation of a labor-organizing project called the Bus Riders Union (BRU), whose membership, drawn from the predominantly low-income, black, Latinx, and Asian mass-transit ridership of Los Angeles, continues to challenge transportation and environmental racism in that city and beyond (Mann 2004). Using mass transit as an organization space and bus riders as an organizing *base*, the BRU successfully sued the Los Angeles County Metropolitan Transit Authority for racial discrimination in its fee and service structure. While primarily organizing bus riders as such, the BRU draws its social power from the dual recognition that bus ridership itself is a condition of being poor and racially marginalized and that the shared space of the bus is an opportune *social* site for organizing in an era of radically atomized working-class life.

From the Freedom Riders to the BRU, bus riders have capitalized on the contradictions of public transit and the role it plays in the work and community life of poor, Latinx and African American communities to transform the dense space and long commutes into an organizing opportunity. They have done this both in spite of and because of the very structural processes through which the bus has become such a paradigmatic racialized and working-class space in the first place, including residential displacement, labor exploitation, and resource scarcity. That so many important historic freedom struggles have coalesced in one way or another around the spaces of the bus thus comes to make sense. As a "'between' of segregated lives" (Gilmore 2007, 236), buses have historically revealed a great deal about the structured inequities of state resource distribution and vulnerability to risk and even offered a (quite literal) platform for the recognition of collective oppression and oppositional politics. The bus thus constitutes a significant political space in that it both expresses the structural organization of racial capitalism within the social landscape and offers, potentially at least, a spatial condition for recognition, reciprocity, and organizing among low-income people of color.

In her own attention to buses carrying the loved ones of prisoners, Gilmore examines how such buses have historically offered a unique site for the organization of poor and working-class people otherwise *disorganized* in the modern economy by segregation and fragmentation. She probes the relationship between organizing and recognition in such spaces by asking: "How do people come actively to identify in and act through a group such that its trajectory surpasses reinforcing characteristics (e.g., identity politics), or protecting a fixed set of interests (e.g., corporatist politics), and instead extends toward an evolving, purposeful social movement (e.g., real class politics)?" (2007, 191). I ask a different but related set of questions, the most central of which is how the socially reproductive labor of prison visiting is experienced and negotiated, within the space of the bus, as a condition of everyday life within neoliberal capitalism. The answer is necessarily contradictory. Indeed, as a zone of ordinary life, the prison bus absorbs lots of incoherence, not least of which is that it can serve not only to aggravate self-isolation but also to facilitate togetherness and common cause. In this way, it resembles the public-transit buses documented by Marisela Norte, a writer who depicts racialized and gendered life on public transit in LA and whom George Lipsitz calls the "bus poet of Los Angeles": "Norte recognizes the bus as simultaneously a site of containment *and* connection, of incarceration *and* affiliation, of solitude *and* sociality" (2004, 512). The prison buses of New York share with LA's public transit an urban, working-class ridership constituted primarily by women of color, but also the social contradictions and fragilities Norte notes. And like most long-distances buses in the United States that carry primarily the poor and working-class, it is experienced first and foremost as the imposition of physical distress.

The Journey and Its Discomforts

The New York State Department of Corrections and Community Supervision (DOCCS) is the state's largest government agency, with an annual budget of $2.5 billion and 31,000 staff spread out across the state. According to DOCCS data, there were approximately 54,142 individuals incarcerated throughout its fifty-four state facilities as of January 1, 2014. Of those prisoners, 49 percent are identified as African American and less than a quarter as white (New York State Department of Corrections and Community Supervision 2014, ii). These prisoners come overwhelmingly from New York City, which is also where their families and loved ones are located. Approximately 62 percent of the state's prisoners hail from the city, with many of those concentrated in just a handful of neighborhoods (Wagner 2003). The vast majority of New York's carceral facilities, however, are located in rural counties upstate. While there are a small number of facilities within relatively short distance from NYC, 87 percent of New York prisoners are incarcerated more than two hours away (Wagner 2003). Many facilities, such Attica and Albion to the west of the state, or Upstate Penitentiary near the Quebec border, are hundreds of miles away from Manhattan, establishing a formidable barrier to those hoping to visit.

The longest running of the private bus and van companies that service visitors to New York's penal facilities is the family-owned Operation Prison Gap (OPG). Founded by a former prisoner named Ray Simmons, OPG was formed after Simmons was released from Attica Prison in 1973. Before Simmons started the company, visitors had no way to get to the facilities other than to take a Greyhound bus, which even then stopped only in town centers, requiring riders to pay additionally for taxis to bring them directly to the facility gates. "In four years [inside] I had four visits," Simmons told me. While many more small-scale operators started running buses and vans beginning in the late 1980s and, in his own words, "business isn't what it used to be," Simmons claims he can still run about twenty buses each weekend.

OPG runs bus services along the two main long distance routes, one travelling due north, toward Upstate Correctional Facility in Malone and nearby facilities, and the other travelling northwest, toward Albion and Orleans correctional facilities. The bus that I took, which travelled the northwest route to Attica, made stops at six different facilities: Groveland and Livingston at about 6 a.m., Wyoming and Attica at about 7 a.m., and then onward to Wende and Albion by the Canadian border. The prison facilities themselves often offer information about the bus companies in their visitors' centers and when people call to ask for information about how they might get there.

Different operators have different pick-up spots and leave through-out the night, depending on where they are going. The most populous depots are at 34th Street and 7th Avenue, on the west side of Manhattan, and at Columbus Circle, where OPG has been picking up riders each Friday and Saturday night for forty years. Both are a formidable distance from the east Brooklyn, Bronx, and Long Island neighborhoods from which the vast majority of the bus riders seem to come. Many riders have already spent between one and three hours just getting to the pick-up spot, travelling by bus, subway, light rail, and in some cases taxi cab in order to get there. Some of the smaller van services will depart from neighborhoods in the outer boroughs of New York, including Brooklyn, the Bronx, and Queens, but their routes are often much more limited.

Prison visits begin at 9 a.m.. Because there is a fair amount of pro-cessing involved before the visitors can get inside the institutions, the buses going the furthest will leave between 9 p.m. and 11 p.m. at night and can take as long as eight or ten hours each way, barring any delays. The bus to Attica is supposed to leave at 10 p.m. but often departs closer to 11 p.m. The cost of a bus ticket to Attica is $65. While the price differs depending on the distance to the facility, tickets tend to cost at least $40 each. Children travel for half price. Expenses can greatly exceed the price of the ticket, as visitors are typically required to spend money travelling to the bus pick-up spot, sometimes relying on car services because public transit, when available, may be less frequent and dependable at the times of night that the visitors are travelling. Additional costs include food and drinks during the twenty-four-hour period of the trip and from the vend-ing machines inside of the prison. Many visitors have also gone shopping for favorite food items, clothing, and cash to bring inside for loved ones.

The prison bus is clearly gendered, with the vast majority of passen-gers being women travelling alone. This observation was corroborated by the women I interviewed as well as two separate bus operators I spoke to, both of whom estimated that about 95 percent of the ridership was female. Some of these women travel with children. When I would ride the bus, I counted six to eight children, ranging from infants to pre-teens. Most of the riders, moreover, are women of color, with African American women constituting the bulk of the ridership. During one journey, from appearances at least, I was the only white person on the bus. When I asked my interviewees about racial composition on the bus, many suggested that all races were represented, including Hispanics, Puerto Ricans, Arab Americans, South Asians, and African Americans, while also acknowledging that white riders were in the minority.

The journey, in my own experience and in the words of my interviewees, is arduous and physically uncomfortable. The chartered buses are low on amenities. Each of them holds between forty-nine and fifty-seven passengers and is equipped with reclining seats, and occasionally a handful of TVs on which movies play throughout part of the ride. During my first ride, one black-and-white movie, difficult to discern and barely audible, played on repeat until we arrived. The buses are often full, and the sheer density of bodies and noises makes it difficult to sleep. Yet, the buses are much preferred to the vans that sometimes come to pick up riders instead, which do not have reclining seats and are without a bathroom, rendering the overnight trip, according to many of those I spoke to, extremely uncomfortable.

This discomfort is experienced for many as more than just incidental inconvenience. For those already worn out by the day-to-day challenges of their lives, which often include inadequate healthcare, responsibility for multiple dependents, and precarious employment, the discomforts of riding the bus further erode already attenuated reserves of energy and goodwill. This bears meaningfully on the risk calculus entailed by investing in others. In other words, riders are already so stressed out, exhausted, and overextended by the time they ride the bus that every additional distress experienced during the journey is exacerbated. Making the journey to visit incarcerated loved ones is a resource-intensive endeavor, costing immense amounts of time, energy, and money. For those riding the bus, most of whom are on the losing side of neoliberalism's widening of the inequality gap, those resources are already scarce. Under such conditions, the activity of engaging with or trusting in others can be felt more as an additional burden than as a source of relief.

Indeed, the material consequences of neoliberalism, as a bundle of policies and organizing rationalities that have transformed the contemporary political and economic landscape of state entitlements, have been unevenly distributed, with women of color bearing the brunt of the shrinkage of social securities (Burnham 2001). The recent period of recession triggered by the 2008 financial crisis has intensified the hardships faced by the lowest strata of the U.S. class and race structures generally, but it has proven particularly devastating for women of color. Black and Latina women today face worse wages and job prospects, higher poverty rates, and greater difficulties in gaining access to health care. As a population, they are significantly worse off than before the economic crisis (Johnson 2013). In 2011, for example, 36 percent of African Americans, including 38.1 percent of black women, were employed in low-wage jobs (earning poverty-level wages or less), compared to 23.4 percent of the white labor force (Mishel et al. 2012). From 2007 to 2011, the percentage of African American female-headed households in poverty grew from 43.9 to 47.3 percent, and for Latina-headed households, from 46.6 to 49.1 percent (Johnson 2013). Jumps in poverty and unemployment rates among these populations, meanwhile, have had direct consequences for healthcare access. Private health-insurance coverage for black women, for example, has dropped from 54.1 to 50 percent, while Latina women have experienced a similar decrease (Johnson 2013).

Berlant writes: "The current recession congeals decades of class bifurcation, downward mobility, and environmental, political and social brittleness that have increased progressively since the Reagan era. The intensification of these processes, which reshapes conventions of racial, gendered, sexual, economic, and nation-based subordination, has also increased the probability that structured contingency will create manifest crisis situations in ordinary existence for more kinds of people" (2011, 11). Life, in other words, has been made harder in the past decade for those who *already* faced difficulties under neoliberal racial capitalism. The result is what Berlant calls "ordinary crisis": the everyday struggle to maintain and manage existence within a context of deteriorating social, economic, and environmental conditions. In other words, the ordinary crisis is the work of social reproduction (maintaining and managing existence) as structured by the provisions of chronic precarity.

The concept of ordinary crisis helps to make sense of the ways the calamities of neoliberal austerity are subjectively registered, socially and affectively, by the already overextended women who regularly ride the prison bus. In the space of the bus, such "manifest crisis situations in ordinary existence" look and feel a lot like the distress of physical discomfort, interpersonal distrust and tension, and deep fatigue. The cumulative impact is a protracted "wearing out" of these bus riders who, in rationing their reserves of time, energy, money, and care into the long overnight bus journeys, often compensate by retreating inward, siphoning their atrophies into privatized experiences of grievance and interpersonal expressions of antagonism and distrust.

The framework of ordinary crisis recasts "crisis" as belonging first in the outside world, as a situation of unevenly disbursed structural precarity, but then also attends to the ways crisis is experienced subjectively and affectively. The experience of crisis as quotidian, whatever else is variegated about the lives of those experiencing it, is that of an extended burden of vulnerability with significant consequences for how and in what shape people imagine reprieve and redress. The prison-bus ridership fits squarely into the demographics tracked by the statistics recounted earlier. Not a single one of the women I interviewed during my research earns more than a few dollars above minimum wage, which in New York State in 2014 was $8 per hour. One rider worked as a janitor, two of them as home-health-care workers (for $12 an hour), another one was out of work due to disability, and another one juggled two jobs, one of them as a call operator for the city's 311 information service. The one white woman I interviewed worked as a corporate travel agent, which she did from home due to a severe swelling in her legs that she attributes to so many years of taking the bus. All spoke in depth about the complicated negotiations of making ends meet, including living periodically or longer-term with other family members, such as sisters and parents, using food stamps as their primary means of feeding themselves and their children, and contending with enormous levels of financial debt. One interviewee spent a long time recounting a story in which her four public-transit metro cards were confiscated by correctional guards, passionately criticizing the rule against bringing metro cards into the visitor's room. In a context like hers, in which she supports herself through disability benefits and has taken her daughter and her daughter's six children into her two-bedroom apartment after they were recently evicted, the handful of dollars distributed among those metro cards is the difference between leaving the house or not on any given day.

Such is the context within which women's preoccupations, frustrations, and anxieties about riding the prison buses must be understood.

Invited to reflect on their experiences of riding the buses, the women I interviewed spoke at length about the physical and psychic agonies experienced there: cramped quarters and impediments to leaning back; snorers and/or crying children; needing to urinate while on vans that refuse to stop; being too hot or too cold; and the various holdups that prolong waiting times both outside and on the bus, including bus breakdowns, drivers getting lost, and companies waiting for more riders to fill their seats. For example, as one woman described to me:

> Everybody gets along until somebody snores too loud in their ear, or hits their feet. Most people complain about the stretching, they can't do anything, stretch or nothing. You can fall asleep but it's very uncomfortable. By the time I get in there, riding 6, 7 hours, by 1 o'clock I'm asleep on the table because I'm so tired. I was so uncomfortable I didn't get proper rest. (Val, interview with author, 2014)

Accounts of physical discomfort were often interspersed, in my interviewee's descriptions, with references to the interpersonal antagonisms they give rise to. This is also a common theme on the online chat rooms frequented by prison riders, such as a popular web forum called "Prison Talk," a platform for loved ones and those in the prisoner support community to communicate about issues and concerns and help support others in similar circumstances. On that site, a well-trafficked thread is devoted entirely to the experiences riders have had on the prison bus and van services in New York State. One commenter named "Ladysmith" writes:

> My first bus ride to Orleans was with Prison Gap. They sent us in a van, which of course had no bathroom and we only stopped once for a bathroom break coming and going. An older woman had to go so bad that she eventually went on herself so then we had to smell that the rest of the way. (Prison Talk n.d.)

Julia, a single mother of three who has been riding the bus for over fifteen years, described some of the tensions that she encounters on her journeys, many of them tethered to competition for the scarce comforts available during long rides:

People fight about seats a lot. They push them all the way back—
and I'm very tall, I'm 5'8", so for the person to push their seat all the
way back, I mean, they're not on a British Airway flight to London,
first class. You have to be kind to the person behind you, you know.
I hear girls fighting in the back about the seats, about who's in that
seat when they get back on the bus. It's horrible, it really is. (interview with author, 2013)

The concept of ordinary crisis helps underscore how a set of quotidian discomforts can radically upend the careful management of scarce
resources, including one's own physical capacities, time, and money. In
the context of the bus riders' multiple stressors, such discomforts are revealed to be not minor at all; indeed, within the context of all-pervading
social and economic insecurity, they bear significantly on the rest of one's
weekend, week, or month, adding further pressures to the exigencies of
everyday life at the bottom of the social class structure. They also significantly delimit the horizons of possibility for those tasked with imagining
how their situations might be improved or how conditions might be
changed. While I deliberately structured my questions to allow my interview subjects to weigh in more broadly on the sense of justice or injustice
of having loved ones incarcerated for such long periods of time, few
women raised overtly critical or political questions about the penal system as a whole. They tended to focus instead on the experience, in all of
its irritating routines and miniature debasements, of riding the bus and
arriving at the prison visitors' centers. For example:

That ride, to Attica, is particularly hard. What's hard about it? Just
in general, people just . . . I don't want to say everybody's rude on
the bus, but you come across a lot of different characters on the
bus, and not everybody gets along, so people fight, they get into
arguments, and then if they have kids on the bus or something it's
hard, you can't always keep them quiet. It's hard to sleep when you
have a kid screaming behind you. (Donna, interview with author,
2014)

Gilmore writes that "prisons wear out places by wearing out people, irrespective of whether they have done time" (2007, 17). The prison buses,
in all their banality, constitute a critical site in and through which non-

prisoners are worn out by the carceral regime. The wearing out is, on the one hand, deeply material, registered by bodies subject to the chronic discomfort, pains, and sleep disruption, ritualized often over many years, that is endemic to the long overnight journeys. Christine, who estimates that she's taken over 500 rides over the twenty years she has spent visiting her husband in various institutions upstate, describes the physical effects of the rides: "I never sleep. I got edema because of this, I have a lump on my left leg because of this, because I'm always sitting down on this sitting position. I went to the doctor and I've got stress and anxiety and high blood pressure; I'm on pills." She told me that her husband has encouraged her to begin visiting once every three weeks, instead of weekly: "Because he doesn't want my health being affected by this. And I did my time, going every week."

"Doing one's time" is a common description of the visitations among bus riders. As a rhetorical construction, it borrows from the familiar euphemism for serving a prison sentence. The analogy is not lost on the women who ride the bus, many of whom see themselves as serving a kind of sentence alongside their loved ones. Ethnographer Megan Comfort, whose work examines the ways female partners of prisoners in California relate to the carceral system through their attachments to the men inside, details the parallels between incarceration and the caretaking of those locked up (2008). Her characterization of the time spent in the liminal spaces of visitation as forms of "secondary prisonization" for the women she studies resonates with my own findings about the prison bus. The exhausting and denigrating experience of contending with arbitrary regulations and restricted rights, the enforced idleness of waiting and lining up for visits, and the physically taxing corporeal confinement of the hallways and waiting rooms in which visitors spend hundreds of hours of their lives parallel, in many ways, the experiences of prisoners doing time in spaces of captivity.

The concept of doing time also points to the temporality of riding the bus, conjuring the notion of "getting by," but also that of "slow death." In the context of everyday crisis, slow death means, for Berlant, "the physical wearing out of a population in a way that points to its deterioration as a defining condition of its experience and historical existence" (2011, 95). Slow death is the condition of being worn out by the sheer effort and endeavor of reproducing life. While, in a sense, the very activity of living makes for a kind of "slow death," it is also true that chronic poverty has long been linked to the probability of shortened life expectancy (Lowrey 2014). When a rider describes, therefore, how she has never once been able to fall asleep during the overnight prison-bus journey to visit her husband, a journey she's been taking bimonthly for fifteen years, there is good evidence to suggest that such cumulative and chronic sleeplessness has adversely effected her *quantity* of life as well its quality. Statistically, we know this of, for example, laborers who work night shifts, whose disrupted sleep over many years has proven to bear out as diminished life expectancy (Blue 2012). As a vessel of austere physical taxation that carries people already at higher risk of chronic illness and inadequate health care by virtue of being poor, the prison bus occupies a role homologous with the penitentiary, long proven to have life-shortening consequences for those in its hold (Patterson 2013).

There is slow death, but there is also quick death, and its specter. Just as the testimonies of prisoners are replete with harrowing accounts of the immediate bodily dangers present in spaces of detention, so too are the testimonies given by those who ride the prison bus, dangers that, whether real or perceived, exact additional stress and psychic toll from riders on an otherwise already arduous journey. The stories bus riders share with one another about the perils encountered while riding the prison buses serve as both supportive warning and an archive of harrowing experiences. One place these stories circulate is the Prison Talk internet forum, where one section devoted specifically to experiences encountered with the two dominant bus companies, OPG and Flamboyant, runs some twenty-five pages (Prison Talk n.d.). The following is a compendium of some of the descriptions posted on the forum of situations in which riders felt acute fear for their safety.

> babyboy421: The ride home was straight out of a horror flick. I got home Sunday morning at 4:00am. If I never prayed before I was sending up some timbers on Saturday. . . . The driver was so tired he started driving off the road. The passengers were screaming for him to stop the bus and rest but he didn't.

> LilBabyL: I rode up to Clinton with Flamboyant from the Bronx about one month ago. . . . The ride was HORRENDOUS!!! I will never ever

take them again. The driver was swerving all over the road and speeding. I really feared for my life. NEVER AGAIN!

Maggiebklyn24: I rode on prison gap back in Nov 19 for that sat visit to Altona. The driver hit a deer then got lost going to Altona.

STB75: It was the worst ride ever. The bus driver was falling asleep. I kept waking up the coordinator she just brushed me off by saying he's alright. He hit the dividers 3 times, the bus was grinding. . . . I kept screaming; a girl was yelling she's a single mom bringing up her kids and wants to get there alive. . . . Sure enough on the return the same thing starting falling asleep the coordinators were long sleeping didn't have a care in the world!! He kept switching lanes I was so afraid for my life I got so many panic attacks a girl nearby me was reassuring me all will be ok. We were all panicking we were so close to falling off the cliff it was terrible. . . . I hope that you guys post this on your website and to please never ride FLAMBOYANT, if you want to stay alive.

Processes by which people are physically and psychically worn out include the stress of feeling acute physical insecurity and impending danger. Indeed, such insecurity is heightened by the social and economic crises that render the bus riders without health insurance in case of accidents and/or without the financial or social resources to bear medical injuries or missed work shifts. Heightened threat can take a variety of forms, from the terror of automobile breakdown to the sleep disturbance of a snoring seatmate. In such a context, one response can be to self-isolate.

Research into the effects of increased policing and state intervention in people's lives suggests they bear destructively on informal networks and relationships of care and mutual support. As Gilmore notes, "people stop looking out for each other and stop talking about anything that matters in terms of neighborly well-being" (2007, 17). Speaking specifically about the disentitlement former prisoners experience from such public institutions as schools, housing, and workplace, she writes: "In such inhospitable places, everybody isolates" (17).

There is much about the scene of the prison bus, from its aggregation of collective experience to its ritualization of shared time and space and its mediating role between the prison and the "outside," that suggests it might provide an ideal space for a collectivization of struggles and solutions among the prison's secondary subjects, the caregivers. Indeed, the examples of bus-based social-justice organizing recounted earlier in this chapter demonstrate how the spatial aggregation of people living with shared conditions of oppression has historically constituted an important property of the bus as a site of mutual recognition and solidarity. Yet interviews with riders and observation during journeys suggest that there is a confluence of forces bearing on the structures of feeling (Williams 1977b) at play that keeps people postured defensively, or just likely to keep to themselves during their time circulating between home and prison.

In some cases, that self-isolation takes the form of distrust or antagonism triggered by the competing needs felt during a physically and psychically arduous journey. Christine, for example, when asked to elaborate in our interview on the fights she said would sometimes break out during long distance trips in particular, described this incident:

> I'm friends with Kathy and two black ladies behind me were starting in with us. And it came to a point where I had my fist in her face, because who's going to tell me that I can't talk on the bus. You know. And I've been taking the bus for years and years and years. And I know the bus driver. And it's just horrible sometimes for women who just want to get up to where they're going, to be safe and to see their husband.

Christine, like other women I interviewed, expressed a preemptive distrust of other riders, seemingly based on previous experiences of betrayal and disappointment:

> There are people I can't get close with, because I have gotten close to other people and have gotten burned. There was one girl I was good friends with. And then all of a sudden she just disappeared. I mean, what happened to her? She and I would sleep in the same bed, go upstate together, and then I just don't hear from her, and she knows my personal business. You know, we were friends! So I just can't have that in my life. (interview with author, 2014)

Val conveyed a similar distrust, telling me: "I get along with people but I mind my own business. You don't know who knows who. You never know who's waiting for you when you get back to Manhattan, so you have to be very careful who you're talking to." Such heightened sense of social risk makes particular sense in the broader context of social abandonment. For many of these women, it is not only their incarcerated loved ones who have been abandoned by others, including their own families, in the process of being stigmatized by criminalization and removed to far away places. Julie, for example, tells me that many of her old friendships have dissipated since she got together with her imprisoned husband: "They don't like the whole prison thing. They think I'm crazy. I have some friends that are just supportive, but they keep their distance. They stay friends but they don't really support." Christine tells me about being kicked out of her house when she decided to marry her incarcerated partner: "My mother said, 'you're not going to live here, if you're going to be with him.'"

Allen Feldman characterizes the practice of arrest as "the political art of individualizing disorder" (1991, 109). He suggests that this isolation extends in concentric rings, beginning with the arrested individual but expanding out to include the family, who must shoulder the privatized burden of undoing or augmenting that detention, as well as the community (97). As Gilmore elaborates, "the larger disorder is then distorted to reflect only a portion of social fragilities, and measured, like unemployment, as though its changing rate in a society were a force of nature" (2007, 235). The fragmentation already produced by the tools of capture and incarceration are easily reproduced under conditions of felt scarcity, competing needs, and the emotionally high stakes of nurturing and performing carework across conditions of carceral control.

While the chronic tribulations of managing scarcity may alone be enough to undermine trust and reciprocity among the beleaguered bus riders, a tendency to self-isolate and view oneself as a solitary agent can also be understood as a manifestation of neoliberal rationality. Indeed, neoliberalism as a political project over the past handful of decades has involved not only the restructuring of space and the state, but a transformation in subjectivity as well (Hall 1988; Katz 2005; Brown 2006). Perhaps most central to the idea of a neoliberal subject is the experience of oneself (and everyone around oneself) as an entrepreneurial agent, a competitive individual who bears both the risks and the responsibilities for her own wellbeing in the world (Rose 1999). Such risks and responsibilities are often calculated within the business rubrics of cost and benefit. As Wendy Brown writes, "while this entails submitting every action and policy to considerations of profitability, equally important is the production of all human and institutional action as rational entrepreneurial action, conducted according to a calculus of utility, benefit, or satisfaction against a microeconomic grid of scarcity, supply and demand, and moral-value-neutrality" (2005, 40). People feel constant pressure to evaluate the value of their actions and expenditures of resources in terms of individualized costs and benefits, and this pressure is only intensified by the retrenchment of social welfare provisions and the imposition of austerity measures.

Such neoliberal logic, once internalized, exacts a particularly acute set of burdens on those at the lowest echelons of the wage-power structure. As Valerie Walkerdine puts it, "the practices of subjectification produce a constantly failing subject who has to understand their position in essentially personal and psychological terms" (2003, 241). Responsibility for self-realization under the caprice of capitalism generally, but the contemporary period of austerity in particular, renders certain low-wage and dispossessed subjects especially vulnerable to experiencing their problems as consequent to personal failure rather than having external, structural causes. A bus rider I interviewed who had reservations about visiting her ex-boyfriend and who had recently taken the bus to visit him with their seven-year-old daughter only at the request of a lawyer who was trying to keep him from being deported, explained her misgivings to me in these terms: "He hasn't gotten any other visits besides mine. I feel bad, but then I don't. When he wasn't incarcerated, he didn't make good choices. He didn't step up and become the man that he needed to be for his child. So it's kind of like, his fault. So I'm not making it my business to accommodate him. Not when I'm being a single mother taking care of his kid." (Gina, interview with author, 2014)

The assumption of a self-interested servicing of ambitions in others can profoundly limit the horizons of political possibility, demarcating the strict contours of trust and distrust, as individuals presume they too are being judged as self-calculating and responsible for their own failures. Indeed, normative attachments to the politics of personal responsibility and judgments to that end do pervade the discourse among bus riders and drivers. Simmons, the African-American founder/operator of OPG (also the company subject to the most complaints within my interviews as well as online), offered a narrative of incarceration and visitation rife with seeming contradiction. On the one hand, for example, Simmons couched his analysis of mass incarceration in terms of structural racism, telling me: "Black and Puerto Rican have always been the majority. That's all by design, because trust me, white people commit just as much crime as black people, they just don't get caught like blacks. Whenever there's too many blacks and Puerto Ricans, they come up with either a war, or they put them in jail." On the other hand, Simmons returned time and again to his theory about bad parents and the resultant abandonment of prisoners by the mothers that used to go visit them. "The parents are just getting high and hanging out. They just don't care. That's why it's more wives and girlfriends now. Parents don't even come, because they don't care like they used to."

With an entrepreneurial outlook, Simmons complained about the increased competition and loss of profitability suffered as other bus companies have entered the prison-visitation market, describing his latest plan to obtain a government subsidy as a means of getting ahead: "So if a fare now is $60, then the government pays $30 and the customer pays $30. With those kind of fares, we knock all of our competition out of the box, because no one's going to be able to take people to Attica for $30." Sometime later in our interview, however, Simmons situated his market ambitions in more systematic and political terms: "I'm going to show you how the system is so against minorities. And by minorities I mean majorities in the prisons. There's a law now, if I go and fill out an application and it comes to the part that asks have you ever been arrested, and I say no, and my parole officer finds out, then I automatically go back to jail for violating parole." As he later describes, with an overt sense of pride:

> I didn't think it was going to turn out to be such a prosperous business. I was able to get my mom out of the projects, buy her a co-op in Yonkers. I was able to get my whole family out of the ghetto. In

my wildest dreams I didn't think that would happen. But it did. My mom is in Yonkers and she has a co-op that's paid off, she doesn't owe a dime on that. And I got my father into a drug program, because he was a drug addict. So I made a difference. If someone had told me I could get my mother out of the projects?! That I could get my father drug free?! Me, the son? So, I made a difference, and that's what I encourage guys now to try and do. I say you can be the one to get your family out of poverty, because I did.

As Simmons's testimony reveals, one can both see oneself as part of a structurally disenfranchised and disentitled population and *also* hold others in that population individually responsible for their own misfortunes. One can also understand the causes of that disentitlement as endemic to a system while conceiving the solutions to that disentitlement in individualist and wholly entrepreneurial terms.

Care and Community in the "In-Betweens" of Carceral Life

Sharing social space doesn't always make for political consciousness, but sometimes it does. Indeed, the prison's politicizing tendencies have long been linked to the space it creates for people of shared social class and experiences of oppression to discover a common cause. Even the very reformers of the eighteenth century who championed the penitentiary as a system of punishment anticipated the threat of insurgency, registering their anxieties that a revolutionary conspiracy might at any moment break out among the condemned by dividing the nation's first prisons into a series of isolation chambers. As texts from the period show, they were obsessed by fears of a kind of political and epidemiological *contagion* within spaces of penal captivity; the same condition of bodily proximity that facilitated the spread of jail fever would also, it was believed, spread the ideology and tactics of riot and rebellion. "The grave problem for reformers of the late eighteenth century," writes literary historian Caleb Smith, "was the 'loathsome communion' of prisoners' bodies and souls, the conspiratorial mingling that threatened to spread from the jail to the public at large, and there to inspire open rebellion" (2011b, 88). French prison reformers Gustave de Beaumont and Alexis de Tocqueville, for example, observed "the contagion of mutual communications," while

Jeremy Bentham lamented the "thronging," "jostling," "confederatings," and "plottings" that plagued British jails (quoted Smith 2011b, 87–88.).

Gilmore has written powerfully about the prison-related organizing of Mothers Reclaiming Our Children (Mothers ROC) in Los Angeles in the early 1990s. She describes how this group of mostly working-class and racialized women transformed their reproductive labor and their care-giving into a project of political solidarity and grassroots activism, suggesting that such transformation began with their recognition of one another in the spaces of the criminal-justice system as "women who work to support their families and to free their loved ones" (2007, 337). She writes that such recognition took on the contours of gender, class and race as the ROCers "identified one another in the tight public spaces between their socially segregated residential living places and the unitized carceral quarters in which their loved ones are caged" (236).

The prison bus constitutes a paradigmatic "in-between" space of segregated lives. Its circulation between the homologous poles of criminalized and disinvested urban neighborhoods and the prison edifice offers a unique window into the carceral lives of nonimprisoned women of color, many of them doing double and triple duty: primary caregivers at home also tasked with maintaining social ties across the isolation and violence of the penal system. The neoliberal economic and social conditions that produce the mass incarceration of millions of Americans are the same conditions under which the ridership of the prison buses struggle to work, raise families, pay rent, and also maintain contact and visits with their loved ones inside. The long bus rides and their attendant discomforts are themselves a labor, one that wears people out at the same time as it brings people together. The scene of the bus demonstrates, in many ways, how structurally inhospitable such conditions can be to the forms of recognition that acts of solidarity and collective organizing seem to require, and which the Mothers ROC so radically exemplified. Yet, just as contradictions abound in capitalism, so too do they in the affective life experienced within its bounds. Inasmuch as my research findings showcased interpersonal distrust, precarity-induced isolationism, and self-serving calculations, they also offered modest but nonetheless significant demonstrations of affiliation, mutual aid, and desire for commonality and support.

Recognition and reciprocity are, of course, complex experiences and can take many forms, including those rife with ambiguity and instability. We are not taught, in the era of neoliberal governance, to trust in interdependency. Yet interdependency is also what people discover in times and spaces of struggle. While women visiting their loved ones argue with each other and the bus drivers, viewing others as competitors and antagonists in the struggle to secure a modicum of comfort and rest, they also acknowledge elements of common cause. As one rider put it to me: "We all share a common bond, really. It's like 'oh, you're visiting your brother, or your sister, or your boyfriend?' and you start talking." While it is not an identification always expressed explicitly in political terms, the prison bus riders *do* recognize each other as people, for example, who have sacrificed too much only to be turned away for inadvertently violating a prison dress code, or who are kept awake by stories of bus drivers falling asleep at the wheel, or who are struggling to figure out how to get their loved ones released from solitary confinement.

Indeed, much of that recognition is expressed implicitly, through incredible acts of solidarity that would sometimes contradict what riders would *verbalize* about their relations with others. One fifty-three-year-old woman I interviewed named Val, who was the wife of a prisoner serving a life sentence, was adamant in her distrust of others, and the bus operators in particular. She told me a story about paying for herself and her three grandchildren to take the bus, only to be told at the pick-up spot that she would only be allowed to bring one child into the visiting room at Attica. As she put it: "I was lied to. They work like that!" She returned to Brooklyn to drop the children off with her daughter and then scrambled to make it back to Columbus Circle so as to not miss her visit. Once there, Val got into an argument with the bus operator, who told her the bus was now full and that she would have to come back next week. "I said I'm not going to come back next week," Val told me. "So then when this woman got out of her seat to go to the bathroom, I jumped right into her seat and I would not move. I told them to get the cops."

Yet Val's expressions of seemingly self-interested ruthlessness and distrust are also mixed with forms of care and sacrifice. Answering my question about the reasons people might get denied visits after they've made the long trip, she told me that she carries around not only an extra set of clothes for herself, but also an extra shirt and set of pants for anyone else who might be found in violation of the numerous rules regarding attire: "When I see people and it's their first time, I try and tell them that they can't wear this or that. I bring extra shirts, extra pants, and I also always carry something for someone else, because they'll be crying if they're turned away."

Another woman, Donna, told me a story meant to illustrate the duplicity of the van operators, recounting being abandoned by the driver she normally relies on in retaliation for making a booking with someone else: "So I was left stuck in Astoria, Queens, at 1:30 in the morning with no van no nothing. . . . Thank God this guy Jeff saw me. His brother ran a bus company, and he drove me to the other side of Bronx to meet this bus at 3am in the morning to take me to Auburn." Her story ended up being about the good will and sacrifice of a stranger who recognized her situation. Still another woman described making one of her closest friendships while taking the bus: "My good friend Enza. I watch her daughter, since I met her at Sullivan [Correctional Facility], and I have almost every weekend when I don't go upstate. And she gives me her daughter when she goes to work."

In my own field notes from my first journey on the bus to Attica in October 2013, I wrote this:

> Behind me two younger women sat and began speaking to each other. They were strangers but immediately began chatting. One woman had travelled from Poughkeepsie on the train and then cab to the bus—so her journey had already begun three or so hours ago. It seemed to be her first time on the bus. She had lots of questions about it that she asked of the other woman, who had travelled from Long Island and hadn't been for a visit since before Christmas of last year, but knew the drill a bit. They spoke a lot about what you can and cannot wear, with the more experienced woman offering all sorts of advice for getting through the visit without encountering trouble.

Such observations are corroborated by a conversation I had with one interview subject at length. Jeanne Ann had just taken the bus for the first time with her seven-year-old daughter: "It was long, and tiring, but it was actually kind of fun because the people on the bus have been doing it a long time, so they give you pointers on what to expect and what not to expect. How to dress, what you can bring when you go to visit him" (interview with author, 2014).

While relationships of trust are often seen as unreliable, they are entered into anyway, and constantly. Indeed, the broader field of the bus journeys reveals a complex mesh of interdependencies. Christine spoke of moving in with her husband's parents just after marrying him while he was incarcerated upstate in the mid-1990s. In those days, she would make the two-hour drive to visit her husband every weekend: "His dad was always nice enough to put gas in my car, always nice enough to help change the transmission, because there was a lot of wear and tear on my car driving from Brooklyn to there."

While one sees fragile demonstrations of reciprocity play out along the harrowing route to and from the upstate prisons, such solidarities are perhaps even more fully visible in the virtual realms where the bus riders make connections and swap survival strategies. Online forums are a particularly popular means of forging social-support networks, perhaps because they operate at a remove from the immediate vicissitudes of the bus and its multiple taxations. On the Prison Talk forum, participants share knowledge and commiserate with each other's harrowing stories, and the site is replete with such exhortations of support and encouragement as "I was holding my breath just reading your post! Thank goodness you are okay" and "glad that you are safe!" and "sorry to hear you experienced that . . . glad you made it home!"

Other online support groups have proliferated. One of the riders I interviewed in 2013, Ana, had actually set up her own online support group on Facebook called "State Greens and Wedding Rings." Her reasons for doing so were expressed in mixed terms of antagonism and solidarity: "I had been on a couple of other ones, and sometimes the women are like evil. Some of them are nice, but they're supposed to be support groups and they end up going after each other and getting into everybody's business." About her own Facebook group, which Ana told me now has about 150 members, she said: "It's online but we also talk offline. A lot of us have exchanged numbers, and we talk on the phone. But the online support is really important too. We just post what we're going through, and everybody rallies around. If somebody needs a phone call, then we call her."

The internet presents a set of social possibilities different from those of the prison bus. Perhaps this is because, as a specific and contingent space in time delicately bridging prisoners to their lifelines outside, the bus is a space in which the stakes of social vulnerability and resource sharing are just too high. Almost all of the riders I spoke to told me that they were their loved one's only visitor, despite, in many cases, the existence of other family members and friends. While prison visits are consistently described in terms that express their emotional value to the women visiting, it is also clear that they feel deeply responsible for the well-being of their loved one inside. More than one person, including Simmons, told me that visits are crucial in safeguarding prisoners from the brutality of guards, who are more likely to engage in violence against those who are seen to have been abandoned by the outside world. As Val put it to me, when I asked her how her husband is holding up five years into his sixteen-to-twenty-five-year sentence:

> As long as he can keep in touch with me and talk with me he feels good. He don't have any family—he had a brother that died of a seizure, he's got another brother that's in doing federal time for guns. And he's in for shooting. His sister she lives in Pennsylvania, she's married to an Italian, owns a restaurant, has two beautiful trucks. And he has a stepbrother that owns his own condo—so they think they're better than us and too good to visit a jail. So he doesn't get no visits except from me.

While much ink has been given to the importance of visiting to "successful prisoner reentry" (Christian 2005, 47), the stakes are often much higher for those making the visits. Indeed, for many, it comes down to whether a loved one will survive incarceration or not, or whether he or she will be victimized by the guards. In this sense, the act of riding the bus constitutes the work of social reproduction in a very literal sense: it is the work of keeping people alive.

The act of care is itself a relation of general social dependency, and the very taking of these buses constitutes an act of solidarity, albeit one often privatized in the family or the couple form. A feminist interpretation of love, however, recognizes that such forms of intimacy also harbor the potential for socialities and solidarities beyond the boundaries of family or coupledom. The state of being in love can offer a glimpse of oneself and one's relations as noninstrumental, magnanimous, and even selfless. Almost all the bus riders I spoke to were unequivocal in their willingness to sacrifice their own immediate well-being for the love and security offered by—and being offered through—the maintenance of visitations with their incarcerated loved ones. Their own happiness was conceived in and through their ability to maintain such relationships.

At the same time, more aspirational desires or conceptions of the good life were rarely articulated, even in specific regard to the traumas of incarceration. When I asked Julie what three things she would change about the prison system if she could, she told me she would: first, make the buses bigger and more spacious, second, add three bathroom stops instead of two, and third, locate the prisons closer to downstate. The modesty of these demands reveals the important political distinction between experience and consciousness, as well as the diminished horizon neoliberal crisis as everyday life lays over the political imagination.

But Julie also said this:

> I just want him to be safe. And you know what I really be scared of? I just wonder if he'll make it out alive. Will I be alive, will his children and grandchildren be alive, will we make it safe and sound? I have a friend, Christopher, he did 35 years in prison, and his wife did that time with him. He's been out five years and then he passed away. They lose a lot of loved ones when they're in prison.

The work of riding the buses constitutes not only care work, but what Marxist feminists in particular have long demonstrated to be the necessary labor of social reproduction (Bannerji 1995; Hochschild 2003; Katz 2001). What this scholarship illuminates is the ways that the daily and generational renewal of human life is itself a labor, one both integral to the reproduction of racial capitalism and rendered invisible by the gendered hierarchies of patriarchy. Indeed, riding the bus can be seen as a means to reproduce life in a context proven to diminish it. Women riding the bus form bonds of support in order to help each other stave off the immediate defeat of missing visits, demonstrating, at the very least, recognition of the high stakes of caring for someone inside prison.

What's at stake in the space of the prison bus is also what's at stake in political life more broadly: the possibility of resisting the isolation and death-dealing of the carceral regime, which is also simultaneously the possibility of resisting the individuation and slow death demanded by the racial capitalist order. Yet Brown, writing about the de-democratizing consequences of neoliberal policies and imaginaries, also warns: "Citizenship, reduced to self-care, is divested of any orientation toward the common, thereby undermining an already weak investment in an *active citizenry* and an already thin concept of a *public good* from a liberal democratic table of values" (2006, 695). It is unclear to what degree community or solidarity are seen, on the bus or elsewhere, as resources for building a more secure bridge out of the crisis of ordinary life. It may be that lending a shirt or offering a warning against a dangerous bus driver may indeed be an entry into forging more collective forms of support and action. Writes Gilmore, optimistically: "It should not be surprising to realize that people who drive long distances to see loved ones will make small talk in parking lots and discover an identity in their immediate purpose. . . . What is surprising, perhaps, is that the temporary camaraderie of those emotional encounters became the basis for trust enabling the newly formed collectives of people with modest resources, mostly women, to do things on a less-than-modest scale" (2007, 234).

My own fieldwork on the prison bus suggests that such transformation, while possible, is not a foregone conclusion, especially not under the prolonged physical and affective attritions that constitute existence in the contemporary neoliberal economy, particularly for women of color. At the same time, that these women are even *riding* the bus is socially significant and should not be underestimated as a form of political action in itself. Cindi Katz, reflecting on the myriad ways in which capitalist production and neoliberal restructuring have pushed people to the limits of their own resilience, reminds us that "social reproduction is precisely not 'revolutionary,' and yet so much rests on its accomplishment, including—perhaps paradoxically—oppositional politics" (2001, 718). In other words, riding the bus might not pose an organized threat to the existing social order in any immediate sense, but it does constitute at least a partial basis of opposition to the fragmentation and isolation of the prison regime.

The prison bus is a space of circulation as well as confinement, of fragmentation and of being together. It is unique in its provision of shared space over a long duration for those loved ones bearing the collateral consequences of mass incarceration. For many, riding the bus represents a spatial and temporal experience analogous to "doing one's time" alongside incarcerated loved ones, as its mostly female ridership also bears the violence of the carceral state. The prison bus thus offers a powerful vantage from which to gauge the ways the crisis of reproducing life is registered by those at the bottom of the class, race, and gender hierarchies and exacerbated by the austerities of neoliberal capitalism.

As a space, the prison bus aggregates its riders' burdens of vulnerability but does not much relieve or redistribute them. It is a site of mass but not necessarily collective endurance. The prison bus often functions simply to aggravate the systematic stresses faced by its riders, wearing them out further and depleting whatever reserves of time, money, energy, and good will to others they have allocated for the ongoing care work of visiting their incarcerated loved ones. While glad and grateful for their visits, bus riders overwhelmingly describe their experiences of *getting there* in terms of physical exhaustion, attenuation of meager incomes, the stress of wasted time, and the unreliability of others. Tensions hewed to the perceived scarcities of comfort, rest, safety, and reprieve within the austere confines of the densely packed buses manifest themselves as sporadic interpersonal antagonisms, producing further fragmentation as each person or household figures out how to endure and survive each journey.

Solidarity on the bus, when it does exist, is fragile, and often contingent. Yet just *being together* on the bus also opens up possibilities for moments of reciprocity and mutual aid. The conglomeration of riders therefore foreshadows the potential for a common alliance built on the recognition of the shared stakes of carceral care work, if not also the shared vicissitudes of class, race, and gender. In the tradition of the long-distance bus more generally, the prison buses aggregate mostly poor women of color, constituting an increasingly rare place for the collectivization of shared time-space in an economy otherwise characterized by the spatial fragmentation of the poor and working class.

Attachments on the prison bus and in the in-betweens of life segregated by the prison system are brittle. The infrastructure of sociality is as contingent as the demonstrated unreliability of transit. Yet the work of keeping life afloat while buffering the abrasions of the prison system on incarcerated loved ones also includes forging small friendships, sharing stories of survival, volunteering advice, and even sharing modest resources. These demonstrations of sociality and solidarity constitute a necessary ballast against what each rider recognizes as the unfathomable risk of their journeys: the possibility of being turned away at the prison gates, making the trip and enduring its sacrifices all for naught. The prison buses and vans are an integral part of the social infrastructure of surviving the prison regime, and a repeated refrain among riders is that they wouldn't know what they would do without them.

Riding the prison bus is also a mode of life building for its passengers. As many riders emphasize, they want to visit their loved ones and they take the bus voluntarily to do so. As Berlant reminds us, however, zones of ordinariness are "where life building and the attrition of human life are indistinguishable" (2011, 95). The neoliberal economic and social conditions of reproducing life, including the labor of care, render meaningful reciprocity difficult to recognize. It does not always resemble revolutionary movement building or even consciousness, but it may still harbor those things. The prison bus is not just any carceral space; it is a distinct and gendered space of circulation, connection, and care work, one that demonstrates how even just the act of riding the bus can constitute at least a partial counterforce to the isolation upon which the prison regime depends.

5
Community Confinements
Social Control in Everyday Life

A satirical sketch on the popular comedy show *Portlandia* showcases an easy fix for profit-seeking artisanal entrepreneurs lacking imagination: "Put a bird on it." Poking fun at the clichéd hipster affection for bird imagery, the skit works on the idea that, just by attaching such an image, any worthless item might be revalued exponentially. Want to sell a rock? Put a bird on it. Want to start a bidding war for your dirty sock? Put a bird on it. In the skit, a picture of a bird is more than just easy value added; it also has the magical power of revalorizing denigrated objects whose worth has been undermined by time or changes in public appetite, or both. The irony, of course, is that the bird is an empty signifier. It does nothing and means nothing more than the public consensus electing it a symbol of virtue.

The equivalent in the realms of police and prison reform might be summed up as: "Add community to it." Both "community policing" and "community corrections" are finding new legs in today's climate of revolt against police brutality and the bloated, increasingly discredited system of mass incarceration for which that brutality serves as a metonym. Community policing, for example, while a strategy originating in 1960s counterinsurgency efforts, is ascendant today as authorities across the country seek appeasement strategies in the context of increased tension between law enforcement and people of color. In May 2015, the *Detroit Free Press* printed a feel-good story about a local precinct's recent acquisition of an ice-cream truck. "The ice cream truck is one part of an Oak Park initiative to bridge the gap between the community and law enforcement," the paper reported, as it then gave numbers to the amount of free ice cream that would be delivered throughout the neighborhood by uniformed police officers (Farrell 2017).

As law professor and activist Justin Hansford notes, the term "community" attached to policing, like a more insidious version of the bird in the *Portlandia* skit, "denotes nothing in particular, but it hints at positive values such as community control and police de-escalation." As he argues, however, not only does community policing do very little to curb violence or decrease tension, but "as an ideological framework it is essential to support [of] broken windows policing, mass incarceration, and America's system of anti-Black state violence" (quoted in Camp and Heatherton 2016). Indeed, the connection to broken-windows policing is not only meaningful, but immediate. George Kelling of broken-windows-theory fame has himself boasted: "For me, broken windows was about community policing" (Pinto 2017).

Community corrections is a similarly trendy concept with a growing roster of champions. Defined at its most basic as the supervision of criminal offenders in the resident population, community corrections as a component of carceral strategy has been given a boost by the recent neoliberal prison-reform movement and its promise to cut spending. The Pew Center on the States, for example, cites the 2008 financial crisis as an opportunity to retool existing penal policies in the name of cost efficiency: "If we had stronger community corrections, we wouldn't need to lock up so many people at such a great cost. By redirecting a portion of the dollars currently spent on imprisoning the lowest risk inmates, we could significantly increase the intensity and quality of supervision and services directed at the same type of offenders in the community" (2009, 3).

Indeed, before the election of President Trump, bipartisan prison reform seemed to be an unstoppable movement among the political classes. The agenda encompassed particular reforms that generally fall into a few areas: addressing "overcriminalization" by amending sentencing laws and reforming pretrial practices, prison release and reentry, and increasing investment in community corrections (Whitlock 2017). As modest sentencing reform and alternatives to incarceration gained traction, states from the East Coast to the West boasted declining incarceration rates for the first time in forty years. In the name of fiscal responsibility, policy makers, prison reformers, and government officials breathed life into new and old technologies of surveillance and control that operate *outside* penitentiary walls and inside communities. Sex-offender registries, exclusion zones and other spatial restrictions, and electronic monitoring are all touted as low-cost alternatives to incarceration that will ensure public safety. Policies enacting them have proliferated in turn. The result is that, even where the numbers of people incarcerated are decreasing, the numbers of those subject to some form of correctional control on the outside are actually going up. In New York, for example, a state that has boasted some modest success in its decarceration efforts, the number of people inside prisons has gone down while the number of people under correctional control has increased. In the nation as a whole, the number of people on probation and parole, the cornerstones of community corrections, has skyrocketed in recent years. Close to 5 million people are now on probation or parole, up from 1.6 million a quarter of a century ago. At the end of 2015, one in every fifty-three adults in the United States was under some form of criminal-justice supervision in the community (Kaeble and Bonczar 2016).

"Community" is a malleable term, at once spatial and social, and invested heavily with normative, even romantic, ideas of virtue, care, and belonging (Joseph 2002). In his entry on the word in his first edition of *Keywords* (1977a), Raymond Williams noted that its most important attribute might be that it "seems never to be used unfavorably." Perhaps this is why the concept does such mollifying work for the institutions of policing and penality. Community always seems to be positioned outside the state, rather than as simply a more local scale of it (Schept 2015). Materialized in space, community is also understood to be where everyday life takes place, interdependence is enacted, and existence is reproduced. James Defilippis and Susan Saegert, for example, define community as "places where people live and work," continuing: "People, places and institutions we encounter in everyday life that provide opportunities and support for our activities as well as barriers and constraints, communities are places of interdependence" (2012, 1). In the context of its appropriation by the central institutions of the carceral state, the term community designates both an ideological strategy of legitimation and a geographic site for action. Both have serious implications for the exercise, reproduction, and transformation of carceral power.

As Stanley Cohen cautioned many decades ago, state initiatives taken in the name of community alternatives often simply usher in new interventions that resemble the old ones in key ways and then "reproduce in the community the very same coercive features of the system they were designed to replace" (1979, 343). Cohen uses the term "community control"' (already confused by its simultaneous but very divergent usage by state authorities and grassroots activists) to describe forms of social control undertaken by the state outside the walls of penal institutions. Reforms enacted over the past decade that might also be considered forms of community control include the expanded use of alternative sentencing protocols and drug courts, certain reentry programming initiatives, and the expansion of electronic monitoring.

In this chapter, I survey the extension of the prison's functions of containment and banishment into spaces aligned with the concept of community, including neighborhoods, homes, and public landscapes. Comprising places where everyday life happens and is reproduced, community is also where people encounter the political and economic structures that produce and uphold the social order. I look at three specific carceral tactics that widen and outsource the reach of the carceral system into communities and whose proliferation can be tracked alongside prison reform initiatives ostensibly designed to downsize prison capacity. These are: sex-offender spatial restrictions, along with the rise of "pocket" (i.e., miniature) parks and other banishment mechanisms; neighborhood-based gang injunctions and the introduction of "safety zones"; and electronic monitoring devices like ankle bracelets. I examine the ways in which these tactics continue the functions of the prison proper, such as controlling movement, fragmenting relationships and isolating individuals, and dispossessing subjects of access to public resources, while simultaneously *absorbing* family, friends, and neighbors into the coercive roles conventionally occupied by police, guards, and parole officers. I do so in order to illuminate the ways community interventions reinforce the carceral system from which they are ostensibly diverting. These tactics and technologies do three particular things simultaneously that belie their reformist promises: they widen the net of carceral power into outside spaces of social life, they authorize increased social control over urban neighborhoods in the service of real estate and other economic interests, and they reinscribe racialized ideologies about who constitutes danger, what activities are criminal, and how safety should be secured.

Civil Gang Injunctions and Contested Neighborhoods

In October 2016, the American Civil Liberties Union (ACLU) filed a federal lawsuit against the Los Angeles Police Department (LAPD) for its deployment of civil gang injunctions. Twenty-two-year-old Peter Arellano, a resident of the rapidly gentrifying neighborhood of Echo Park, is one of the litigants represented by the ACLU. Arellano is subject to an injunction initially secured for six gangs, with the names of additional individuals appended at the discretion of the LAPD. He grew up in Echo Park and has witnessed its transformation into a trendy neighborhood for young professionals with disposable incomes. He was standing in the street with his father in 2016 when an LAPD officer stopped and arrested him, accusing him of vandalism a few blocks away. Within minutes Arellano was served with a gang injunction, restricting where he could go in public and with whom he could associate. Among those he is restricted from visiting is his own father.

A gang injunction is a civil court order filed against a group of people identified or construed as a "public nuisance" prohibiting them from participating in certain activities within a designated area. These activities might include being outside after an evening curfew, wearing colors identified by police as signaling a particular street organization, or appearing in public with a person police have labeled a "gang member," even if that person is not him or herself named in the injunction. An injunction is obtained by the city or district attorney, who asks a judge to declare a particular gang a public nuisance and then imposes permanent restrictions on the targeted individuals' daily lives within a designated area. As civil proceedings, injunctions face a lower legal standard than required by the criminal-justice system, therefore allowing police to label people gang members and restrict their liberties without actually having to present any evidence or charge someone with a crime. What they actually do is make otherwise legal, innocuous activities—from loitering to possessing paraphernalia identified with graffiti art—illegal for those people targeted and named by an injunction.

The ACLU's lawsuit argues that the city's civil gang injunctions violate the right to due process of thousands of city residents, effectively subjecting them to house arrest without legal cause. Because gang injunctions begin as civil proceedings, they can be imposed without the due processes afforded those subject to the criminal-justice system, but they turn into criminal matters once their provisions are breached. Those found in violation of their injunctions, perhaps by wearing certain colors while in a gang injunction zone or being found outside after curfew, can thus be charged with contempt and face up to six months in jail. The ACLU argues that, because the injunctions restrict liberties without offering an opportunity for those named under them to prove that they are not actually gang members, they infringe on the constitutionally protected right to challenge legal orders.

Legal experts compare gang injunctions to being subject to the restrictions of probation or parole without actually being convicted of a crime. Police officers are authorized to decide whom to serve with an injunction at their own discretion (Caldwell 2010). In addition to naming a handful of specific people on a given injunction, prosecutors are also allowed to list hundreds of "John Does," to be identified at a later point. As subjects of a civil rather than criminal proceeding, those named are not entitled to a public defender if they chose to appeal their order. While getting added to an injunction list or a gang database is easy, moreover, given the low burden of proof and discretionary power accorded to police, getting oneself removed from the lists is remarkably difficult. Of the almost 10,000 Angelinos subject to gang injunctions, fewer than fifty have managed to get off the list, according to legal advocates (Flores 2017).

As of October 2016, the city of Los Angeles was enforcing forty-six separate injunctions against approximately 10,000 people putatively suspected to be gang members, barring them from engaging in certain activities in areas of the city designated as "safety zones." Los Angeles has more gang injunctions than any other city in the United States. At last count, at least seventy-two neighborhoods were under a gang injunction, with one of those injunctions covering an entire sixteen-square-mile radius. Combined, the enforcement areas covered seventy-five square miles, or 15 percent of Los Angeles. In California, being named in an injunction also means having one's personal information, social contacts, and even tattoo details entered into a massive statewide surveillance registry called the CalGang database. By 2012, CalGang contained the names of more than 200,000 individuals who police had identified as "gang members," some as young as ten years of age. The lists, critics point out, tend to disproportionately target people of color. One in ten of all African Americans in Los Angeles County between the ages of 20 and 24 is on the list, and 66 percent of those named are Latinx (Alarcón 2015).

Once an area is under a gang injunction, police authority expands exponentially. Because enforcement depends almost entirely on the visual identification of alleged gang membership or of broadly defined activities deemed associated with gang membership, gang injunctions serve police a vast amount of discretionary power. That power can intensify the racial discrimination already proven to accompany urban policing more generally. Gang injunctions tend to lead to increased harassment of people who "fit the description" of anyone on the lists, often resulting in racial profiling of African American and Latino young men. The effect is not only to further criminalize people of color and expand police power against them but also to stigmatize and socially control whole neighborhoods predominately made up of black and brown residents. Olu K. Orange, a civil rights lawyer who won a lawsuit against the city of Los Angeles in 2016 for unconstitutionally imposing curfews in twenty-six gang injunctions, described the effect of the curfews as turning Los Angeles "into a Jim Crow-era 'Sundown Town' forcing several thousand black and brown residents indoors on a nightly basis" (quoted in Flores 2017).

Los Angeles has been the test case for gang injunctions, becoming the first city to enact the then novel policing tactic in 1987. Since then, and especially from the 1990s onward, gang injunctions have increased in popularity throughout both the state and the nation. At least seven states other than California have imposed civil gang injunctions in their cities. The injunctions are part of a trend in law-and-order politics that has seen the incorporation of criminal law into administrative legal processes in ways that enhance state carceral power (Beckett and Murakawa 2012, 224). Indeed, gang injunctions are just one of a myriad of civil and administrative alternatives to conventional criminal-justice techniques that municipalities have created to extend official control over urban space.

Historically, control over the urban poor has been exercised by a wide variety of mechanisms putatively outside the criminal-justice system, such as zoning regulations and neighborhood redlining. But municipalities have also relied heavily on specific criminal-justice mechanisms, such as criminal-vagrancy and loitering statutes, to govern and constrain their most socially marginal residents. In a series of decisions throughout the 1960s and 1970s, the U.S. Supreme Court ruled these statutes unconstitutional, finding that they penalized people for behaviors that were based on the status of being poor, rather than behaviors over which they could ostensibly exercise control. While municipal ordinances that penalize people for so-called crimes of poverty (e.g., panhandling, sleeping on public benches) have continued to proliferate under new forms and legal guises, court rulings against vagrancy and loitering statutes pushed city bureaucrats to search out new, more broadly applicable, malleable, and often legally "hybrid" tools. These tools are now on the ascendance as popular policing methods for the production of social "order" in urban spaces and the social control of their most marginalized residents (Beckett and Herbert 2010).

Legally, gang injunctions operate as just such a tool. Injunctions entail a civil order to comply with certain spatial restrictions, but they are ultimately underwritten by the criminal-justice system and its punitive capacities. Those found in violation of a civil gang injunction can be arrested and convicted under criminal law. Like no-contact orders and innovations in trespass law that authorize the exclusion of individuals perceived as disorderly from urban space, gang injunctions involve a merger of civil and criminal law, effectively undermining the rights of those subject to them while strengthening the power of the state. As such, civil gang injunctions are precisely the kind of institutional innovations that Katherine Beckett and Naomi Murakawa point to as enhancing carceral power in the present political era through the development of a kind of "shadow carceral state" (2012). By "carceral state power," they mean specifically "the capacity of governments to incarcerate and otherwise curtail the liberty and mobility of subjects" (232). Insofar as the gang injunctions are operationalized and legitimated within a so-called "administrative" realm of criminal justice that is putatively distinct from a "real" criminal punishment regime, they not only restrict freedom and movement (both defining characteristics, notably, of incarceration itself) but also create new spatial criteria for criminalization proper. What is notable about civil injunctions is not just *who* they control, but *where* such control is deemed useful and productive to authorities. The vast majority of civil gang injunctions, like other regulations that empower officials to exclude people perceived as disorderly from urban spaces, are enacted in cities undergoing or aspiring toward rising property values and urban revitalization projects. Insofar as gang injunctions authorize law enforcement to remove identified individuals from public space, and those individuals tend disproportionately to be low-income youth of color, they both parallel and elaborate on the broken-windows tactic of policing. Within the logic of broken-windows theory, small acts of disorder, such as loitering, informal vending, and graffiti, supposedly create an environment conducive to more serious crimes. In practice, such logic simply expands discretionary police power, serving less to resolve harm than to shore up real estate values and bolster gentrification efforts.

Criticism of gang injunctions from rights-advocacy organizations and social-justice groups abounds. Gang injunctions have been found to drain community resources, facilitate processes of gentrification, increase police harassment (especially against residents of color), and divide and fragment communities. At the same time, they actually *fail* to reduce harm and violence within historically underserved neighborhoods. The Oakland chapter of the prison abolition group Critical Resistance, for example, has organized extensively and successfully against the application of civil gang injunctions in the Bay Area, issuing reports on their findings on the injunctions' costs and consequences. While accurate information is difficult to find, Critical Resistance estimates that Oakland's first injunction cost the city $430,000 in legal fees alone. The group also gathered evidence demonstrating that, rather than being instituted in the most violent neighborhoods of the cities in which they are applied, gang injunctions tend to be enacted in poor, predominantly black and brown neighborhoods that border white or gentrifying neighborhoods (Critical Resistance Oakland 2011).

Indeed, lessons from the Oakland case are instructive. In February 2009, Oakland City Attorney John Russo announced plans to file gang injunctions throughout the city, following through a year later with a temporary injunction in North Oakland, a second proposed for East Oakland, and the threat of eleven more to come. The first of these, enacted in June 2010, named fifteen African American men and created a "safety zone" across a 100-block area within which the named individuals were prohibited from conducting a variety of activities, including loitering, being outside between 10 p.m. and 5 a.m., and possessing paraphernalia associated with graffiti, such as felt tip markers. As the ACLU points out, police often label people gang members based on things like how they dress and whom they know, a fully discretionary and arbitrary means of delineating affiliation not subject to due legal processes of evidentiary corroboration. Close scrutiny of Oakland's two gang-injunction lists revealed a long catalogue of individuals who have never actually associated themselves with any gang (Critical Resistance Oakland 2011, 5). Meanwhile, maps showing the location of Oakland's redevelopment-project areas during the period of Russo's gang injunctions reveal the close proximity between areas targeted by the gang injunctions, both in North Oakland in East Oakland, and areas targeted for economic revitalization (6).

The socioeconomic profile of gang injunctions nationwide suggests that they are often applied in poor neighborhoods of color in urban areas targeted by state and economic actors alike for gentrification and commercial development (Alonso 1999; Barajas 2007; Caldwell 2010). The imposition of the gang injunction in Echo Park, the historically Latinx area of Los Angeles where Arellano is fighting his injunction restrictions, occurred at a time of declining crime rates in which the area was also seeing an influx of white and more affluent residents. As local scholar Ana Muniz has demonstrated, this is in keeping with LA's gang-injunction history (2014). Looking back at the city's very first injunction, instituted in 1987 in the Cadillac-Corning neighborhood, she found that prosecutors and police had targeted the area because the neighborhood and others near it were undergoing a demographic transformation that threatened nearby property values. "With the 1987 injunction in Cadillac-Corning," she writes, "authorities sought to control black youth in an early version of broken windows policing" (232). Its implementation in that area specifically, she notes, had less to do with crime or violence than with counteracting the dissolution of existing neighborhood boundaries of class and race.

The imperative to banish the poor in the service of urban property markets continues. The racialized figure of the gang member offers a useful cover story in these efforts. To that point, it is worth noting the possible new and unanticipated applications of gang injunctions, which are extensive. As the *New York Times* reported early in the presidency of Donald Trump, for example, gang membership and the databases cataloguing it could be used to help deport unauthorized migrants that the federal administration considers criminals, even if they have no criminal record (Medina 2017). En route to the presidency, Trump consistently vowed to immediately deport two to three million unauthorized migrants. Immigration lawyers with experience representing accused gang members against deportation orders say that inclusion in state databases leads to an exponentially more difficult process fighting deportation proceedings. Meanwhile, immigrant detention has never been included in the agenda for bipartisan prison reform, nor does it seem likely any time soon, given the rhetoric coming out of the Trump White House.

Sex Offender Spatial Restrictions and the Punishable Subject

In July 2013, Harbor Gateway, a 5.14-square-mile working-class neighborhood running north–south in the southern region of Los Angeles, cut the ribbon on the smallest park in the city. At one fifth of an acre, the park has barely enough room for the tiny jungle gym that constitutes its only playground infrastructure. Enclosed inside a code-secured metal gate and located on a busy intersection at the edge of a set of train tracks, the park appears inhospitable, even inaccessible, to the children and residents who might be expected to enjoy its public provisions. The site, however, was never actually intended for enjoyment as such. Instead, the park—what planners call a "pocket park" because of its diminutive size—was constructed for the sole purpose of forcing thirty-three registered sex offenders to move out of a nearby apartment building. It can have such power because a state statute known as Jessica's Law prohibits sex

The Harbor Gateway park in Los Angeles, built to force thirty-three registered sex offenders to move out of a nearby halfway house. Photograph by Ava Berkovsky.

offenders in the state of California from living within 2,000 feet of a park or school.

The brainchild of Joe Buscaino, the local city councilor and a former LAPD officer, Harbor Gateway's pocket park cost over $300,000 to build and took over three years to plan (Jennings 2013). In public statements, Councilor Buscaino has been unequivocal about the park's purpose as a technical strategy to displace and recapture otherwise law-abiding residents with sex-offender status. As he described his goals to one radio broadcaster: "We need to be strategic in addressing this quality of life issue. Anything that has an opportunity to cause fear in the community, we need to stand with the parents and the kids. . . . As a police officer, I visited that location, and checked on compliance, and we netted some arrests for non-compliance" (Mantle 2013).

The location referred to by Councilor Buscaino is actually a halfway house, one of the few structures of secure housing available to people with registered sex-offender status. Because of spatial restrictions across the country like those operationalized under Jessica's Law, secure housing is one of the most serious challenges facing parolees with sex-offender status once they are released from prison. According to reports from the Ex-Offender Management Board, the number of homeless sex offenders in California has tripled since 2006, which is when the latest residency restrictions were passed. A third of people with sex-offender status on parole are now homeless (Lovett 2013).

In some cities across the United States, spatial restrictions are so vast in scope and severe in their consequences that whole residential areas have been rendered off limits. The result has been the proliferation of homeless encampments across the country, many of which have large concentrations of registered sex offenders. In one high-profile case in Miami, dozens of homeless people with sex-offender status were found to be camped under a bridge, where they remained until the encampment was broken up by city police. Elsewhere in the city, dozens of registered sex offenders were forcibly dispersed from the sidewalk they had been sleeping on when a city commissioner named Marc Sarnoff had three anti-sex-offender pocket parks built in the neighborhood (Lovett 2013). The sex-offender-registry spatial restriction in Miami is a formidable 2,500 feet. For perspective, a football field is about 300 feet by 160 feet.

The *New York Times* reports the proliferation of such pocket parks across the country in recent years. A Houston-based playground installation company even advertised its park-building services to homeowner associations as a means of keeping sex offenders away (Lovett 2013). It is in this context that such parks must be examined, for here they function less as spaces of leisure and play (if at all) than as physical expressions of contemporary penal power enacted and extended into the community in the disguise of a public good. Just by existing in the landscape, the Harbor Gateway pocket park operates as both a technical and an ideological mechanism for sending former prisoners back to prison as so-called recidivists. It is, in this function, itself a carceral space.

The category of "sex offense" has proven historically elastic, and Sex Offender Registries (SORs) specifically have a long and sordid record in American life. The nation's first SOR law was enacted in California more than seventy years ago, in 1947. Its primary purpose at the time was as a sociolegal tool for the police harassment of gay men. It required people to register with the police for such "crimes" as consensual adult sodomy and gay solicitation (Jacobson 1999, 2432). Indeed, consensual sodomy was a crime punishable by life imprisonment in California until 1975, and much later in many states. Sex offense as a category of crime has also historically included interracial marriage. The last state law prohibiting black–white marriage was not struck down until 1968. The category of sex crime has also included, variously, contraception, adultery, oral and anal intercourse even between spouses, and the perusal of pornography (Wacquant 2009a, 210).

Today, California's SOR laws cover a broad range of offenses, from the consensual to the injurious, including noncontact activities such as public urination, streaking, and "sexting," as well as some consensual teen sex. While offenses also include deeply harmful violations such as sexual assault, the point here is that such laws neither differentiate nor track responsively to actual evidence of fluctuations in sexual injury. California law, meanwhile, requires that all sex offenders, even those whose crimes were not violent or against children, register for life. It is one of only four states for which the SORs are lifelong, with little to no possibility of removal.

Over the past two decades especially, SORs have assumed an increasingly restrictive and high-profile character, first with the passage in the 1990s of "Megan's Laws," and then in the 2000s with the passage of "Jessica's Laws" in states across the country. Megan's Law is the informal umbrella term for a slew of state statutes that require law enforcement to make personal information about registered sex offenders publicly available. The specifics of what information is included and how it is distributed are at the discretion of individual states; the offender's name, photograph, and address are commonly made public. That information can often be accessed on public websites, but it may also be published in newspapers or disseminated through other channels like neighborhood pamphlets. At the federal level, Megan's Law is officially titled the Sexual Offender Act of 1994, which requires people convicted of sex offenses to notify local law enforcement of any change of address or employment for at least a ten-year period, or in some cases permanently. Failure to register or to update personal information, including home address, counts as a felony offense and can be prosecuted as such.

The first of what are commonly referred to as Jessica's Laws was enacted in Florida in 2005. More than forty states have introduced versions of Jessica's Law since then. California's version of Jessica's Law, also known as the Sexual Predator Punishment and Control Act, was voted into law in 2006 through Proposition 83, a statute supported by 70 percent of California voters as well as by Governor Schwarzenegger and law-enforcement agencies throughout the state, despite vigorous opposition by California Attorneys for Criminal Justice, among other groups. The law bars convicted sex offenders from living within 2,000 feet of a school, park, or any other place where children ostensibly congregate. Its provisions also increased penalties for sex offenders, broadened the definition of certain sexual offenses, and allowed the civil commitment of a sex offender (meaning preemptive indefinite detention) with a minimum of one victim and any previous criminal history. It further increased court-imposed fees on sex offenders, prohibited probation for certain crimes, eliminated good-time credits for early release of certain offenders, and provided for lifelong GPS monitoring of high-risk sex offenders. In 2010, the Supreme Court of California ruled that the residency requirements of Jessica's Law could be applied retroactively.

Anti-sex-offender pocket parks, like the one built in Harbor Gateway, function as a spatial enactment of carceral power at two interrelated registers. The first is as a technical, administrative mechanism for the return of formerly incarcerated people back into prison, literally expanding prison holdings and the nation's rate of incarceration. By geographic design, the park works to impede registered sex offenders from settling in the area, or expels those who are already there by materializing the spatial prohibitions applied to them in the state of California. Failure to abide by this restriction, whether accidentally or intentionally, can result in a revocation hearing. Revocation hearings are administrative proceedings that shadow the formal criminal-justice system, in which correctional officers present evidence of a *technical* violation (rather than evidence of a commitment of a new offense) that may, and in fact often does, lead to reincarceration.

Revocation hearings are not actually construed as criminal legal processes requiring due-process standards. As Beckett and Murakawa note, "the construction of revocation hearings as administrative (rather than criminal) in nature has therefore had important consequences for the nature and strength of parolees rights protections, and has significantly enhanced carceral state power" (2012, 227). In the state of California, which already has the largest population of prisoners in the country, some 64 percent of all parolees are returned to prison within three years. Of those, 39 percent are reimprisoned for a technical or administrative violation, such as a violation of one's settlement restrictions (Grattet et al. 2008, 5). These numbers point to a larger trend obscured by the dominant discourse, which is the degree to which growing "recidivism" rates are driven by tighter controls and regulations, rather than by an increase in criminal activity on the part of people on parole. In 1980, parole revocations represented 18 percent of U.S. prison admissions. That number nearly doubled in just twenty years. By 2000, 34 percent of all prison admissions were triggered by parole violations (Beckett and Murakawa 2012, 227). A 2011 study by the Pew Center on the States showed that 25 percent of people released in 2004 went back to prison on technical violations within three years (Pew Center on the States 2011, 10).

Secondly, anti-sex-offender parks and the spatial restrictions they enforce also operate as a material terrain of ideological practice, which is to say a site for the enactment and reenactment of particular and often hegemonic ideas about safety, danger, and the geographies of risk. The anti-sex-offender pocket park normalizes in space two interrelated narratives about the contested category of the "sex offender": first, a moral panic around the prevalence of "stranger danger"; and second, the belief that protection, or safety from such danger, is productively achieved through transformations in geography, and specifically through tactics of spatial banishment. In the latter sense, the park serves ideologically to veil the illogic of prisons and other banishment spaces (their evidenced *failure* to secure community safety or reduce harm) with the appearance of logic. The park's ideological work is thus also to reproduce commonsense epistemologies regarding the sex offender himself as an especially irredeemable and abhorrent subcategory of "criminal." The marking off of the category of the sex offender in terms that exceptionalize the threat he or she poses in turn serves to expand and cement carceral state power.

As critical feminist Rose Corrigan argues (2006), the passage of Megan's Laws across the United States actually works to undermine feminist efforts to challenge sexual violence by excluding many of its most common perpetrators from their legal and ideological purview. The laws deflect attention from offenses committed by family and friends of victims, despite the fact that those offenses constitute the bulk of sexual assaults, and instead focus almost exclusively on the category of the "deviant stranger." Statistically, when it comes to sexual violence against children and women, the "deviant stranger" actually poses the *least* significant risk (Bureau of Justice Statistics 2000). Research suggests that the overwhelming majority of survivors of sexual assault know their attackers. This is especially true of children: it is estimated that approximately 90 percent of child victims know their offenders, as do 80 percent of adult victims (Kilpatrick et al. 1992).

Public *perception* of "stranger danger" is not only amplified by the logics and restrictions embedded in contemporary sex-offender laws but also has had enormous implications for the organization of public space and production of disposable subjects. Erica Meiners writes: "The rampant fear of stranger sexual assault on children requires sex offender-free neighborhoods. These fears reshape public and private spaces, expand the punitive functions of the state, and also produce identities" (2009, 43). Like SORs generally, the anti-sex-offender park is not designed to monitor or prevent violence by family members or acquaintances, the populations most likely to engage in the sexual assault of children and adults alike. Nor does it offer protection from sexual violence committed within intimate, often domestic spheres, where such violence is most likely to happen. Of all reported sexual assaults against children, 70 percent are actually committed in a home, usually the victim's own residence (Bureau of Justice Statistics 2000).

The emphasis within these anti-sex-offender strategies on *public* spaces thus suggests that a political purchase is at play other than the protection of women and children from violence. As a material and symbolic social space, the park itself mediates the production and reproduction of beliefs about what kinds of spaces are dangerous, what social proximities are to be impeded, which categories of people are defensible, and which need to be defended *against.* SORs and spatial restrictions disproportionately impact the poor and link intimately to racialized stereotypes of deviance and danger (Meiners 2009). As Meiners argues, the constitution of the "dangerous" stranger "functions to erase the reality of the much more prevalent threat of violence in the family, a space that is conceptualized as both natural and safe" (2009, 41). This ideological construction serves to absolve society and the state of any responsibility in the production of actual danger structured, for example, through relations of patriarchy, homophobia, and misogyny and directed at those most often vulnerable to sexual violence. There is little actual data to suggest that SORs reduce violence against women and children. On the contrary, the registries would seem to participate in the continued mystification of the patriarchal family as a central site of violence, sexualized or otherwise. The unevenness by which anti-sex-offender schemes target specific individuals and spaces thus contributes to a tautology identified by Corrigan: "All sex offenders will come to be seen as sexual predators, but only those defendants who fit the preconceived profile of a sexual predator will be recognized as sex offenders" (2006, 306).

The point here is *not* to further bifurcate those that fall under the category of sex offender into new divisions of guilt and innocence, real or fictitious, or more or less *bad*. Rather, it is to point out that even those spaces that enact and ritualize the logic of punishment and punishability are fraught with so many contradictions as to belie almost entirely their claims to be productive solutions to the problem of sexual violence. Their productive work is better understood as operating at the level of symbolism and popular thought: they produce the very idea of the punishable (and thus disposable) subject while harnessing aspirations for harm reduction to enactments of punishment against certain categories of people and in certain kinds of places.

As a visible index of which places and people pose dangers to be preempted within the landscape of sexual violence, the anti-sex-offender park mimics the logic of prisons themselves. The anti-sex-offender park further reifies the demonstrably false idea of the prison as a solution to violence by exemplifying, and thus ritualizing, the idea that *spatial banishment* constitutes a sensible means of protection from sexual danger. Prisons have always been used, as Angela Davis writes, as "a way of disappearing people in the false hope of disappearing the underlying social problems they represent" (2003, 41). Anti-sex-offender parks operate on—and reproduce—the same organizing logic. Like prisons, anti-sexoffender parks and the legal restrictions they activate "don't pretend to change anything about people except where they are" (Gilmore 2007, 14).

Yet their increasing popularity suggests the existence of an alternative political investment in geographical displacement and disappearance.

Meanwhile, while sex offenders themselves tend more likely than other felony offenders to be white, middle-class, and married (Corrigan 2006, 280), Harbor Gateway is a predominantly working-class neighborhood of color. As such, it is in keeping demographically with other neighborhoods disproportionately targeted for surveillance by the criminal-justice system and law enforcement. It is worth noting that Councilor Buscaino, the former LAPD officer now representing Harbor Gateway, was among the park's main champions and easily won reelection to the city council a month after the park's February 2013 groundbreaking. Two more pocket parks are in the works for another neighborhood in Buscaino's district (Lovett 2013).

Meiners points out: "Privatizing public spaces and institutions has long required the production of disposable identities. . . . These identities become integral to the reconfiguration of public institutions and state resources" (2009, 43). While other racialized categories of disposability such as the "welfare queen" and the "illegal alien" have justifiably provoked vast bodies of critical literature (see, respectively, Hancock 2004 and Nevins 2002), the "sex offender" appears to be a more challenging category of "bad" for even radical activists and scholars to ally themselves with, especially those active in ongoing struggles against sexual assault and gender-based violence. The sex offender is seemingly indefensible, and is thus continuously constructed as such. But, as Meiners argues, the feelings of disgust, fear, and anger harnessed in both the enactment and enforcement of sex-offender laws "become rationalizations to expand the punitive arm of the state and to contract its social-service functions." She continues: "The fearful feelings invite tough love, a defensive and protective 'daddy' state, while the feelings of anger fuel more accountability from the public sphere and justify the dismantling of public programs" (2009, 43). Such spaces, in addition to cementing moral consensus around the punishability of the sex offender, further actualize and legitimate state tactics of dispossession and social exclusion. By heightening the judicial vulnerability and public isolation of people with sex-offender status, spatial restrictions further consolidate public opinion on the disposability of such individuals. Sex offenders, in other words, become ideal targets for the public performance of tough-on-crime politics.

It is precisely because "the sex offender" operates as such a powerful placeholder or "mobile artifact," as Meiners puts it (36), for the worst of the worst in both the general and the activist imaginations that it poses such a great ideological impediment to conceptually challenging the conflation of incarceration with punishment, and thus the relationship between prisons and crime. Whatever else it does, the category of sex offender shores up deep and visceral attachments to the affective logic of punishment, thus reinforcing the common sense idea of incarceration as a *response* to crime and the punitive feeling that such putatively heinous acts elicit in people. In contrast to the other carceral spaces explored in this book, the anti-sex-offender park does actually ritualize the ideology of punishment, while also mystifying the other social relations and imperatives at work in the production and siting of such spaces. In so doing, it demonstrates another reason for abolitionists to refuse the partitioning of some carceral subjects as legitimate targets of state intervention: perhaps more than another other category of "criminal," the sex offender is produced in such a way as to make *affective sense* out of the desire to punish, the practice of incarceration, and thus the production of indefensible and disposable life.

It is in this sense that the anti-sex-offender park does such effective work to shore up the legitimacy of the prison system. This is not a merely theoretical observation. Undertaking a comprehensive study of criminal-justice law and policy between 2000 and 2006, Beckett and her collaborators found that many states continued to enact "tough" anti-crime legislation through the onset of the recession and that much of it was aimed at sex offenders (2014, 15). Between 2007 and 2013, there were zero progressive reforms aimed at or inclusive of sex offenses. In other words, as they put it, "the punitive trend vis-à-vis violent and sex offenders remains untouched and, in some states, has continued to intensify" (17). Indeed, current reform efforts have already begun to demonstrate a bifurcation in the populations deemed deserving and undeserving of imprisonment, with reform initiatives aimed at lessening sentences or facilitating releases of some prisoners often purchased at the expense of increasingly restrictive sentences and conditions for other prisoners, usually those cast as violent or sex-related.

Scholars have crunched the numbers to demonstrate that mass incarceration will be impacted only if we reduce sentences for long-term "violent offenders" and "sex offenders" as well (Beckett et al. 2014; Gottschalk 2015). It is thus conceivable that current prison-reform efforts might contribute to a long-term entrenchment of mass incarceration, insofar as they deepen the political commitment to severely treating and intensively confining undeserving prisoners. Sex offenders are almost always constructed, within such partitions, as undeserving, irredeemable, and indefensible. Refusing the idea that prisons and other like structures are *legitimate* in the case of these populations and rejecting those strategies and policies organized by such logic, including the production of banishment spaces within the community, thus constitute important means of interrupting the logics and tactics through which the carceral state is actively reproduced.

The Electronic Ball and Chain

On any given week, about 125,000 people in the United States go about their day with an ankle bracelet affixed to their leg. On that ankle bracelet is a transmitter that sends a continuous location-tracking signal to a monitoring center, assuring the constant supervision of the monitored person's movement. The ankle bracelet, in other words, operates as a kind of electronic ball and chain, one whose capacity to enact spatial control and bodily surveillance is only getting more sophisticated. With the development of global-positioning-system (GPS) technology, corrections supervisors are privy to increasingly detailed information about a subject's whereabouts: on what street corner, in what building, at what precise spot on a digital map. Many monitors are also currently programmed to incorporate "exclusion zones" into their GPS tracking of individuals. These are areas deemed prohibited and whose GPS coordinates are built into the capacity of the device, which is then set to trigger an alarm and alert authorities if a person enters the prohibited area. The slightest travel delay, battery fritz, or accidental stroll into an exclusion zone can authorize a supervisor to find a monitored person in violation of their restrictions. For those subject to electronic monitoring, the margin of error for rearrest is so low and the control capacity so high that they render this putative "alternative" to incarceration little more in actuality than an extension of incarceration into the community. Rather than set people free, in other words, electronic monitoring simply turns the home into a prison.

While electronic monitoring (EM) has been a part of the U.S. criminal-justice system for more than two decades, its use has been rising in recent years. In 2005, only 53,000 people were subject to electronic monitoring. According to a recent survey conducted by the Pew Charitable Trusts, the number of people accused and convicted of crimes who are monitored with electronic tracking devices has risen by nearly 140 percent in the decade since (Public Safety Performance Project 2016). EM is often trumpeted as a popular alternative to incarceration that offers a means of reducing penal costs while maintaining public safety. Its proponents tout it as an affordable way for officials to conduct active monitoring outside of the penitentiary. In the prison-reform era of fiscal crisis and revalorized community corrections, EM seems poised to proliferate. For example, in Wisconsin in 2013, GPS monitoring was projected to expand by nearly 50 percent over the next two years. Republican Governor Scott Walker's proposed austerity budget that year recommended $10 million in new funding for expanded use of GPS tracking in fiscal years 2014 and 2015 (Koran 2013). The introduction of user fees for most people on EM means that proponents can claim it to be not only cost-effective, but income-generating as well, even when administered publicly through state correctional departments. In many jurisdictions, it is common for a monitored person to pay as much as $105 to the state in fees every week. This leads some to speculate that politicians will be tempted to order GPS monitoring for those who would not otherwise be incarcerated as well as those who would (Saletan 2005).

Meanwhile, the net of EM use is widening. Juveniles, individuals on pretrial release, and immigrants awaiting adjudication are all new populations for the application of EM. Their numbers expand the existing categories to which EM has traditionally been applied: people on parole or probation, those with sex-offender status, people found guilty of DUIs and traffic offenses, those charged with minor transgressions such as municipal ordinance violations or trespassing, and individuals involved in cases of domestic violence. Within these realms, the extension of punitive measures within the law often means an increase in EM deployment. The expansion of SORs in many states is often accompanied by the rise of EM and other mandatory surveillance devices. Due in no small part to Jessica's Law and Chelsea's Law, for example, which mandate lifetime GPS supervision for many people with sex-offender status, the state of California currently operates the largest EM program in the nation (Gottschalk 2015, 2010).

As a popular supervision technique that is playing an increasingly important role in many community corrections programs, EM works in various ways to extend and intensify networks of carceral power. It expands carceral power spatially through exclusion zones, de facto house arrest, and movement restrictions. And it tightens the hold of that control through relaxed legal parameters. Indeed, legislation governing the use of technological incapacitation is decidedly lacking, in contrast to that for its architectural counterpart, the prison. As legal scholar Erin Murphy writes, "across legal doctrines, courts erroneously treat physical deprivations as the archetypal 'paradigm of restraint' and thus largely overlook the significant threat to liberty posed by technological measures" (2008, 1323). Rather than circumscribe use, legal frameworks tend instead to further *empower* authorities to use EM and penalize those who breach its rules. Under California's legal code, for example, supervising officers are allowed to take an individual into custody for violation of parole if he/she finds that person to be in contravention of the rules or conditions set forth for the use of EM. No warrant of arrest is deemed necessary (California Penal Code 2010, 3010.7). With such unregulated parameters, the house becomes a site of incarceration and supervising authorities obtain almost unlimited power. If your supervision officer decides, for example, to institute a "lockdown" and deny all requests to leave the house for any reason, there is no means of appealing that decision or contesting its duration (Staples and Decker 2011; Kilgore 2013).

The extensive power granted authorities in cases where someone has been found to breach the restrictions on their movement becomes especially problematic in light of the enormous technical glitches EM devices have already evidenced. As well as being cumbersome and conspicuous, these devices are also notoriously prone to technical difficulties, such as misfiring in public. Even those responsible for their manufacture concede that their technical limitations are numerous. Signals can be lost, for example, due to weather conditions, car travel, and even the presence of tall buildings (Koran 2013). James Kilgore recounts the case of a man whose device kept losing the satellite signal the GPS needed in order to track his movements, a common failing in many such devices. When the man's efforts to restore the signal failed, he was told by his parole officer that he would simply have to find a new place to live, which is already a tremendously difficult undertaking for those with felony status. He was forced to impose on an aunt who was reluctant to have him stay and soon found himself again scrambling to find a new residence (Kilgore 2016).

Kilgore has not only studied the proliferation and consequences of EM; he has himself been subject to it. He edits a website called Voice of the Monitored that collects information about the experiences of people subject to electronic monitoring through their encounters with the criminal-justice system. His findings corroborate other existing surveys that have found EM to bear considerably on two areas central to a person's economic and social wellbeing: work and relationships. EM control puts increased pressure on a person's relationships with family and loved ones, especially those with whom one shares a home, and it often compromises a person's ability to find and maintain employment (Bales et al. 2010).

The kind of caregiving intimates must perform to keep their loved ones safe *while* incarcerated often becomes intensified and integrated with the security regime once a loved one is out and attached to a monitor. Alongside the labor of earning an income and conducting domestic chores like cooking, cleaning, and childrearing, there is the extended burden of providing the support services once performed by social workers, case managers, and parole officers. Frequent visits by authorities expand the scope of surveillance and control to all of those residing in the home, including children. Rather than experiencing a sense of freedom upon release from prison, many people on monitors report feeling that the house arrest and curtailed movement to which they are subjected instead turn their homes and neighborhoods into a new kind of prison. As well as still feeing unfree, they also bear the guilt of having brought the carceral apparatus with them into the lives of their families and neighbors (see Kilgore 2013; Staples and Decker 2011).

GPS and other forms of electronic monitoring transform the domestic spaces where parolees live, including their relationships with those they might cohabit with. Even probation officers have recognized this consequence. In a study by the Justice Department, 89 percent of officers surveyed felt that being monitored transformed a person's relationship to their significant others (Nation Institute of Justice 2011). Indeed, electronic monitoring often has the effect of *transferring* the control and supervision functions of prison staff to the loved ones and family members of a person on EM. Kilgor writes: "As the default position is house arrest, already overextended family are landed with an often angry, frustrated individual occupying space in their home virtually 24 hours a day. . . . There may be no spare bedroom or extra bathroom to cater to their needs. Their transition to civil life often takes place in the public space of the house, severely disrupting the normal routine" (2012, 131).

In some states where GPS is employed, individuals are required to remain at home for six hours per day in order to recharge their devices. For many, this spatial restriction means that they are subjected to de facto house arrest. A curfew of 2 p.m. (to take a common example) creates an immense barrier to participation in the job market, school events, or community activities. Depending on the restrictions, even the movement of those allowed to leave their homes is highly restricted, with all stops requiring authorization. One advocate recounts the example of a person on a monitor who wanted to get a job mowing lawns. The conditions of his electronic monitor required him to get permission from his parole officer for every residential address that he wanted to visit. His job as a lawn cutter, by definition, would necessitate travelling to at least thirty or forty different houses. The amount of paperwork involved in being cleared to visit all of those homes was undoable, time-wise, for both the parolee and his parole officer (Kilgore 2014b).

As for employment, something already rendered more difficult by felony status, EM produces formidable obstacles for those under its charge. Not only is a person wearing an ankle bracelet subject to strict limitations on their movement outside of the home; their mobility outside of that sphere also becomes dependent on the discretion of their supervision officer, rendering the monitored person that much more dependent on the officer's availability and will. This severely limits a person's ability to secure work that demands travel or movement between various locations (such as house cleaning), changes in schedule, short notice given for job interviews, or the need for flexibility in daily hours worked, all conditions common to the kind of low-wage employment in the service economy that people with convictions are more likely to obtain.

Journalist Maya Schenwar (2015) calls the ankle bracelet "an imprisonment device attached to the body at all times." Framing EM as an extension of rather than an alternative to the prison points to the enormous, life-altering consequences such surveillance has for those monitored, their families, and their neighbors. To underscore this point, Kilgore characterizes EM as a kind of privatized, remote-control incarceration or a form of virtual incarceration that outsources costs to families while transforming homes into spaces of isolated captivity and surveillance. He also highlights how EM functions even more insidiously as a reformist technological innovation in the ongoing project of producing a "humanist" carceral state retrofitted for the age of austerity. In the name of costs savings and prison reform, EM adds a whole new mesh of complex, even unknowable, controls to the lives of those subject to its surveillance. Access to medical care, intimate relationships, and participation in the labor force are all areas of life fundamentally impeded by these controls, not to mention the climate of fear, suspicion, and self-censorship that the virtual and mostly unregulated monitoring of their lives produces.

As Joan Petersilia argues, "the ability to arrest, confine and, in some cases, re-imprison the parolee for violating conditions of the parole agreement makes the parole agent a walking court system" (2003). When that ability is augmented by GPS satellite technology, battery-life issues, twenty-four-hours-per-day surveillance, and the electronic delineation of exclusion zones, that walking court system becomes more like a walking prison system. Like spatial exclusions and gang injunctions, the exclusion zones enforced through location tracking and EM reproduce a key property of the prison regime: banishment. The prison's function as a space of disappearance for people and social problems alike is carried over and into the community through the production of exclusion zones and the exile of particular people and activities from those spaces. In this sense, EM fits into a larger devolution of imprisonment back to communities. One expression of this devolution is the increased importance of county jails to the prison industrial complex, as the numbers inside them expand even while state prison populations shrink (see for example Hinds and Norton 2018). Penal devolution, however, also encompasses the relocation of carceral authority from spaces of detention to the churches, homes, schools and local nonprofits currently tasked with everything from reentry programming to the surveillance of movement and behavior.

Civil gang injunctions, SORs and their spatial banishment mechanisms, and EM are all powerful tools enacted outside of prison walls for law enforcement and other authorities to exert control over particular people and places. Much like the Brownsville alternatives described in chapter 2, they are also all decidedly *geographic* interventions that serve to shore up the legitimacy of the penal state under the guise of community corrections. In this way, they operate alongside and in concert with a whole host of initiatives, some explicitly reformist and some not, that currently serve to support or legitimize the expansion of the carceral state. This means more people, rather than fewer, enmeshed in an ever-expanding matrix of control, confinement, and responsibilization, all of which serve to destabilize relationships and undermine participation in civic and social life. In these instances of carceral power, space is used strategically, just as law is.

The term "transcarceration" has been used to describe the kinds of nonprison tactics of socially controlling former and would-be prisoners outlined in this chapter, as well as the neoliberal reorganization of prison facilities and other like structures themselves (Schept 2013b; Hallett 2012). Beckett and Murakawa, meanwhile, use the term "the shadow carceral state" to describe those activities *outside of* but effectively undergirding more visible institutions of criminal law and criminal justice, or as they put it, the "more submerged, serpentine forms of punishment that work in legally hybrid and institutionally variegated ways" (2012, 222). These include emerging processes such as the expansion of civil and administrative pathways to incarceration, the creation of civil alternatives to invalidated criminal-social-control tools, and the incorporation of criminal law into administrative legal processes in ways that enhance state carceral power, for example civil gang injunctions (224). Both concepts (transcarceration and shadow carceral state) are useful frameworks for anticipating and recognizing the reproduction of carceral power, often in the name of prison reform and under the sign of community.

The expansion of carceral technologies out of prisons and into homes and communities penetrates all aspects of daily life, including intimate and community relations. For those subject to parole, probation, or "pre-crime" surveillance, such as those named under gang injunctions, all aspects of life on the *outside* continue to be governed and regulated. This includes everything from where one lives and who one befriends to whether one is permitted to carry a cell phone or have a drink at the end of the day. But these technologies and tactics also perform the ideological work of the carceral state and the prison regime, insofar as they reproduce hegemonic ideas and feelings about who is dangerous and where danger happens. They neither dislodge the surveillance apparatus through which authorities maintain control over certain people and certain places nor disturb the logics through which the carceral state maintains legitimacy, including the idea of the prison as the ultimate repository of danger. Indeed, by invoking community, whether in the context of "community corrections" or more generally during the implementation of gang injunctions and banishment spaces in the name of keeping communities safe, these tactics work only to mask the widening of a shadow penal regime. These activities, while seemingly outside and beyond the prison and sometimes situated within civil law, serve both to further carceral logics and to enhance state carceral power insofar as they effect punitive bodily control and create new criteria for criminalization proper.

Stuart Schrader extends the caution against what he calls "the romance of the community," borrowing from the title of Miranda Joseph's *Against the Romance of Community* (2002). In response to the reemergence of community policing, he warns: "Community is the terrain of intervention for police, shaped by police. It does not preexist police and it does not provide a bulwark against police power. . . . Community and police double-back on each other under present social arrangements, to maintain and reproduce present social arrangements" (Schrader 2006). The reproduction of existing social arrangements is indeed what is at stake in current debates about prison reform and the role of community corrections as a so-called decarceration strategy.

As Ruth Wilson Gilmore reminds us, prison reform has historically, as now, opened the door to the expansion of the prison under the guise of social improvement (2009, 82). A half century ago, André Gorz offered this useful distinction between reformist and nonreformist reforms:

A reformist reform is one which subordinates its objectives to the criteria of rationality and practicality of a given system and policy. Reformism rejects those objectives and demands—however deep the need for them—which are incompatible with the preservation of the system. On the other hand, a not necessarily reformist reform is one which is conceived not in terms of what is possible within the framework of a given system of administration, but in view of what should be made possible in terms of human needs and demands. (1967, 7–8)

In the context of the prison system, therefore, nonreformist reform can be understood as "changes that, at the end of the day, unravel rather than widen the net of social control through criminalization" (Gilmore 2007, 242). Gilmore further underscores how reformist reform is particularly crucial to the way that neoliberalism operates. Its very ability to adapt to and incorporate itself into critique is part of what makes neoliberalism, with the structures of violence it enacts, so dangerous to the project of prison abolition. Prison reforms forged in the context of unabated neoliberal restructuring and state austerity, even those measures that seem to get people out of prisons and into the communities ostensibly outside their walls, are especially important to appraise with a critical eye precisely because, as Williams noted a decade after Gorz (1977a), the notion of community is so rarely viewed unfavorably. Even the prison boosters of eastern Kentucky invoke community in order to characterize the penitentiaries they want to build as an unassailable social good.

If we are indeed witnessing the unfolding demise of America's regime of hyperincarceration, then it is necessary to extend the critiques lodged against jails and prisons to those *other* spaces of everyday social life where the carceral state may be repackaging and reinstantiating itself. Differentiating between reformist reform and nonreformist reform in practice, however, can be a difficult challenge. It requires vigilance and an expansive analytical frame to decipher whether initiatives funded and propagated under the sign of community have the effect of making lives better, or instead structure further immobility, displacement, and racialized immiseration into our existing social order. Even while the prison remains the state's privileged spatial fix, the invention and proliferation of new, community-based instruments of social and geographic control signal a crises of legitimacy for the carceral state, even while they also reinforce its power and continue its work. This suggests that, in the spaces of transference between one mode of carceral control and another, there is also organizing potential. The community, after all, is also where everyday life is reproduced, and thus also where people will fight to survive and work to be free.

Conclusion
Freedom Struggles and the Future of Carceral Space

The very idea of precariousness implies dependency on social networks and conditions, suggesting that there is no "life itself" at issue here, but always and only conditions of life, life as something that requires conditions in order to become livable life and, indeed, in order to become grievable.

—JUDITH BUTLER, *FRAMES OF WAR*

What is, so to speak, the object of abolition? Not so much the abolition of prisons but the abolition of a society that could have prisons.

—FRED MOTEN AND STEFANO HARNEY,
"THE UNIVERSITY AND THE UNDERCOMMONS"

The United States operates the largest archipelago of jails and penitentiaries in the world. And yet it can be hard to find the prison in today's landscape. Prisons are, after all, by design and definition, spaces of disappearance. They disappear (or attempt to disappear) the people inside them. And they are themselves increasingly disappeared from the dense social spaces where many of us live and move around. Prisons today are built far away from urban areas, often invisible from major thoroughfares. Some facilities are redacted from Google Maps. Others are so disguised in their built form that they are commonly mistaken for warehouses or logistic compounds, thus blending seamlessly into the bleak scenery of rural and peri-urban deindustrialization.

But prisons are disappeared in other ways as well. They are disappeared behind common ideas, exploited anxieties, and persistent mythologies, including the fantasy that prisons keep us safe by holding those who pose us danger apart and far away. In this sense, not only are they themselves disappeared, but they perform a disappearing trick of their own. For, as well as disappearing people, prisons also disappear the social crises that they are tasked, in practice, with resolving: poverty, unemployment, political dissent, inequality, uneven development, and other social calamities inscribed in the landscape by racial capitalism.

One concept that usefully encapsulates this phenomenon of disappearance is *reification*. Reification and ideology are closely related, but if ideology is the interpretation in thought of social relations, reification is the mystification of those social relations into "things"—things that appear to us as pregiven and self-contained but whose historical formations and social contingencies are thoroughly obscured. The prison is just such a thing: its built form betrays little of the historical conditions that produced it in the first place or for which it now serves. Wedded in "common sense" and legal logic to the problem of crime, the prison as a building in the landscape mystifies the underlying social formations, those gendered, racialized, capitalist relations, that actually produce and reproduce the carceral state in our lives.

The problem, politically, with the reified world is that it robs the conditions of existence of their collective action. It seeks to turn injustice into tragedy. The Marxist critic Georg Lukács theorized the reified world as "the only possible world, the only conceptually accessible, comprehensible world vouchsafed to us humans" (1971, 119). Prisons endure, at least in part, because of their reified status in the social landscape. Just by existing, they seem to have always been part of our lives. They mask their own contingency, concealing their emergence out of particular struggles, debates, and crises that are themselves rooted in (relatively recent) historical transformations. The problem of reification and the politics of prison abolition are thus intimately connected: the latter becomes possible only once the prison is deconstructed and perceived not as a "thing" or as "fact," but as the ossification of a set of social relations, or relationships of power, that could, in fact, be arranged otherwise. The question, therefore, is not simply how to close down existing spaces of detention, but also how to transform the kind of society for which the prison is required in the first place.

Prison abolition is a movement aimed at changing the relationships that produce the kinds of events and behaviors for which prison seems to be the solution. Within this framework, the goal of dismantling penal facilities necessarily coexists with the seemingly disparate aims of, for example, providing stable housing, interrupting interpersonal violence, or guaranteeing access to wealth and resources, for these are all social problems for which the prison currently serves as a surrogate solution. Demystifying the prison, then, is at once both about revealing the place of the prison system within the larger social fabric and about recuperating the transformative power of people as agents of collective action. Such work, it follows, includes identifying those forces that function ideologically as counterproductive to that power.

One argument of this book is that, since ideology is always mediated through space (Goonewardena 2005), we should expand the geographies within which we investigate the contemporary prison system and its social functions. The spatial move as analytic move has precedence within critical thought. Karl Marx was already deep into writing *Capital* when he decided to include a chapter on the working day. In order to describe and understand the market, he realized, one had to actually *turn away* from the marketplace and peer instead into the factory floor, for it is within the walls of the factory that actual relations between people are transformed into commodities (Ross 2015, 80). So it is with the prison and the broader task of understanding and deconstructing carceral power. It is the social relations and social processes invested in the production of the prison regime that tell us how the system works, and why. Discerning those relations and processes requires, at times, a shifting of perspective.

While this book is, on one hand, about the production and operation of carceral spaces as landscapes of power, it is also about how geographic or spatial inquiry can yield new frameworks for understanding the work that prisons do and how things might be otherwise. New frameworks are frequently the lifeblood of critical thought, but they are especially needed in the field of penal studies, where the criminal-justice system is too often treated as a closed circuit of laws and policies within which tautological claims and logics then circulate unchallenged. The most hegemonic of such claims is that prisons are a response to crime and/or criminals, with the normative choice then being limited to whether we see them succeed or fail in this function. A central ambition of this book has been to challenge this claim. To do so, I have invited you, as readers, to journey outward with me in search of the prison in the peripheries of our frame. To see the prison clearly, and therefore differently, I suggest, we might do well to cast our gaze, at least for a period, everywhere but the actual penitentiary.

Prison Land attempts to interrupt the work of reification by resituating the prison in everyday landscapes (some urban and some rural, some in transition and some in motion) that may not immediately appear to us as carceral. "Carceral space," as I have elaborated in these pages, designates both the exterior sites that make up the whole continuum of the prison system itself and also those social relations, like property and waged labor, and geographic processes, like gentrification and resource enclosure, through which racial capitalism reproduces itself and for which the state's capacities of containment and social control are put to use. Making that case opens up new sites for intervention and the making of demands. The political stakes revolve around the possibility of a world without prisons, and a world in which the violence that prisons perform is not continued by other means or through new spatial arrangements. This is the challenge provoked by neoliberal prison reform, which, among other things, holds us to the myth that mass incarceration simply reflects the sway of punishment within public opinion. The political project of rethinking the practice of incarceration altogether and abolishing prisons and other like structures of captivity and premature death will fail so long as the terms we use to describe or even denounce imprisonment hinge on the assumption that prisons emerge out of the logic of punishment, rather than vice versa.

The expanded framework of carceral space reveals new terrains of contingency for prison reformers and abolitionists to intervene and transform our social landscape, helping us connect across discretely organized struggles and disciplines. It also helps us think about how these *places* are themselves connected across space. The most salient organizing features of the prison regime, as found in Detroit's downtown real-estate corridor and eastern Kentucky's impoverished coalfields, for example, have to do with property, waged labor, and race. It is through the production and cognition of *those* social relations, rather than any overwhelming drive to punish, that the carceral order is reproduced. For example, the recognition that the prison system is intimately bound up with the capitalist reification of work—"the fact that at present one must work to 'earn a living' is taken as part of the natural order rather than as a social convention," as Kathi Weeks describes it (2011, 3)—helps further the case for centering the problem of waged labor and dispossession as necessary facets of abolitionist struggle. Whether this means making demands on the state for a more robust system of public goods, or control over the social surplus and the means of producing it, or the redistribution of wealth and resources, or something else entirely, is up to us, though it is the suggestion of this book that all constitute necessary abolitionist demands.

Similarly, recognition of the property relation at the heart of carceral logic helps us connect today's racialized struggles in urban spaces against police violence, criminalization, and securitization to the ideology of settler colonialism as a historical and ongoing state project. Making just such a connection after the death of Trayvon Martin and the release of his killer, George Zimmerman, the historian Robin D. G. Kelley (2014) instructs us to be clear:

> The point is that justice was always going to elude Trayvon Martin, not because the system *failed,* but because it worked. Martin died and Zimmerman walked because our entire political and legal foundations were built on an ideology of settler colonialism—an ideology in which the protection of white property rights was always sacrosanct; predators and threats to those privileges were almost always black, brown, and red; and where the very purpose of police power was to discipline, monitor, and contain populations rendered a threat to white property and privilege. This has been the legal standard for African Americans and other racialized groups in the U.S. long before ALEC or the NRA came into being. We were rendered property in slavery, and a threat to property in freedom.

Kelley invites us to look beyond the killing itself to the suburban real estate that was securitized to exclude people like Trayvon Martin, whose blackness marked him as a threat to those properties. Indeed, the modality of race and the ordering logic of white supremacy structure the form and character of all the carceral geographies explored in this book. If the ideologies of race and racism live on today, it is because we continue to create them today. As Barbara Fields suggests, we reritualize them to fit our own terrain. That terrain is a neoliberal racial order in which the production of a permanent surplus labor force and the terrorization of that labor force through wagelessness and incarceration condition the possibility of continued accumulation by dispossession (Harvey 2004). The social vocabulary that helps such practices "make sense" includes crime, property, individual responsibility, and race. This does not mean there is anything natural or necessary about any of these categories. Quite the contrary. But it is precisely because these concepts bear so meaningfully and materially on the world, and for some violently so, that we must continue to ask how they are socially constructed, and to what ends.

The *punishable subject* is itself an ideological product of carceral space, one that bears intimately on the production of difference and disposability. The question of who can be punished is also a question about whose labor has value, or who can be housed near toxic waste, or who can be killed. Retrieving these as genuine questions available for democratic debate and transformation is part of the work and the challenge of fighting for economic and racial justice within the context of unbridled carceral state power. This work will require a broad rethinking of the property and labor relations that currently organize the social order and the legitimizing cover racial categories give the inequities of that order. But it will also require including in an abolitionist politics those "indefensible" categories of criminal, such as the sex offender, upon which the prison's promise to punish holds strongest purchase across the spectrum of public opinion. Such a politics is in keeping with the abolitionist commitment to recovering effective and empowering (rather than surrogate) strategies against harm, including sexual violence.

Feelings of vindication in the aftermath of harm are no evidence of justice's triumph, however much they may be desired or even deserved. Similarly, the shift from exclusion to inclusion does not in and of itself necessitate any form of structural or systemic change to a given system. An example can be found in President Obama's passage of the Matthew Shepard and James Byrd Jr. Hate Crimes Prevention Act. Introduced in response to the mainstream LGBT community's appeals in the wake of a number of bias-motivated murders, the measure expanded the 1969 U.S.

federal hate-crime law to include crimes motivated by a victim's actual or perceived gender, sexual orientation, gender identity, or disability. Like hate-crime legislation generally, this act is strictly concerned with retribution through the criminal-justice system. It authorizes expanded powers of policing, persecution, and punishment and effects greater severity of treatment under the law of those individuals engaging in acts of hate against identified groups of people. There is little, however, to suggest that hate laws appealed to on the basis of *bad feeling* offer anything more substantial than emotional catharsis. What they do instead, like all carceral strategies, is legislate the disappearance of the perpetrators while, at the same time, reproducing the social conditions that give rise to such violence by failing to express them as anything other than individual. Retributive politics makes such violence somehow bearable, yet it does little for the struggle to reshape collective life.

The case studies investigated in this book have shown geographies of economic abandonment, real-estate accumulation, and devalued labor power (including caregiving) functioning alongside the neoliberal logic of individual responsibility to undermine the project of collective life-building at every turn. Capitalist fantasies about failure and scarcity continue to underwrite the banishment of some and the self-isolation of others. The anti-sex-offender park, for example, demonstrates the role of carceral space in producing privileged categories of deviance even within the already stigmatized arena of criminality, reinforcing the common-sense belief that carceral spaces protect people from harm through dispossession and banishment, while also shoring up affective attachments to the punishment functions of the state. In the case of the long-distance prison bus, the geographic isolation of faraway prisons compounds and conditions the secondary prisonization of visiting loved ones, most of whom are women of color, already bearing the extended physical and psychic burdens of neoliberal austerity. Under such conditions, self-isolation is both an affective condition of internalized neoliberal logic and a coping mechanism against risk in the high-stakes game of caretaking across prison walls.

Together, these spatial investigations demonstrate how a variety of capitalist social relations seemingly outside the aegis of the criminal-justice apparatus, including property, waged labor, and race, powerfully animate and legitimate the penal regime. It is in this sense that a radical deconstruction of carceral space serves not only to demystify the prison itself as a social construction but also to assemble an alternative analytical framework that disarticulates crime from punishment. The imperative to punish is a *product*, not a cause, of the practice of incarceration, one best challenged by closing down prisons and interrupting the very relations that make penal institutions and disposable subjects useful in the first place.

Penal-reform initiatives forged under the neoliberal auspices of fiscal responsibility will fail to ensure an abolitionist future precisely because they do not and cannot challenge the social relations for which prisons are put to work. One consequence of appealing to neoliberal rationale is a remade carceral apparatus retrofitted for the age of austerity, one in which the social- and racial-control functions of the modern prison are outsourced to new or revitalized institutions within the scene of class-fortified urban space or the sacrifice zones of urban and rural abandonment. In the wake of a new and self-stylized "law and order" president in Donald Trump, however, the ostensible beacon of neoliberal prison-reform will, for many, take on an extra glow.

Where We Are Now

The election of right-wing stalwart and revanchist demagogue Donald Trump as president of the United States in 2016 threw the period's great elite hope of bipartisan prison reform into a tailspin. Promising to stamp out "the crime and gangs and drugs that have stolen too many lives and robbed our country of so much unrealized potential" (what he also dubbed "American carnage"), Trump staked his political legacy firmly on the claim of law and order, a gainful political strategy for such past presidential aspirants as Richard Nixon and Bill Clinton. Complicating things for those invested in the idea of an unassailable bipartisan reform movement was the fact that some of the movement's key figureheads, such as "Right on Crime" founder Newt Gingrich, stumped openly for Trump and currently advise him. Laments now abound that the right–left coalition in support of criminal-justice reform is on the verge of collapse. As the nonprofit news site The Marshall Project put it in a piece published in collaboration with *The New Yorker*: "Left and right came together on criminal justice reform. Then Trump happened" (George 2017). Indeed, the Trump presidency, while still in its early days as of this book's writing, already forecasts much to be alarmed about, including rollbacks to sentencing-reform measures, the revocation of limits to federal use of private prisons, decreased oversight of local police, and increased immigration enforcement and detention (Grawert and Camhi 2017).

The appointment of career racist Jeff Sessions to the position of Attorney General under President Trump sounded another alarm. Despite crime rates nearing historic lows, Sessions reinvigorated the war on drugs, calling on all federal prosecutors to "charge and pursue the most serious, readily provable offense" for federal crimes in a memo titled "Department Charging and Sentencing Policy" (U.S. Attorney General 2017). The memo resurrected the emphasis on mandatory-minimum-sentencing requirements within federal drug law and built on other initiatives historically integral to the massive buildup of our carceral facilities. Trump and Sessions actively stoked racist and white-nationalist antagonisms. Even though Sessions resigned his position as Attorney General in November 2018, Trump's policies continue to pose real and immediate threats to many already marginalized and some not-so-marginalized groups. The Trump administration thus gives us much to worry about and fight against. The danger, however, is that, in focusing on the Trump administration as the key adversary to a decarcerated future, one may mistake the bipartisan reform movement that it putatively tramples for a liberatory politics with substantive social justice promise. It is not.

This book points to some of the ways that, under the pretext of bipartisan prison reform, the capacities of the carceral state may be retrofitted for the current conjuncture, producing new spatial fixes for managing surplus life. Such findings are in keeping with the history of prison reform. Scholars have offered examples throughout U.S. penal history of reform efforts that have failed to stem either the growth or the increased racialization of U.S. prisons, in some cases having even engendered more austere and punitive conditions (Rothman 1971; Foucault 1977; Gottschalk 2006; Reiter 2012). Indeed, recent scholarship shows that reformist appeals to a more "rehabilitative" approach to incarceration have actually helped facilitate the building of *more* carceral spaces in the guise of "justice campuses" (Schept 2013a) and "gender-responsive prisons" (Braz 2006).

Recent reform efforts forged within the active zone of neoliberal state-building appear to be continuing the punishment system's coercive management of people of color and urban poverty while rendering the system as a whole more flexible and cost-effective. The rise of electronic monitoring as a so-called alternative to incarceration, for example, figures crucially in the rebranding of the carceral state. As an extension of mobility control at the urban scale, such monitoring forms part of the penal-reform landscape that is refashioning cities into sites of carceral control. Likewise, Proposition 47 in California, a reform initiative passed in 2014, purchases the decarceration of certain low-level drug and property offenders at the cost of those convicted of so-called violent and sex offenses, whom it promises to keep sentencing severely. It also mandates and financially underwrites the proliferation of police officers in schools, furthering the degree to which the public education system in America figures as a locus of carceral power (Meiners 2011). While prison reform at the federal scale may thus be in a holding pattern, many of the nation's financially beleaguered states are continuing to beat the drum of bipartisan prison reform. Animated by fiscal pressures and framed through neoliberal rationalities, many of these reform strategies widen the net of carceral control while reproducing the racialized inequalities, exploitative capitalist relations, and social crises that produced mass incarceration in the first place.

If neither tough-on-crime policies (whether issued from the political right or the political left) nor bipartisan neoliberal prison reform (championed by Republicans and Democrats alike) offer a meaningful justice or freedom from harm, then what is to be done? The answer, as always, can be found on the ground.

Learning from Movements

During the writing of this book, a powerful set of events was unfolding in the United States. In cities and towns across the country, demonstrators took to the streets in coordinated and spontaneous actions against violence and systemic racism. One of the flashpoints for these uprisings occurred in the predominantly poor and African American suburbs of St. Louis, Missouri. In communities like Jennings and Ferguson, where I began at the opening of this book, decades of economic disinvestment and racial segregation have coalesced to produce a situation of almost daily harassment and police violence for local residents. In August 2014, one of those residents, an eighteen-year-old Ferguson man named Michael Brown, was fatally shot by a white police officer who fired twelve rounds of ammunition at the teenager's body. In late November, a grand jury failed to indict the officer who killed Brown, sparking sustained social protests in the streets and sidewalks of Ferguson and adjacent municipalities. A short week later, a separate grand jury in New York also sided with law enforcement in a verdict of nonindictment against the NYPD officers who had choked to death Eric Garner, a forty-three-year-old black man whose livelihood depended on selling loose cigarettes in Staten Island. The protests that erupted in anger around these killings and the nonindictments of the police officers responsible grew quickly into a nationwide uprising. Responding not just to the news of Mike Brown and Eric Garner but also the deaths of Trayvon Martin, Jordan Davis, Rekia Boyd, Renisha McBride, and countless other unarmed African Americans killed by police and vigilantes, tens of thousands of people across the United States took to the streets not only to proclaim but also to demand that "Black Lives Matter."

Under this mantle, sustained protests and actions have united around the issues of police violence, systemic racism, and vulnerability to premature death. At the core of this uprising is the assertion that black life has value, despite and against a societal backdrop in which it is constantly and actively rendered valueless. In today's context of unfettered racial capitalism, black life is life structurally degraded by and within an economic system that requires a permanent, differentiated class *that does not appear as a class* so that those people can more easily be exploited as laborers, expropriated from resource-rich territories or profitable real estate, and banished or killed if unabsorbable or threatening to the social order (Linebaugh 2015). Class, of course, is not a fixed identity, but a relation, which is why we can acknowledge the prison's role in upholding and naturalizing a racial order even while recognizing that those identified as "white" represent 39 percent of the people currently held in America's prisons and jails (Wagner and Rabuy 2017). Inequality as a whole has increased in the United States to levels not seen in a hundred years. This means that life for almost everyone is getting worse, even while African American, indigenous, and Latinx people bear the brunt of economic hardship disproportionately. Following previous black-liberation struggles, Black Lives Matter has enabled us to think through the economic dispossession of, state violence against, and premature deaths of Latinx, Native, Muslim, poor white, queer, and other marginalized populations together, not just as an aberration of black suffering but as part of a shared condition of economic exploitation and systemic violence.

Black Lives Matter demonstrates a dialectical expansion of activism in our current moment, inviting us to pivot from the sites of police violence to a reimagining of an entire apparatus. As the poet and scholar Fred Moten argues, the police killings of Brown and Garner were both deadly manifestations of broken-windows policing. As a theory and model of intensive policing of working-class African American communities that itself builds on a longer history of black criminalization, broken-windows theory encourages police to intervene in low-level, so-called quality-of-life issues, such as Garner's selling of loose cigarettes. The official purpose of broken-windows policing is to prevent more serious crime, but its effects have been mainly to intensify police dragnets in neighborhoods and communities of color. Moten extends his analogy further: "What they made clear, is that we *are* the broken windows. We constitute this threat to the already existing normative order" (2014). In other words: some lives are deemed valuable to the existing order while others can be abandoned, and even killed.

In everything that comes out of the Black Lives Matter movement, I see the prison. In every prisoner struggle I participate in or read about, I hear people declaring that black lives matter. The statistic (widely touted over the past few years) that tells us that a black person is killed by law enforcement or vigilantes every twenty-eight hours on average (Malcolm X Grassroots Movement 2012) is part of the same story as the fact that one in three young African American men is currently under the control of the criminal justice system, either in prison, in jail, on probation, or on parole (Alexander 2010, 9). This is not to say that prisons and other spaces of carceral control are a neat and inevitable continuation of other modes of racial state violence, such as Jim Crow laws. Rather, it is to assert that the production of black criminality in particular serves, like all regimes of systemic racism, to naturalize the social wreckage of a capitalist order and to legitimize the state violence required to quell the contradictions endemic to it.

What Donald Trump calls "American carnage" the historian Khalil Muhammad calls the production of "black criminality." Invented after the Reconstruction by white sociologists, the idea of black criminality differed from "white criminality," Muhammad argues, in that black criminality was supposedly impervious to remedy through government policy because it was reflective of so-called black culture, or even a black biology. Black criminality, according to Muhammad, thus became a "tool to measure black fitness for citizenship" and to "shield . . . white Americans from the charge of racism, helping to determine the degree to which whites had any responsibility to help black people" (Muhammad 2011, 139). In other words, white criminality, as it emerged in this period, was considered society's problem, but black criminality was the affliction and liability of black communities alone. In this way, the concept of black criminality served—and still serves—to naturalize black poverty and disinvestment from the social wage, even while legitimizing massive state expenditure in a growing punitive apparatus for containment and control.

Carceral spaces, including the prison, do not *respond* to criminality, black or otherwise, so much as they help produce and reproduce black criminality as an ideological construct. Banishment spaces and containment sites, from the neighborhood exclusion zone to the police holding van, demonstrate to a wider public that danger is nearby, that it is predominantly black or brown, poor and working class, and that those labeled as dangerous are socially disposable. In this way, they also undermine and occlude the shared material basis for solidarity that should exist among ordinary people whose living conditions continue to worsen under neoliberal capitalism. As Keeanga-Yamahtta Taylor reminds us, "solidarity is only possible through relentless struggle to win white workers to antiracism, to expose the lie that Black workers are worse off because they somehow choose to be" (2016, 215). The case studies in this book reveal how carceral space produces and manages disposability in various ways: by individualizing social problems and disorganizing collectivized counterpower; by dispossessing urban residents of public space, social resources, and state entitlements; and by responsibilizing people into neoliberal subjects. It does so perhaps most meaningfully, however, by producing the *criminal* as a class of human being, one that overlaps and provides ideological cover for other racial classifications and class divisions. The category of the criminal may be the paradigmatic vehicle for antiblackness in the United States today, even while it also enshrines other racial and gendered identities as indexes of danger, risk, and un-grieveable life. So, when we see so-called alternatives to the prison, like the Brownsville Youth Courts, continuing to construct certain people as criminal subjects, they are actually reproducing a central function of the prison system. They do so at the same time as they *recuperate* the carceral state by making it seem responsive to waning public support for mass incarceration.

One thing I have tried to do in this book is show the ways in which the production of surplus life is braided within the organization of carceral space. The concept of surplus life suggests something more complicated than just the production of superfluous labor in reserve or its intimate relation to the contemporary "warehouse" prison, though that too is relevant (Irwin 1980; Wacquant 2009a). To be sure, capital accumulates not just through the laboring body but also through the coerced idling of those whose labor is deemed extraneous. In the context of the Black Lives Matter movement, however, surplus life also recalls something more closely akin to what Judith Butler calls "precarious life": the ideological and material practices of class production through which some lives are rendered grievable and others are not: "These normative schemes operate not only by producing ideals of the human that differentiate among those who are more and less human. Sometimes they produce images of the less than human, in the guise of the human, to show how the less than human disguises itself, and threatens to deceive those of us who might think we recognize another human there" (2004, 146). The racialized category of the "criminal" continues to operate as one such powerful cover, as we witnessed in the cases of Garner and Brown. In mainstream-media coverage of both deaths, debates about police culpability hung not on the recklessness and harmfulness of the uniformed perpetrators, but instead on the putative criminality of their victims.

Much ink was spilled in the national press on the question of whether Brown was indeed shoplifting from a convenience store just before his murder, while Garner's hawking of loose cigarettes had made him a target of police harassment for many years. In a country where over seven million people are under some form of state supervision by the criminal-justice system, the massive reach and potency of "criminality" as camouflage for the less-than-human is almost ungraspable. For Butler, this necessitates that we challenge all political forms that exclude the conditions of a livable life for so many. It is mass criminalization *and* mass incarceration that require immediate dismantling. But we must also challenge the continued enclosure of the commons, the structures of private property that limit access to the means of survival, like housing, water, and food, and the relations of power that force people to labor at the lowest possible wages only so that others can profit from that labor.

Black Lives Matter is a movement against the creation and oppressive management of surplus life. It is also a movement for radical black sociality in a context of such aggressive neoliberalization that sociality itself constitutes a kind of insurgent threat. Moten puts it powerfully: "When we say that Black lives matter I think what we do sometimes is obscure the fact that in fact it's Black *life* that matters; that insurgent Black social life still constitutes a profound threat to the already existing order of things" (2014). Communalized survival and collective struggle have always been both an object of and a threat to capitalist relations and carceral power. For this reason, the external geographies and afterlives of the prison matter. They point to our progress toward an abolitionist future, irrespective of whether we are in a moment defined by the elite bipartisanship of criminal-justice reform or the law-and-order revanchism of Donald Trump. Financial disinvestment from penal institutions, while critical as a demand, does not by itself portend the end of the production and management of surplus life. In fact, as we have seen throughout the history of prison-reform movements, and especially in the past decade, such disinvestments can facilitate new spatial fixes for that surplus life out of the carceral state's own crisis of legitimacy and under the guise of penal critique.

The project of *Prison Land* has been to demonstrate that what is at stake in both the prison regime and prison reform is the production of dispossession and disposability, the development of new carceral spaces and new penal mechanisms. The prison is but one spatial technology within a larger state regime of organized racial capitalism. By recasting the prison as a set of social relationships and exploring the landscapes within which those relationships play out, we also discover its vulnerabilities. We cannot interrupt the growth and transformation of imprisonment without looking, clear-eyed, at the present conjuncture: renovations in contemporary practices of statecraft and political economy, restructurings of urban and rural space, and the shifting terms and terrain of systemic racism and its discontents.

Transformations in carceral space are signals of crisis. Our current juncture exemplifies Stuart Hall and Bill Schwartz's observation that "crises occur when the social formation can no longer be reproduced on the basis of the preexisting system of social relations" (quoted in Gilmore 2007, 54). The systemic change necessary to resolve such crises, Ruth Wilson Gilmore reminds us, must be determined through struggle: "Crisis means instability that can be fixed only through radical measures, which include developing new relationships and new or renovated institutions out of what already exists" (26). The afterlives—and afterspaces—of the prison are already being determined in the present. The gentrifying urban neighborhood is one site where we can see how the current period's preoccupation with prison reform as an exercise in corrections-budget recapture is being translated on the ground into a widening, rather than downsizing, of the carceral regime. In this case, the economic imperatives and neoliberal initiatives that drive urban gentrification dovetail productively with reified narratives of individualized black criminality. Stitched onto poor, black urban neighborhoods, these practices effectively render the space of the neighborhood a legitimate target of increased state and economic intervention under the liberal guise of justice reinvestment and prison reform.

We cannot predict, exactly, the future of criminal justice under President Donald Trump. Unfolding power battles within the White House and elite turmoil within both major political parties render the immediate future of penal policy, at least at the federal level, still unclear. Just as this book was being completed, the Department of Justice released its 2018 budget, within which it *rescinded* its request for the $444 million needed to construct the long-planned federal prison in Letcher County, Kentucky. Members of Congress with vested interests in the new construction project, most vocally U.S. Representative Hal Rogers, are livid at the betrayal and are spoiling for a fight. What we do know, however, is that the current administration is explicitly and unflinchingly hostile to unions, immigrants, women, and the poor. Every Trump policy and budgetary initiative thus far forecasts a continued dismantling of the social wage and further fomenting of the social and economic crises for which prisons have long served as the surrogate solution.

Taking a longer view, we also know that the neoliberal processes by which the carceral state is remaking and respatializing itself, whether under the sign of prison reform or a revanchist doubling down on tough-on-crime politics, offer important terrain for continued research and vigilant organizing. The prison's afterlives and afterspaces are being forged at the elite level in terms that ensure the continued expansion of the carceral state: producing new means and spatial configurations through which to control and contain, to degrade and destroy those rendered surplus and/ or threatening to the capitalist economy; deepening the fracturing of the social and obliterating the commons; and generating new cover stories to legitimate the abandonment and containment of some lives and not others. The category of the criminal is itself an uneven ontological field in that regard: as the freedom of low-level and drug offenders is increasingly purchased through appeals to relative innocence, those labeled by the state as violent or sex offenders pay the high price of the carceral regime in the form of longer and harsher sentences.

Even while the concept of "punishment" may be a misleading framework for making sense of the prison's ideological traction, an effective abolitionist challenge to the carceral regime must include precisely those categories of prisoner or criminal who seem so legitimately *punishable.* For, even while the carceral state is actually expanded through normative appeals to the sanctity of property, the responsibilizing ethic of work, and a racial ordering of valuable life, its camouflage remains the spurious promise that it and it alone can keep us from harm. The task, then, is to disinvest from the economy of guilt and innocence altogether, which is also to insist, without caveat, that black life matters.

Under the mobilizing mantle of Black Lives Matter, important links are being forged across the arenas that constitute the "matter" of life, in particular between economic well-being and freedom from state violence. Activists from Black Lives Matter have called for an economic program that resurrects from previous black-liberation struggles such demands as a freedom budget, universal healthcare, and good housing for all. Expressing a clear vision of how economic precarity undergirds state violence, authors of the "Ferguson Action Demands" write: "Inability to access employment continues to marginalize our communities, ready us for imprisonment, and deny us of our right to a life with dignity" (Ferguson Action 2014). In Ferguson, residents who are fighting against ongoing police violence understand that work to include abolishing the entrenched practice of bankrolling local municipalities though traffic stops and poverty fines. In other words, they understand their fight to be about economic justice as well as racial justice; theirs is a class struggle for living wages and desegregated housing as much as it is also about freedom from police brutality.

Moten, meanwhile, continues on the theme of black life as broken windows: "Part of what's at stake is that to fix a broken window is to fix *another* way of imagining the world; to literally fix it, to destroy it, to regulate it, to exclude it, to incarcerate it. But also at the same time, to incorporate it, to capitalize upon it, to exploit it, to accumulate it" (2014). The prison as a set of relations is just such a fix, and when we go looking for it through this frame, we find it materialized as much in the rural industrial sacrifice zone or the urban no-trespass area as in the cell block and the solitary-confinement unit. The demand that black lives matter is radical and transformative precisely because the capitalist status quo requires that they do not. The existing order of things cannot continue if they do. This is not a claim about the essentialism of race or racism, but rather precisely the opposite. It is a reminder to remain vigilant in our efforts to map the consolidations of racial capitalism and carceral power, as well as the challenges against that power. To insist that black lives matter is to struggle to remake, out of the intertwined crises of police violence, mass incarceration, and economic inequality, a new system of social relations altogether. It is a demand for freedom, without exception.

Acknowledgments

This book is dedicated to the many people in prisons, sent home from prisons, or on their way to visit prisons who gave their time to speak with me and whose struggle inside inspires me to struggle outside. I want especially to acknowledge my friend James Perez, who has spent more than two decades in solitary confinement at the supermax penitentiaries in Pelican Bay and Corcoran in California.

I want to thank my mother, Jane Story, who is always quick to remind me that "problematic" is not a noun and who put the first book into my greedy little hands. Her love of reading and commitment to social justice were passed on to me at an early age and have shaped the course of my life. Thank you also to too many dear friends to name, but especially to my friend John Hodgins, the smartest human being I know. He long ago assured me that resenting rich people can, in fact, be a starting point for struggle, and for that and more, I have endless thanks. James Cairns believed I could do this from the start and diligently read many, many drafts. My political education was honed out of many years of conversations and direct actions taken alongside good friends and devoted comrades in the three main cities of my adult life: Montreal, Toronto, and New York. I want to thank all of the antipoverty and antiracism activists and radical media makers I've had the privilege of working with in those places who continue to do the work, to refuse despair, and who fight to win.

This book began as a PhD dissertation completed while a student in the Department of Geography and Planning at the University of Toronto. While there, I was lucky to meet some of the most wonderful colleagues and friends, including the incomparably brilliant Shiri Pasternak and the absurdly talented Alexis Mitchell. Thanks especially to my reading group companions, with whom I've had the pleasure of working through many dense texts while also taking care to gossip and eat well: Katie Mazer, Patrick Vitale, Laura Pitkanen, Prasad Khanolkar, Caitlin Henry, Martin Danyluk, Martine August, and Kanishka Goonewardena. Sue Ruddick, Scott Prudham, Phil Goodman, Matt Farish, Judy Han, Victor Lorentz, James Nugent, Lisa Freeman, Lia Frederiksen, and David Seitz at the University of Toronto have read drafts, shown up at talks to ask hard questions, and proven themselves to be fabulous colleagues along this journey.

Thank you to my graduate committee, Matt Farish, Kanishka Goonewardena, Emily Gilbert, Phil Goodman, and Deb Cowen, and to my external examiners, Michelle Brown and Eric Cazdyn, for their careful reading and generous support. This work has also benefited enormously from the friendship and feedback of Judah Schept, Jack Norton, Orisanmi Burton, Lisa Guenther, Sarah Armstrong, Anne Bonds, Micol Seigel, Annie Spencer, Pascal Emmer, and Jenna Loyd, and many others from whom I continue to learn so much about abolitionist scholarship and practice.

I am very grateful to have participated in the legendary Center for Place, Culture, and Politics Seminar at the City of New York Graduate Center during a postdoctoral fellowship. The lively weekly discussions and engaged research and writing of the seminar's participants consistently challenged me to think harder and better about the work, and also reminded me why it matters.

Thank you especially to Ruth Wilson Gilmore, who generously supported my work as a postgraduate scholar and a filmmaker but even more important demonstrates a model of all that politically engaged scholarship can and should be. To say that her work has been enormously influential to my own is a gross understatement. She is one of the most brilliant and politically committed thinkers I have ever had the privilege to learn from and call a friend.

Thank you to the anonymous readers who did such diligent work to point out the flaws, omissions, and elisions that pervaded the first draft of this book. I also owe much thanks to the University of Minnesota Press, in particular to my editor, Pieter Martin, who has been an unflinching champion of this book, and editorial assistant Anne Carter. My experience with them has been nothing but rewarding throughout this process. I also thank my research assistant Jen Atalla, who helped manage the chaos of putting this book together, and Colin Beckett, who so skillfully edited a version of this manuscript.

I had the enormous pleasure and the privilege of workshopping this book in its final stages as part of the New Directions in American Studies Manuscript Workshop at Barnard College. I thank Christina Heatherton, Jordan T. Camp, Don Mitchell, and Manu Vimalassery for reading its pages so generously and holding its arguments and evidence to account politically and intellectually. I am enormously grateful and humbled to have had the opportunity to learn from such sharp scholars and interlocutors.

This book may not have been completed if Jason Fox had not provisioned my life with morning coffees and endless snacks. His loving companionship and political incisiveness have made my thinking sharper and my days better. I, too, believe love and struggle are necessarily bound together.

Finally, I thank my friend and graduate supervisor Deb Cowen. Any attempt to express how much her support has meant throughout this process will fall short. Suffice it to say that I have never met a better teacher: rigorous and encouraging, politically uncompromising in action as well as ideas, and generous beyond all measure.

Notes

Introduction

1 See, for example, Harvey 1973; Soja 1980; Lefebvre 1974; Massey 1994.

2 By "common sense," I am specifically invoking Antonio Gramsci's notion of *senso commune,* which lays emphasis on those elements of belief that are shared or held in "common" and refers to "the conception of the world which is uncritically absorbed by the various social and cultural environments" (1971, 419). Following Gramsci, I hold common sense to be always partial and contradictory, even while it works to render aspects of the status quo normal and even inevitable. Gramsci thus argues that common sense offers clues about "the source of the problems" that critical analysis "sets out to study and resolve" (330).

3 This book builds on this important body of research and contributes specifically to a growing literature concerned with "contexts that challenge traditional understandings of the penal realm" (Hannah-Moffat and Lynch 2012, 119). This work includes the identification of a "shadow carceral state" comprised of ostensibly nonpunitive "civil" law mechanisms (Beckett and Murakawa 2012) and increased attention to the burgeoning field of prisoner-reentry programming as an expanding arena of responsibilization and social control (Miller 2013; Hallett 2012).

4 On 2016 Republican presidential contenders and criminal-justice reform, see Blakinger 2015, Campbell 2015, and O'Keefe 2014. George Kelling (2015) has written recently of how broken-windows policing was misinterpreted by police departments. On the dismantling of the welfare state by the people now discussing reform, see Bauer 2014. On private prisons and reentry, see Takei 2014. On bipartisanship and the carceral state more broadly, see Gottschalk 2015.

5 Analytically, this book is guided by political-economic theories of mass incarceration that attribute the growth of prisons to the ascendance of neoliberal global capitalism, the reconfiguration of the post-Keynesian state, and the deindustrialization of urban space and labor since the 1970s. This approach views the prison as an expression of shifting state strategy in the management of urban, racialized poverty (Simon 1993; Beckett and Western 2001; Camp 2011). Key to my theoretical approach is the geographic analysis of the prison as a "spatial fix" for the multiple and intersecting crises of surplus labor, surplus state capacity, and racialized social unrest (Gilmore 2007). My own contribution seeks to build on those interpretations of the prison system to ask how contemporary shifts in state strategy involve restaging space and spatial tactics, including (but not limited to) prison infrastructure, toward the production and management of surplus populations. This includes, for example, resituating the social and racial control functions of the prison to the embattled space of the urban neighborhood. I draw insight from critical race scholarship (Davis 2003; Rodriguez 2006) and economic geography (Harvey 1996; Peck 2003; Gilmore 2007) to also ask how new racial and spatial fixes are being formed out of the most recent financial crisis and the emerging crisis of state legitimacy.

1. The Prison in the City

1 The "book" can be found at quickenloanscareers.com/about-us/culture/.
2 See Smith 1996; Coulthard 2014; Dunbar-Ortiz 2014.
3 See detroithistorical.org/learn/encyclopedia-of-detroit/uprising-1967.

2. Neighborhood Watch

1 A new subfield within urban studies scholarship known as the "neighborhood effects" literature emerged as a key trend in the 1990s and gained particular influence in the second half of the decade (see Jencks and Mayer 1990; Ellen and Turner 1997). Robert Sampson and colleagues note that "the mid 1990s to the year 2000 saw more than a doubling of neighborhood studies to the level of about 100 papers per year" (Sampson et al. 2002, 444). The field of neighborhood effects seeks to link the life chances of particular urban residents to their neighborhood conditions, almost exclusively in regard to high-poverty neighborhoods and the *ill* effects considered consequent to their concentrated poverty. Key variables within this putatively causal relationship are almost always reduced to matters of culture and individual behavior and seen as pathologically incubated by the space of the neighborhood itself.

2 During this small group interview, a project staff member was present and the interviewees were preselected by the project director.

3 Enormously influential theories attempting to account for persistent poverty and low levels of educational attainment were famously promoted by figures like Oscar Lewis (1961; 1966) and Daniel Patrick Moynihan, who was President Nixon's Secretary of Labor. In a controversial and now widely criticized report he authored in 1965, Moynihan argued that black American families were in a crisis due to their social reproduction of particularly self-sabotaging and pathological behavioral traits, such as laziness and hyper-sexuality (see Rainwater and Yancey 1967). As the report argued, the recycling of these cultural and behavioral traits via the family unit is what prevented the children of these families specifically, and black people more broadly, from succeeding in mainstream society. Within the popular "culture of poverty" framework, it was the family unit (and black women in particular, whom Moynihan accused of emasculating black men) that was the dominant unit of blame, and therefore the site for state intervention. Deeply racist, sexist, and classist core assumptions were coded behind references to an urban "underclass" and informed analyses of the persistence of "under-privilege" across a variety of indexes.

3. Rural Extractions

1 In national media discourse, Appalachia is often used as a stand in for what is referred to as the "white working-class." While, of course, the working class in the United States is actually very racially diverse, this is also true in parts of Appalachia. Indeed, poor people of color in the region were often the first to lose their jobs to automation. For more, see Elizabeth Catte's *What You are Getting Wrong about Appalachia* (2018).

2 Consider, for example, Haney 2010.

Bibliography

Achenbach, J., and D. Keating. 2017. "New Research Identifies a 'Sea of Despair' among White, Working-class Americans." *The Washington Post*, March 23. washingtonpost.com/national/health-science/new-research-identifies-a-sea-of-despair-among-white-working-class-americans/2017/03/22/c777ab6e-oda6-11e7-9b0d-d27c98455440_story.html?utm_term=.79367a96oa9f.

Akers, J. 2013. "Decline Industry: The Market Production of Detroit." PhD diss., University of Toronto.

Akers, J. 2017. "The Actually Existing Markets of Shrinking Cities." Metropolitics.eu, April 18. metropolitiques.eu/The-Actually-Existing-Markets-of.html.

Alarcón, D. 2015. "How Do You Define a Gang Member?" *The New York Times*, May 27. nytimes.com/2015/05/31/magazine/how-do-you-define-a-gang-member.html.

Alexander, M. 2010. *The New Jim Crow: Mass Incarceration in the Age of Colorblindness*. New York: The New Press.

Allegretti, M. 2013. "Addressing Detroit's Crime Problem." *Real Clear Policy*, September 3. realclearpolicy.com/articles/2013/09/03/addressing_detroits_crime_problem_635.html.

Alonso, A. A. 1999. "Territoriality among African-American Street Gangs in Los Angeles." Master's thesis, University of Southern California.

American Civil Liberties Union. 2013. "ACLU Urges Detroit to End Illegal Practice of 'Dumping' Homeless People outside City Limits, files DOJ Complaint." ACLU, April 18. aclu.org/news/aclu-urges-detroit-end-illegal-practice-dumping-homeless-people-outside-city-limits-files-doj.

Appalachian Land Ownership Task Force. 1982. *Who Owns Appalachia? Land Ownership and Its Impact*. Lexington: University of Kentucky Press.

Austin, J., E. Cadora, et al. 2013. *Ending Mass Incarceration: Charting a New Justice Reinvestment.* The Sentencing Project. sentencingproject.org/doc/Charting %20a%20New%20Justice%20Reinvestment%20FINAL.pdf.

Avila, E. 2014. *The Folklore of the Freeway: Race and Revolt in the Modernist City.* Minneapolis: University of Minnesota Press.

Bain, J., and M. Gartland. 2013. "Postal Workers Too Scared to Deliver Mail in Crime-ridden Brownsville, Brooklyn." *New York Post,* May 5. amren.com/news /2013/05/postal-workers-too-scared-to-deliver-mail-in-crime-ridden -brownsville-brooklyn/.

Bales, W., et al. 2010. *A Quantitative and Qualitative Assessment of Electronic Monitoring: Report Submitted to the Office of Justice Program National Institute of Justice U.S. Department of Justice.* ncjrs.gov/pdffiles1/nij/grants/230530 .pdf.

Balko, R. 2014a. "How Municipalities in St. Louis County Profit from Poverty." *The Washington Post,* September 3. washingtonpost.com/news/the-watch/wp /2014/09/03/how-st-louis-county-missouri-profits-from-poverty/.

Balko, R. 2014b. "Why We Need to Fix St. Louis County." *The Washington Post,* October 16. washingtonpost.com/news/the-watch/wp/2014/10/16/why-we-need -to-fix-st-louis/.

Bannerji, H. 1995. *Thinking Through: Essays on Feminism, Marxism, and Anti-racism.* Toronto: Women's Press.

Barajas, F. P. 2007. "An Invading Army: A Civil Gang Injunction in a Southern California Chicana/o Community." *Latino Studies* 5, no. 4: 393–417.

Bauer, S. 2014. "How Conservatives Learned to Love Prison Reform." Mother Jones, March/April. motherjones.com/politics/2014/02/conservatives-prison -reform-right-on-crime.

Becker, B. 2016. "The Prison Builder's Dilemma: Economics and Ethics Clash in Eastern Kentucky." Ohio Valley Resource, July 29. ohiovalleyresource.org /2016/07/29/the-prison-builders-dilemma-economics-and-ethics-clash -in-eastern-kentucky/.

Beckett, K., and B. Western. 2001. "Governing through Social Marginality: Welfare, Incarceration, and the Transformation of State Policy." *Punishment and Society* 3, no. 1: 43–59.

Beckett, K., and S. Herbert. 2008. "Dealing with Disorder: Social Control in the Post-industrial City." *Theoretical Criminology* 12, no. 1: 5–30.

Beckett, K., and S. Herbert. 2010. *Banished: The New Social Control in Urban America.* Oxford: Oxford University Press.

Beckett, K., and N. Murakawa. 2012. "Mapping the Shadow Carceral State: Toward an Institutionally Capacious Approach to Punishment." *Theoretical Criminology* 16, no. 2: 221–44.

Beckett, K., et al. 2014. "The End of an Era? The Contradictions of Criminal Justice Reform." Unpublished paper delivered at the Realigning Corrections workshop, University of California, Irvine, October 16–18.

Bellafante, G. 2013. "Resurrecting Brownsville." *The Nation,* May 6. thenation.com /article/173886/resurrecting-brownsville#.

Bello, G. 2016. "Abolishing Private Prisons Is the Biggest Lie since Economic Recovery." The Mockingbird. mockingbirdpaper.com/content/abolishing-private -prisons-biggest-lie-economic-recovery.

Berger, D. 2010. "We Are the Revolutionaries: Visibility, Protest, and Racial Formation in 1970s Prison Radicalism." PhD diss., University of Pennsylvania.

Berger, D. 2014, *Captive Nation: Black Prison Organizing in the Civil Rights Era (Justice, Power, and Politics).* Chapel Hill: University of North Carolina Press.

Berger, J. 2012. "As Brooklyn Gentrifies, Some Neighborhoods Are Being Left Behind." *The New York Times,* July 8. nytimes.com/2012/07/09/nyregion/as -brooklyn-gentrifies-some-neighborhoods-are-being-left-behind.html.

Berlant, L. 2000. "The Subject of True Feeling: Pain, Privacy, and Politics." In *Feminist Consequences: Theory for the New Century,* edited by E. Bronfen and M. Kavka, 126–60. New York: Columbia University Press.

Berlant, L. 2007. "Nearly Utopian, Nearly Normal: Post-Fordist Affect in *La Promesse* and *Rosetta.*" *Public Culture* 19, no. 2: 273–301.

Berlant, L. 2011. *Cruel Optimism.* Durham, N.C.: Duke University Press.

Billings, D., and K. M. Blee. 2000. *The Road to Poverty: The Making of Wealth and Hardship in Appalachia.* New York: Cambridge University Press.

Blakinger, K. 2015. "Rand Paul Is Playing with Fire: The Shockingly Reasonable Ideas That Could Doom Him with Republicans." Salon, April 20. salon.com /2015/04/20/rand_paul_returns_to_the_scene_of_the_crime_drug_war _crusade_takes_him_back_to_howard_university/.

Blomley, N. 2004. *Unsettling the City: Urban Land and the Politics of Property.* New York: Routledge.

Blue, L. 2012. "It's Called the Graveyard Shift for a Reason." *Time Magazine,* July 27. healthland.time.com/2012/07/27/its-called-the-graveyard-shift-for-a -reason/.

Bonds, A. 2009. "Discipline and Devolution: Constructions of Poverty, Race, and Criminality in the Politics of Rural Prison Development." *Antipode* 39: 416–38.

Bonds, A. 2012. "Building Prisons, Building Poverty: Prison Sitings, Dispossession, and Mass Incarceration." In *Beyond Walls and Cages: Prisons, Borders, and Global Crisis,* edited by J. M. Loyd, M. Mitchelson, and A. Burridge, 129–42. Athens: University of Georgia Press.

Bonds, A. 2013. "Economic Development, Racialization, and Privilege: 'Yes in My

Backyard' Prison Politics and the Reinvention of Madras, Oregon." *Annals of the Association of American Geographer* 103, no. 6: 1389–1405.

Bonds, A. 2018. "Race and Ethnicity I: Property, Race, and the Carceral State." *Progress in Human Geography,* January, 1–10.

Braz, R. 2006. "Kinder, Gentler, Gender Responsive Cages: Prison Expansion Is Not Prison Reform." *Women, Girls & Criminal Justice,* October–November, 87–91.

Brice, M. 2014. "Brownsville: What Will NYPD 'Impact' Changes Mean?" *City Limits,* March 27. citylimits.org/2014/03/27/brownsville-what-will-nypd-impact -changes-mean/.

Brown, W. 2005. *Edgework: Critical Essays on Knowledge and Politics.* Princeton, N.J.: Princeton University Press.

Brown, W. 2006. "'American Nightmare: Neoliberalism, Neoconservatism, and De-democratization." *Political Theory* 34, no. 6: 690–714.

Brownsville Community Justice Center. n.d. "Brownsville Anti-Violence Project." *Brownsville Community Justice Center* (blog). brownsvillejusticecenter.blogspot .mx/p/brownsville-anti-violence-project.html.

Bryan, B. 2000. "Property as Ontology: On Aboriginal and English Understand-ings of Ownership." *Canadian Journal of Law and Jurisprudence* 13, no. 1: 3–32.

Bureau of Justice Statistics / U.S. Department of Justice. 2000. *Sexual Assault of Young Children as Reported to Law Enforcement: Victim, Incident, and Of-fender Characteristics in 2000.* bjs.gov/content/pub/pdf/saycrle.pdf.

Burnham, L. 2001. "Welfare Reform, Family Hardship, and Women of Color." *An-nals of the American Academy of Political and Social Science* 577 (September): 38–48.

Butler, J. 2004. *Precarious Life.* New York: Verso.

Butler, J. 2009. *Frames of War: When Is Life Grievable?* London: Verso.

Byrd, R. 2013. "'Punishment's Twin': Theorizing Prisoner Reentry for a Politics of Abolition." PhD diss., University of Washington.

Cadora, E. 2014. "Civics Lessons: How Certain Schemes to End Mass Incarcera-tion Can Fail." *Annals of the American Academy of Political and Social Science* 651 (January): 277–85.

Cadora, E., L. Kurgan, and Spatial Information Design Lab / Columbia Univer-sity Center for Spatial Research. 2006. *Architecture and Justice.* spatialinformationdesignlab.org/sites/default/files/publication_pdfs/PDF _04.pdf.

Caldwell, B. 2010. "Criminalizing Day-to-Day Life: A Socio-legal Critique of Gang Injunctions." *American Journal of Criminal Law* 37, no. 3: 241–90.

California Penal Code. 2010. Article 2: "Electronic Monitoring" (section 3010-2010.9). law.justia.com/codes/california/2010/pen/3010-3010.9.html.

Camp, J. T. 2016. *Incarcerating the Crisis: Freedom Struggles and the Rise of the Neoliberal State.* Berkeley: University of California Press.

Camp, J. T., and C. Heatherton. 2016. *Policing the Planet: Why the Policing Crisis Led to Black Lives Matter.* New York: Verso.

Campbell, C. 2015. "How Republican Presidential Candidates Want to Reform the Criminal Justice System." *Business Insider.* businessinsider.com/how-2016 -candidates-want-to-reform-criminal-justice-2015-4.

Center for Court Innovation. 2012. "Officials Announce Funding for the Brownsville Anti-violence Project." September. courtinnovation.org/research/officials -announce-funding-brownsville-anti-violence-project.

Center for Court Innovation and New York State Senate. 2012. "Brownsville Community Justice Center Seeking Program Coordinator." *The New York State Senate.* October 9. nysenate.gov/newsroom/articles/martin-malav%C3%A9-dilan /brownsville-community-justice-center-seeking-program.

Catte, E. 2018. *What You Are Getting Wrong about Appalachia.* Cleveland, Ohio: Belt.

Cheves, J. 2014. "House Adds Nursing Home for Felons to Kentucky Budget; Likely Location Is in Stumbo's District." *Lexington Herald Leader,* March 12. kentucky.com/news/politics-government/article44476179.html.

Christian, J. 2005. "Riding the Bus: Barriers to Prison Visitation and Family Management Strategies." *Journal of Contemporary Criminal Justice* 21, no. 1: 31–48.

Clear, T. 2007. *Imprisoning Communities: How Mass Incarceration Makes Disadvantaged Neighborhoods Worse.* Oxford: Oxford University Press.

Clear, T., and N. A. Frost. 2013. *The Punishment Imperative.* New York: New York University Press.

Cohen, S. 1979. "The Punitive City: Notes on the Dispersal of Social Control." *Contemporary Crises* 3, no. 4: 339–363.

Comfort, M. 2008. *Doing Time Together: Love and Family in the Shadow of the Prison.* Chicago: University of Chicago Press.

Corrigan, R. 2006. "Making Meaning of Megan's Law." *Law & Social Inquiry* 31, no. 2: 267–312.

Coulthard, G. 2014. *Red Skin, White Masks: Rejecting the Colonial Politics of Recognition.* Minneapolis: University of Minnesota Press.

Cowen, D., and A. Siciliano. 2011. "Surplus Masculinities and Security." *Antipode* 43, no. 5: 1516–41.

Critical Resistance Oakland. 2011. "Betraying the Model City: How Gang Injunctions Fail Oakland." stoptheinjunction.files.wordpress.com/2010/03/cr _ganginjunctionsreport-1.pdf.

Cullors-Brignac, P., and D. Zuniga. 2014. "A Mental Health Jail is an Oxymoron; Diversion Is What's Needed: Guest Commentary." Opinion, *Los Angeles Daily News*, June 24. dailynews.com/opinion/20140624/a-mental-health-jail-is-an -oxymoron-diversion-is-whats-needed-guest-commentary.

Dalla Costa, M., and S. James. 1973. *The Power of Women and the Subversion of the Community.* 2nd ed. Bristol, UK: Walling Wall.

Davies, L. A. 2013. "A First Look inside Dan Gilbert's Multimillion-dollar Security Hub." *Deadline Detroit,* October 11. deadlinedetroit.com/articles/6760/a _first_look_inside_gilbert_s_downtown_multi-million_dollar_security_hub #.VCQwqyiY3bz.

Davis, A. 2003. *Are Prisons Obsolete?* New York: Seven Stories.

Davis, M. 1990. *City of Quartz: Excavating the Future in Los Angeles.* London: Verso.

De Lissovoy, N. 2012. "Conceptualizing the Carceral Turn: Neoliberalism, Racism, and Violation." *Critical Sociology* 39, no. 5: 739–55.

Defilippis, J., and S. Saegert. 2012. *The Community Development Reader.* New York: Routledge.

Detroit People's Water Board, Blue Planet Project, Food & Water Watch, and Michigan Welfare Rights Organization. 2014. *Submission to the Special Rapporteur on the Human Right to Safe Drinking Water and Sanitation Regarding Water Cut-offs in the City of Detroit, Michigan.* June 18. blueplanetproject.net /wordpress/wp-content/uploads/Detroit-HRTW-submission-June-18-2014 .pdf.

Drum, K. 2014. "In Ferguson, Cops Hand Out 3 Warrants Per Household Every Year." Mother Jones, August 21. motherjones.com/kevin-drum/2014/08/ferguson -cops-hand-out-three-warrants-household-every-year.

Dunaway, W. A. 1995. "Speculators and Settler Capitalists: Unthinking the Mythology about Appalachian Landholding, 1790–1860." In *Appalachia in the Making: The Mountain South in the Nineteenth Century,* edited by Mary Beth Pudup, Dwight B. Billings, and Altina Waller, 50–75. Chapel Hill: University of North Carolina Press.

Dunbar-Ortiz, R. 2014. *An Indigenous Peoples' History of the United States.* New York: Beacon.

Eason, J. 2016. *Big House on the Prairie: Rise of the Rural Ghetto and Prison Proliferation.* Chicago: University of Chicago Press.

Ellen, I. G., and M. A. Turner. 1997. "Does Neighborhood Matter? Assessing Recent Evidence." *Housing Policy Debate* 8, no. 4: 33–66.

Eller, R. D. 2008. *Uneven Ground: Appalachia since 1945.* Lexington: University Press of Kentucky.

Eller, R. 1982. *Miners, Millhands, and Mountaineers: Industrialization of the Appalachian South, 1880–1930*. Knoxville: University of Tennessee Press.

Estep, B. 2013. "Steve Beshear and Hal Rogers Propose Summit to Revive Eastern Kentucky's Economy." *Lexington Herald-Leader,* October 28. kentucky.com/news /politics-government/article44451084.html.

Estep, B. 2014. "Eastern Kentucky Ranks Last in National Survey of Well-being." *Lexington Herald-Leader,* April 5. kentucky.com/news/politics-government /article44481810.html.

Farrell, P. A. 2017. "Oak Park Police Department Gets Its Own Ice Cream Truck." *Detroit Free Press,* May 2. freep.com/story/news/local/michigan/oakland/2017/05 /02/oak-park-police-ice-cream-truck/101195192/.

Federal Reserve. 2014. "Annual Report, 2014." Board of Governors of the Federal Reserve System. federalreserve.gov/publications/annual-report/2014-federal -reserve-banks.htm.

Feldman, A. 1991. *Formations of Violence: The Narrative of the Body and Political Terror in Northern Ireland.* Chicago: University of Chicago Press.

Ferguson Action. 2014. "Demands." Ferguson Action. fergusonaction.com /demands/.

Fields, B. 1990. "Slavery, Race and Ideology in the United States of America." *New Left Review* 181, no. 1 (May–June): 95–118.

Flores, A. 2017. "A Court Made It Illegal for This Guy to Be Seen with His Dad in Public and Now He's Fighting Back." *Buzzfeed News,* March 14. buzzfeed.com /adolfoflores/life-under-a-gang-injunction?utm_term=.vcwMwYLqR#.fbDeL gonq.

Foucault, M. 1977. *Discipline and Punish: The Birth of the Prison.* Translated by A. Sheridan. New York: Vintage Books.

Garland, D. 2001. *Culture of Control: Crime and Social Order in Contemporary Society.* Chicago: University of Chicago Press.

George, J. 2017. "Can This Marriage Be Saved?" The Marshall Project, June 6. themarshallproject.org/2017/06/06/can-this-marriage-be-saved#.4HDU sqzaP.

Gilmore, R. W. 1994. "Capital, State and the Spatial Fix: Imprisoning the Crisis at Pelican Bay." Unpublished paper, Rutgers University.

Gilmore, R. W. 2007. *Golden Gulag: Prisons, Surplus, Crisis, and Opposition in Globalizing.* Berkeley: University of California Press.

Gilmore, R. W. 2009. "Race, Prisons, and War: Scenes from the History of U.S. Violence." *Socialist Register* 45: 73–87.

Gilmore, R. W. 2014. "Mass Incarceration, Deportation, Stop and Frisk: The Urban Ecology of the Prison-Industrial Complex." Third Annual Robert Fitch Memorial Lecture, City University of New York, May 6. vimeo.com/98395694.

Gilmore, R. W. 2015. "The Worrying State of the Anti-prison Movement." *Social Justice,* February 23. socialjusticejournal.org/the-worrying-state-of-the-anti -prison-movement/.

Gilmore, R. W., and C. Gilmore. 2008. "Restating the Obvious." In *Indefensible Space: The Architecture of the National Insecurity State,* edited by M. Sorkin, 141–62. New York: Routledge.

Goldstein, J., and J. D. Goodman. 2013. "Frisking Tactic Yields to a Focus on Youth Gangs." *The New York Times,* September 18. nytimes.com/2013/09/19 /nyregion/frisking-tactic-yields-to-a-focus-on-youth-gangs.html.

Goodman, P. 2008. "'It's Just Black, White, or Hispanic': An Observational Study of Racializing Moves in California's Segregated Prison Reception Centers." *Law & Society Review* 42, no. 4: 735–70.

Goonewardena, K. 2005. "The Urban Sensorium: Space, Ideology, and the Aestheticization of Politics." *Antipode* 37, no. 1: 46–71.

Gorz, A. 1967. *Strategy for Labor.* Boston: Beacon.

Gottschalk, M. 2006. *The Prison and the Gallows: The Politics of Mass Incarceration in America.* Cambridge: Cambridge University Press.

Gottschalk, M. 2015. *Caught: The Prison State and the Lockdown of American Politics.* Princeton, N.J.: Princeton University Press.

Gramsci, A. 1971. *Selections from the Prison Notebooks.* Edited and translated by Q. Hoare and G. N. Smith. New York: International.

Grattet, R., et al. 2008. *Parole Violations and Revocations in California: Report Submitted to the U.S. Department of Justice.* ncjrs.gov/pdffiles1/nij/grants /224521.pdf.

Grawert, A., and N. Camhi. 2017. "Criminal Justice in President Trump's First 100 Days." Brennan Center for Justice, April 20. brennancenter.org/publication /criminal-justice-president-trumps-first-100-days.

Gross, A. 2014. "Detroit's New Policing Strategy Is Stop-and-Frisk on a Massive Scale." *Vice,* September 18. vice.com/read/detroit-broken-windows-policing-918.

Hacking, I. 2002. *Historical Ontology.* Cambridge, Mass.: Harvard University Press.

Hackman, R. 2014. "Bratton-style Policing Means More Fines and Arrests for Black Residents of Detroit." *The Guardian,* September 7. theguardian.com /money/2014/sep/07/safer-detroit-fines-racial-profiling-black-residents.

Hall, S. 1988. "The Toad in the Garden: Thatcherism among the Theorists." In *Marxism and the Interpretation of Culture,* edited by C. Nelson, 35–73. Urbana: University of Illinois Press.

Hall, S., et al. 1978. *Policing the Crisis: Mugging, the State, and Law and Order.* New York: Holmes and Meier.

Hall, T. 2000. "Habits/Bedford-Stuyvesant; Finding a Townhouse with a Sense of History." *The New York Times,* April 30. nytimes.com/2000/04/30/realestate /habitats-bedford-stuyvesant-finding-a-town-house-with-a-sense-of-history .html.

Hallett, M. 2012. "Reentry to What? Theorizing Prisoner Reentry in the Jobless Future." *Critical Criminology* 20, no. 3: 213–28.

Hancock, A. 2004. *The Politics of Disgust: The Public Identity of the Welfare Queen.* New York: New York University Press.

Haney, L. 2010. *Offending Women: Power, Punishment, and the Regulation of Desire.* Berkeley: University of California Press.

Hannah-Moffat, K., and M. Lynch. 2012. "Theorizing Punishment's Boundaries: An Introduction." *Theoretical Criminology* 16, no. 2: 119–21.

Harcourt, B. 2001. *Illusion of Order: The False Promise of Broken Windows Policing.* Cambridge, Mass.: Harvard University Press.

Harcourt, B. 2010. "Neoliberal Penality: A Brief Genealogy." *Theoretical Criminology* 14, no. 1: 74–92.

Harney, S., and F. Moten. 2013. *The Undercommons: Fugitive Planning & Black Study.* New York: Minor Compositions.

Harvey, D. 1973. *Social Justice and the City.* Baltimore, Md.: The Johns Hopkins University Press.

Harvey, D. 1990. *The Condition of Postmodernity.* Cambridge: Blackwell.

Harvey, D. 1996. *Justice, Nature, and the Geography of Difference.* Oxford: Blackwell.

Harvey, D. 2004. "The 'New' Imperialism: On Spatio-temporal Fixes and Accumulation by Dispossession." *The Socialist Register* 40: 63–87.

Harvey, D. 2005. *A Brief History of Neoliberalism.* Oxford: Oxford University Press.

Herbert, S., and E. Brown. 2006. "Conceptions of Space and Crime in the Punitive Neoliberal City." *Antipode* 38, no. 4: 755–77.

Hinds, O., and J. Norton. 2018. "Crisis at the Crossroads of America." Vera Institute of Justice. vera.org/in-our-backyards-stories/crisis-at-the-crossroads-of -america.

Hochschild, A. 2003 [1989]. *The Second Shift.* Toronto: Penguin.

Hooks, G., et al. 2010. "Revisiting the Impact of Prison Building on Job Growth: Education, Incarceration, and County-level Employment, 1976–2004." *Social Science Quarterly* 91, no. 1: 228–44.

Huling, T. 2002. "Building a Prison Economy in Rural America." In *Invisible Punishment: The Collateral Consequences of Mass Imprisonment,* edited by M. Mauer and M. Chensey-Lind, 197–213. New York: New Press.

Irwin, J. 1980. *Prisons in Turmoil.* Boston: Little, Brown.

Jacobson, R. L. 1999. "Megan's Laws: Reinforcing Old Patterns of Anti-gay Police Harassment." *Georgetown Law Journal* 87, no. 7: 2431–73.

Jay, M. 2017. "Policing the Poor in Detroit." *Monthly Review,* January, 21–35.

Jay, M., and P. Conklin. 2017. "Detroit and the Political Origins of 'Broken Windows' Policing." *Race & Class* 49, no.2: 26–48.

Jencks, C., and S. Mayer. 1990. "The Social Consequences of Growing Up in a Poor Neighborhood." In *Inner City Poverty in the United States,* edited by L. Lynn and M. McGeary, 111–86. Washington, D.C.: National Academy Press.

Jennings, A. 2013. "L.A. Sees Parks as a Weapon against Sex Offenders." *Los Angeles Times,* February 28. articles.latimes.com/2013/feb/28/local/la-me-parks -sex-offenders-20130301.

Johnson, M. 2013. "Why America's Women of Color Have Lost Ground since the Great Recession." Scholars Strategy Network, July. scholars.org/sites/scholars /files/ssn_basic_facts_johnson_on_how_women_of_color_fared_during_the _great_recession.pdf.

Joseph, M. 2002. *Against the Romance of Community.* Minneapolis: University of Minnesota Press.

Kaeble, D., and T. P. Bonczar. 2016. "Probation and Parole in the United States." Bureau of Justice Statistics, December 21. bjs.gov/index.cfm?ty=pbdetail&iid =5784.

Katz, C. 2001. "Vagabond Capitalism and the Necessity of Social Reproduction." *Antipode* 33, no. 4: 708–27.

Katz, C. 2005. "Partners in Crime? Neoliberalism and the Production of New Political Subjectivities." *Antipode* 37, no. 3: 623–31.

Kelley, R. D. G. 2013. "The U.S. v. Trayvon Martin: How the System Worked." *The Huffington Post,* July 15. huffingtonpost.com/robin-d-g-kelley/nra-stand-your -ground-trayvon-martin_b_3599843.html.

Kelling, G. 2015. "Don't Blame My Broken Windows Theory for Poor Policing." *Politico Magazine,* August 11. politico.com/magazine/story/2015/08/broken -windows-theory-poor-policing-ferguson-kelling-121268.

Kenney, M. R. 2001. *Mapping Gay L.A.* Philadelphia: Temple University Press.

Kentucky Energy and Environment Cabinet. 2016. *Kentucky Quarterly Coal Report, January–March.* eec.ky.gov/Pages/OpenRecords.aspx.

Kentucky Office of Energy Policy. n.d. "Expanded Online Kentucky Coal Facts." *Kentucky Coal Education.* coaleducation.org/Ky_coal_facts/.

Kilgore, J. 2013. "Progress or More of the Same? Electronic Monitoring and Parole in the Age of Mass Incarceration." *Critical Criminology* 21, no. 1: 123–39.

Kilgore, J. 2014a. "Repackaging Mass Incarceration: The Rise of Carceral Humanism and Non-alternative Alternatives." *Counterpunch,* June 6–8. counterpunch .org/2014/06/06/repackaging-mass-incarceration/.

Kilgore, J. 2014b. "Interview with Monica Jahner." Voice of the Monitored, May 6. voiceofthemonitored.com/2014/05/06/interview-with-monica-jahner -northwest-initiative-lansing-mi/.

Kilgore, J. 2016. "E-Carceration: The Problematic World of Being on an Electronic Monitor." Voice of the Monitored, October 20. voiceofthemonitored .com/2016/10/27/e-carceration-the-problematic-world-of-being-on-an -electronic-monitor/.

Kilpatrick, D. G., et al. 1992. *Rape in America: A Report to the Nation.* Arlington, Va.: National Victim Center.

Koran, M. 2013. "Lost Signals, Disconnected Lives." WisconsinWatch.org, March 24. wisconsinwatch.org/2013/03/lost-signals-disconnected-lives/.

Lefebvre, H. 1974 [reprinted 1991]. *The Production of Space.* Translated by D. Nicholson-Smith. Oxford: Blackwell.

Lefebvre, H. 1976. "Reflections on the Politics of Space." Translated by M. Enders. *Antipode* 8, no. 2: 31–37.

Lewis, O. 1961. *The Children of Sanchez.* New York: Random House.

Lewis, O. 1966. *La Vida: A Puerto Rican Family in the Culture of Poverty—San Juan and New York.* New York: Random House.

Li, T. 2009. "To Make Life or Let Die? Rural Dispossession and the Protection of Surplus Populations." *Antipode* 41: 66–93.

Linebaugh, P. 2004 [reprinted 2006]. *The London Hanged.* Cambridge: Cambridge University Press.

Linebaugh, P. 2015. "Police and Plunder." *Counterpunch,* February 13–15. counterpunch.org/2015/02/13/police-and-plunder/.

Lipsitz, G. 2004. "Learning from Los Angeles: Another One Rides the Bus." *American Quarterly* 56, no. 3: 511–29.

Lockwood, F. E. 2002. "Kentucky Federal Prison Sinking Even before It's Finished." *Lexington Herald-Leder,* July 24. highbeam.com/doc/1G1-89580357.html.

Logan, J. R., and B. J. Stults. 2011. "The Persistence of Segregation in the Metropolis: New Findings from the 2010 Census." US2010 Project, March 24. s4.ad.brown.edu/Projects/Diversity/Data/Report/report2.pdf.

Lovett, I. 2013. "Neighborhoods Seek to Banish Sex Offenders by Building Parks." *The New York Times,* March 9. nytimes.com/2013/03/10/us/building-tiny-parks -to-drive-sex-offenders-away.html.

Lowrey, A. 2014. "Income Gap, Meet the Longevity Gap." *The New York Times,* March 15. nytimes.com/2014/03/16/business/income-gap-meet-the-longevity -gap.html.

Lukács, G. 1971. *History and Class Consciousness: Studies in Marxist Dialectics.* Translated by R. Livingstone. Cambridge, Mass.: MIT Press.

Malcolm X Grassroots Movement. 2012. *Operation Ghetto Storm: 2012 Annual Report on the Extrajudicial Killing of Black People.* April. mxgm.org/wp-content/uploads/2013/04/Operation-Ghetto-Storm.pdf.

Manhattan Institute. n.d. "Motor City Implements Proven 'Broken Windows' Policing Strategy." Manhattan Institute for Policy Research, On the Ground. manhattan-institute.org/on-the-ground/detroit-policing-strategy.

Mann, E. 2004. "Los Angeles Bus Riders Derail the MTA." In *Highway Robbery: Transportation Racism and New Routes to Equity,* edited by R. D. Bullard, G. S. Johnson, and A. O. Torres, 33–47. Cambridge, Mass.: South End.

Mantle, L. 2013. "Harbor Gateway's Pocket Park Solution to Sex Offenders." Interview: Joe Buscaino, Janice Bellucci, Angel Jennings, and Janet Shour. Air Talk, March 1. scpr.org/programs/airtalk/2013/03/01/30735/harbor-gateway-s-pocket-park/.

Marx, K. 1976 [originally 1876, reprinted 1990]. *Capital: A Critique of Political Economy.* Volume 1. Translated by B. Fowkes. New York: Vintage.

Massey, D. B. 1994. *Space, Place, and Gender.* Minneapolis: University of Minnesota Press.

Mauer, M. 2011. "Sentencing Reform: Amid Mass Incarcerations—Guarded Optimism." *Criminal Justice* 26: 27–39.

McNally, D. 2011. *Global Slump: The Economics and Politics of Crisis and Resistance.* Oakland, Calif.: PM Press.

Medina, J. 2017. "Gang Database Criticized for Denying Due Process May Be Used for Deportations." *The New York Times,* January 10. nytimes.com/2017/01/10/us/gang-database-criticized-for-denying-due-process-may-be-used-for-deportations.html.

Meiners, E. R. 2009. "Never Innocent: Feminist Trouble with Sex Offender Registries and Protection in a Prison Nation." *Meridians: Feminism, Race, Transnationalism* 9, no. 2: 31–62.

Meiners, E. R. 2011. "Ending the School-to-Prison Pipeline/Building Abolition Futures." *Urban Review: Issues and Ideas in Public Education,* no. 4: 547–65.

Miller, R. J. 2013. "Devolving the Carceral State: Race, Prisoner Reentry, and the Micro-politics of Urban Poverty Management," *Punishment & Society* 16, no. 3: 305–35.

Mishel, L., et al. 2012. *The State of Working America.* 12th ed. Ithaca, N.Y.: Cornell University Press.

Moten, F. 2014. "Do Black Lives Matter? Robin D. G. Kelley and Fred Moten in Conversation." *Critical Resistance,* December 13. vimeo.com/116111740.

Mountain Eagle Staff. 2012. "Training for Prison Jobs Coming." *The Mountain Eagle*, December 19. themountaineagle.com/articles/training-for-prison-jobs -coming/.

Muhammad, K. G. 2011. *The Condemnation of Blackness: Race, Crime, and the Making of Modern Urban America.* Cambridge, Mass.: Harvard University Press.

Muniz, A. 2014. "Maintaining Racial Boundaries: Criminalization, Neighborhood Context, and the Origins of Gang Injunctions." *Social Problems* 61, no. 2: 216–36.

Murphy, E. 2008. "Paradigms of Restraint." *Duke Law Journal* 57: 1321–411.

Nagourney, A. 2016. "Aloha and Welcome to Paradise. Unless You're Homeless." *The New York Times,* June 3. nytimes.com/2016/06/04/us/hawaii-homeless -criminal-law-sitting-ban.html.

National Institute of Justice / U.S. Department of Justice. 2011. *Electronic Monitoring Reduces Recidivism.* September. ncjrs.gov/pdffiles1/nij/234460.pdf.

National Institute of Justice / U.S. Department of Justice. 2016. "Race, Trust, and Political Legitimacy." National Institute of Justice, July 14. nij.gov/topics/law -enforcement/legitimacy/Pages/welcome.aspx.

National Law Center on Homelessness & Poverty. 2014. *NO SAFE PLACE: The Criminalization of Homelessness in U.S. Cities.* nlchp.org/documents/No_Safe _Place.

Nevins, J. 2002. *Operation Gatekeeper: The Rise of the "Illegal Alien" and the Remaking of the U.S.–Mexico Boundary.* New York: Routledge.

New York City Department of Health and Mental Hygiene. 2015. *Community Health Profile, Brooklyn Community District 15: Brownsville (Including Broadway Junction, Brownsville, and Ocean Hill).* nyc.gov/assets/doh/downloads /pdf/data/2015chp-bk16.pdf.

New York Civil Liberties Union. 2018. "Stop-and-Frisk Data." NYCLU. nyclu.org /en/stop-and-frisk-data.

New York State Department of Corrections and Community Supervision. 2014. *Under Custody Report: Profile of Under Custody Population as of January 1, 2014.* doccs.ny.gov/Research/Reports/2014/UnderCustody_Report_2014.pdf.

Newman, J. 2011. "In Judge Nikkia's Court: A Response to Teen Crime." The Brooklyn Ink, July 20. brooklynink.org/2011/07/20/26623-in-judge-nikkias -court-a-response-to-teen-crime/.

Norton, J. 2016. "Little Siberia, Star of the North: The Political Economy of Prison Dreams in the Adirondacks." In *Historical Geographies of Prisons: Unlocking the Usable Carceral Past,* edited by Karen Morin and Dominique Moran, 168–84. New York, Routledge.

Norwood, K. J. 2015. *Ferguson Fault Lines: The Race Quake That Rocked a Nation.* Chicago: American Bar Association.

O'Keefe, E. 2014. "Cory Booker, Rand Paul Team Up on Sentencing Reform Bill." *The Washington Post,* July 8. washingtonpost.com/news/post-politics/wp/2014 /07/08/cory-booker-rand-paul-team-up-on-sentencing-reform-bill/.

Pager, D. 2003. "The Mark of a Criminal Record." *American Journal of Sociology* 108, no. 5: 937–75.

Parenti, C. 1999. *Lockdown America: Police and Prisons in the Age of Crisis.* London: Verso.

Parks, K. 2013. "'Reflection Cottages': The Latest Spa Getaway or Concrete Solitary Confinement Cells for Kids?" ACLU, April 29. aclu.org/blog/reflection -cottages-latest-spa-getaway-or-concrete-solitary-confinement-cells-kids.

Pasternak, S. 2010. "Property in Three Registers." *Scapegoat: Architecture, Landscape, Political Economy,* no. 00 (Fall): 10–17.

Patterson, E. J. 2013. "The Dose-Response of Time Served in Prison on Mortality: New York State, 1989–2003." *American Journal of Public Health* 103, no. 3: 523–28.

Peck, J. 2003. "Geography and Public Policy: Mapping the Penal State." *Progress in Human Geography* 27, no. 2: 222–32.

Peck, J., and N. Theodore. 2008. "Carceral Chicago: Making the Ex-offender Employability Crisis." *International Journal of Urban and Regional Research* 32, no. 2: 251–81.

Petersilia J. 2003. *When Prisoners Come Home: Parole and Prisoner Reentry.* New York: Oxford University Press.

Pew Center on the States. 2009. *One in 31: The Long Reach of American Corrections.* Washington, D.C.: The Pew Charitable Trusts.

Pew Center on the States. 2011. *State of Recidivism: The Revolving Door of America's Prisons.* Washington, D.C.: The Pew Charitable Trusts.

Pinto, N. 2016. "NYPD Watchdog Shatters Bratton's 'Broken Windows'—Now What?" *The Village Voice,* June 28. villagevoice.com/2016/06/28/nypd -watchdog-shatters-brattons-broken-windows-now-what/.

Potter, M. 2009. "Prescription Drug Abuse Ravages a State's Youth." NBCNEWS .com, July 6. msnbc.msn.com/id/31707246/ns/health-addictions/t/prescription -drug-abuse-ravages-states-youth/.

Prison Talk. n.d. "Flamboyant / Prison Gap Bus Services Info and Experiences." Prison Talk Forum. prisontalk.com/forums/archive/index.php/t-178558.html.

Public Safety Performance Project and Pew Charitable Trusts. 2016. *Use of Electronic Offender-tracking Devices Expands Sharply.* September 7. pewtrusts .org/en/research-and-analysis/issue-briefs/2016/09/use-of-electronic -offender-tracking-devices-expands-sharply.

Purser, G. 2012. "'Still Doin' Time': Clamoring for Work in the Day Labor Industry." *The Journal for Labor and Society* 15: 397–415.

Rainwater, L., and W. Yancey. 1967. *The Moynihan Report and the Politics of Controversy.* Cambridge, Mass.: MIT Press.

Reiter, K. 2012. "The Most Restrictive Alternative: A Litigation History of Solitary Confinement in U.S. Prisons, 1960–2006." In *Studies in Law, Politics, and Society* 57: 71–124.

Rhodes, L. A. 2004. *Total Confinement: Madness and Reason in the Maximum Security Prison.* Berkeley: University of California Press.

Roberts, S. 2011. "Striking Change in Bedford-Stuyvesant as the White Population Soars." *The New York Times,* August 4. nytimes.com/2011/08/05/nyregion /in-bedford-stuyvesant-a-black-stronghold-a-growing-pool-of-whites.html.

Robinson, C. 1983 [reprinted 2001]. *Black Marxism: the Making of the Black Radical Tradition.* London: Zed Books.

Rodriguez, D. 2006. *Forced Passages: Imprisoned Radical Intellectuals and the U.S. Prison Regime.* Minneapolis: University of Minnesota.

Rose, N. 1999. *Powers of Freedom: Reframing Political Thought.* Cambridge, Mass.: Cambridge University Press.

Ross, K. 2016. *Communal Luxury: The Political Imaginary of the Paris Commune.* New York: Verso.

Rothman, D. J. 1971 [reprinted 2002]. *The Discovery of the Asylum: Social Order and Disorder in the New Republic.* Hawthorne, N.Y.: Aldine de Gruyter.

Rousseau, M. 2009. "Re-imaging the City Centre for the Middle Classes: Regeneration, Gentrification, and Symbolic Policies in Loser Cities." *International Journal of Urban and Regional Research* 33, no. 3: 770–88.

Ryerson, S. R. 2010. "Prison Progress . . . Neocolonialism as a Relocation Project in 'Post Racial' America: An Appalachian Case or Listening to the Canaries in the Coal Mine." Honors thesis, Wesleyan University.

Ryerson, S. 2013. "Speak Your Piece: Prison Progress?" *The Daily Yonder,* February 20. dailyyonder.com/speak-your-piece-prison-progress/2013/02/12/5651 #comments.

Saletan, W. 2005. "Call My Cell: Why GPS Tracking Is Good News for Inmates." *Slate,* May 7. slate.com/articles/health_and_science/human_nature/2005/05 /call_my_cell.html.

Sampson, R., et al. 2002. "Assessing 'Neighborhood Effects': Social Processes and New Directions." *Annual Review of Sociology* 28: 443–78.

Sante, L. 1991. *Low Life.* New York: Farrar, Straus and Giroux.

Schenwar, M. 2015. "Your Home Is Your Prison: How to Lock Down Your Neighborhood, Your Country, and You." *TruthDig,* January 19. truthdig.com/report /item/your_home_is_your_prison_20150119.

Schept, J. 2013a. "'A Lockdown Facility . . . with the Feel of a Small, Private College': Liberal Politics, Jail Expansion, and the Carceral Habitus." *Theoretical Criminology* 17, no. 1: 71–88.

Schept, J. 2013b. "Rejecting Future Prisons." Reclaim Justice Network, July 2. downsizingcriminaljustice.wordpress.com/2013/07/02/rejecting-future -prisons/.

Schept, J. 2014a. "(Un)seeing Like a Prison: Counter-visual Ethnography of the Carceral State." *Theoretical Criminology* 18, no. 2: 198–223.

Schept, J. 2014b. "Prison Re-Form: The Continuation of the Carceral State." Tennessee Studies and Educators for Social Justice, July 15. tnsocialjustice .wordpress.com/2014/07/15/prison-re-form-the-continuation-of-the -carceral-state/.

Schept, J. 2015 *Progressive Punishment: Job Loss, Jail Growth, and the Neoliberal Logic of Carceral Expansion.* New York: New York University Press.

Schept, J. 2017, "Sunk Capital, Sinking Prisons, Stinking Landfills: Landscape, Ideology, and the Carceral State in Central Appalachia." In *Routledge International Handbook of Visual Criminology,* edited by Michelle Brown and Eamonn Carrabine, 497–513. New York: Routledge.

Schrader, S. 2016. "Against the Romance of Community Policing." Stuart Schrader (blog), August 10. stuartschrader.com/blog/against-romance-community -policing.

Scott, R. 2010. *Removing Mountains: Extracting Nature and Identity in the Appalachian Coalfields.* Minneapolis: University of Minnesota Press.

Segal, D. 2013. "A Missionary's Quest to Remake Motor City." *The New York Times,* April 13. http://www.nytimes.com/2013/04/14/business/dan-gilberts -quest-to-remake-downtown-detroit.html.

Simon, J. 1993. *Poor Discipline: Parole and the Social Control of the Underclass, 1890–1990.* Chicago: University of Chicago Press.

Simon, J. 2003. *Governing through Crime: How the War on Crime Transformed American Democracy and Created a Culture of Fear.* New York: Oxford University Press.

Singh, N. P. 2003. *Black Is a Country: Race and the Unfinished Struggle for Democracy.* Cambridge, Mass.: Harvard University Press.

Slaven, J. 2004. "Pine Knot Penitentiary Dedicated, Inmates Will Arrive Soon." *McCreary County Record,* April 6.

Smith, C. 2011a. "The Carceral Continuum" (interview with Silence Opens Doors online magazine). April 13, 2011. Select video at youtube.com/watch?v =YXEQRffaEm4 (3:17) and youtube.com/watch?v=NUXSBl445lM (3:55). Textual introduction by George Jackson at web.archive.org/web/20160525062153

/http://www.silenceopensdoors.com/2011/04/13/the-carceral-continuum
-interview-with-caleb-smith/.

Smith, C. 2011b. *The Prison and the American Imagination.* Yale Studies in English. New Haven, Conn.: Yale University Press.

Smith, N. 1984. *Uneven Development: Nature, Capital, and the Production of Space.* Oxford: Blackwell.

Smith, N. 1996. *The New Urban Frontier: Gentrification and the Revanchist City.* New York: Routledge.

Smith, N. 2002. "New Globalism, New Urbanism: Gentrification as Global Urban Strategy." *Antipode* 34, no. 3: 427–50.

Smith, S. J. 2013. "Closing in on Brownsville: Brooklyn Gentrification Nears the Final Frontier." *The New York Observer,* May 14. observer.com/2013/05/closing -in-on-brownsville-brooklyn-gentrification-nears-the-final-frontier/.

Soja, E. W. 1980. "The Socio-spatial Dialectic." *Annals of the Association of American Geographers* 70, no. 2: 207–25.

Sorge, M. 2013. "Dan Gilbert and Rock Ventures Own or Control 30 Properties Downtown." *Detroit Unspun,* July 17. blog.thedetroithub.com/2013/07/17 /dan-gilbert-and-rock-ventures-own-or-control-more-than-30-properties -downtown/.

Staples, W., and S. Decker. 2011. "Between the 'Home' and 'Institutional' Worlds: Tensions and Contradictions in the Practice of House Arrest." *Critical Criminology* 18: 1–20.

Stein, D. 2014a. "Keyword: Labor." Panel presentation, annual meeting of the American Studies Association, Los Angeles, November 6–9.

Stein, D. 2014b. "Full Employment for the Future." *Lateral,* no. 3. http://csalateral .org/issue3/theory/stein.

Stein, D. 2014c. "Fearing Inflation, Inflating Fears: The End of Full Employment and the Rise of the Carceral State." PhD diss., University of Southern California.

Story, B. 2016. *The Prison in Twelve Landscapes.* 90:00. Grasshopper Films.

Story, B., and J. Schept. Forthcoming. "Against Punishment: Centering Work, Wages, and Uneven Development in Mapping the Carceral State." *Social Justice.*

Takei, C. 2014. "Prisons Are Adopting the Wal-Mart Business Model." *Huffington Post: The Blog,* September 29. huffingtonpost.com/carl-takei/prisons-walmart -business-model_b_5900964.html.

Taylor, K-Y. 2016. *From #BlackLivesMatter to Black Liberation.* Chicago: Haymarket.

Teal, C., and T. Lessin. 2014. "The Next Phase of the Koch Brothers' War on

Unions." *The Daily Beast,* December 12. thedailybeast.com/articles/2014/12/22/the-next-phase-of-the-koch-brothers-war-on-unions.html.

Travis, J. 2007. "Reflections on the Reentry Movement." *Federal Sentencing Reporter* 20, no. 1: 84–87.

Travis, J., and B. Western, eds. 2014. *The Growth of Incarceration in the United States: Exploring Causes and Consequences.* Washington, D.C.: National Academies Press.

U.S. Attorney General. 2017. "Memorandum for All Federal Prosecutors Re: Department Charging and Sentencing Policy." *The Washington Post,* May 10. apps.washingtonpost.com/g/documents/national/jeff-sessionss-criminal-charging-policy/2432/.

U.S. Bureau of the Census. 2010. *Decennial Census of Population and Housing, 2010.* census.gov/programs-surveys/decennial-census/decade.2010.html.

U.S. National Advisory Commission on Civil Disorders. 1968. *Report of the National Advisory Commission on Civil Disorders.* Washington, D.C.: United States Federal Government, 1968.

Van Parijs, P., ed. 1992. *Arguing for Basic Income: Ethical Foundations for a Radical Reform.* London: Verso.

Vanhemert, K. 2013. "The Best Map Ever Made of America's Racial Segregation." *Wired,* August 26. wired.com/2013/08/how-segregated-is-your-city-this-eye-opening-map-shows-you/#slideid-210281.

Vera Institute. 2018. "People in Prison 2017." Vera Institute of Justice, May. vera.org/publications/people-in-prison-2017.

Vitullo-Martin, J. 2013. "Is Brownsville Brooklyn Ready for Its Jane Jacobsian Comeback?" *Untapped Cities,* January 17. http://untappedcities.com/2013/01/17/brownsville-brooklyn-ready-for-comeback/.

Wacquant, L. 2002. "From Slavery to Mass Incarceration: Rethinking the 'Race Question' in the US." *New Left Review* 13: 41–60.

Wacquant, L. 2009a. *Punishing the Poor: The Neoliberal Governance of Social Insecurity.* Durham, N.C.: Duke University Press.

Wacquant, L. 2009b. *Prisons of Poverty.* Minneapolis: University of Minnesota Press.

Wagner, P. 2003. "The Prison Index: Taking the Pulse of the Crime Control Industry." Prison Policy Initiative. prisonpolicy.org/prisonindex/variation.html.

Wagner, P., and R. B. Rabuy. 2017. "Mass Incarceration: The Whole Pie 2017." Prison Policy Initiative. March 14. prisonpolicy.org/reports/pie2017.html.

Walkerdine, V. 2003. "Reclassifying Upward Mobility: Femininity and the Neoliberal Subject." *Gender and Education* 15, no. 3: 237–48.

Walsh, M. 2010. "Gender on the Road in the United States: By Motor Car or Motor Coach?" *The Journal of Transport History* 31, no. 2: 210–230.

Weeks, K. 2011. *The Problem with Work.* Durham, N.C.: Duke University Press.

Western, B., and K. Beckett. 1999. "How Unregulated Is the U.S. Labor Market? The Penal System as a Labor Market Institution." *American Journal of Sociology* 104, no. 4: 1030–60.

Whitlock, K. 2017. "Endgame: How 'Bipartisan Criminal Justice Reform' Institutionalizes a Right-wing, Neoliberal Agenda." Political Research Associates, June 6. politicalresearch.org/2017/06/06/endgame-how-bipartisan-criminal -justice-reform-institutionalizes-a-right-wing-neoliberal-agenda.

Williams, E. J. 2011. *The Big House in a Small Town: Prisons, Communities, and Economics in Rural America.* Santa Barbara, Calif.: Praeger.

Williams, R. 1977a. *Keywords: A Vocabulary of Culture and Society.* New York: Oxford University Press.

Williams, R. 1977b. "Structures of Feeling." In *Marxism and Literature,* 128–36. Oxford: Oxford University Press.

Winsa, P. 2008. "Lock-'em-up Laws Infect Entire Neighborhoods." *The Toronto Star,* July 24. thestar.com/news/crime/crime/2008/07/24/lockemup_laws_infect _entire_neighbourhoods.html.

Index

BRETT STORY is assistant professor at the School of Image Arts at Ryerson University and director of the award-winning documentary film *The Prison in Twelve Landscapes.*